THOMAS AQUINAS ON
FAITH, HOPE, AND LOVE

THOMAS AQUINAS ON
FAITH, HOPE, AND LOVE

*Edited and Explained
for Everyone*

CHRISTOPHER KACZOR

FOREWORD BY
PETER KREEFT

Sapientia Press
of Ave Maria University

Requests for permission to make copies of any part of the work should be directed to:

Sapientia Press
of Ave Maria University
5050 Ave Maria Blvd.
Ave Maria, FL 34142
888-343-8607

Cover Design: Eloise Anagnost

Cover Image: *The Triumph of St. Thomas Aquinas* (tempera on panel), Gozzoli, Benozzo di Lese di Sandro (1420–97) © Louvre, Paris, France / Lauros / Giraudon / The Bridgeman Art Library

Printed in the United States of America.

Library of Congress Control Number: 2008941957

ISBN: 978-1-932589-50-4

Amicus Amicis

~~

To
Michael and Catherine Pakaluk
and
Bob and Liz Crnkovich

~~

In thanksgiving
for your abundant hospitality and inspiring example

TABLE OF
CONTENTS

Vices Opposed to Hope

The Nature, Objects, and Order of Charity

FOREWORD

~~~~~~~~~~~~~~~~~~~~~~~~~

THE SUBJECT of this book, the three "theological virtues" of faith, hope, and charity, is nothing less than the greatest thing in the world. And the author of this book, St. Thomas Aquinas, was nothing less than the greatest theologian in the history of the world. This book, therefore, is—well, use your own British understatement.

There is a great advantage to reading St. Thomas himself rather than any of the hundreds of excellent disciples (Gilson, Maritain, Pieper, McInerny) or any of the thousands of disciples of his disciples, like myself and Dr. Kaczor, who are useful even though two steps removed from the great master.

What advantage? It is like breathing clean, unperfumed air, or drinking pure water. It is also a lot like drinking single malt scotch rather than blended whiskey. It is an acquired taste, but one well worth acquiring. Therefore this book is for amateurs and beginners as well as professionals and scholars. Dr. Kaczor has made it more accessible by judicious footnoting, thus proving that even disciples of disciples of St. Thomas can be very useful if they have the humility to be "dwarfs standing on the shoulders of giants," to quote a favorite medieval image.

St. Thomas himself did this: his typically medieval method of quoting "authorities" was not mere fashion or personal penchant, like our current fashion and penchant for defying all authorities. Rather, it was a key to his success and a source of his greatness to be open to all the great sources. There is absolutely nothing but silly social fashions and petulant personal penchants to stop us from using exactly the same key. That is why we should all be "peeping Thomists" (to steal Ralph McInerny's imperishable pun), or "tasting Thomists."

That is why this introduction means only to introduce, to match-make, to point, to invite, like the Psalmist's "taste and see." A Psalmist and a Thomist are only a syllable apart, after all. Our Lord Himself used the same method: "Come and see." I am very proud to be so slavish and unoriginal as to imitate the method of these masters.

Christopher Kaczor was one of the best students I have had at Boston College. Here he does for the *Summa*'s treatment of the three theological virtues the very thing I did in my *Summa of the Summa* for its central philosophical passages. My advertisement for it here is simply that it works. Students learn from Aquinas. So do teachers. I have learned more from Aquinas than from any other philosopher or theologian. Perhaps most important of all, I have learned the habit of philosophizing from him, by example, more than from anyone else. So has Dr. Kaczor. So can you.

Far more important is that this book can actually help you to live by faith and hope and charity. One is helped to live these virtues in two ways: first, by consciously understanding them more deeply through this opus, and also by unconsciously imitating them in Aquinas's soul as they guided his *operatio*, his actions of thinking and teaching, which shine through their product, the *Summa*. We see the artist through the art, the poet through the poem, the finger through the fingerprints. The *Summa* is the fingerprints of a saint and a sage. The act of writing it was structured by faith and hope and charity. This book makes them present to us as objects of our knowledge only because they were first present to Aquinas as objects of his knowledge, but they were present to him in such depth as objects only because they were first present to him subjectively, as virtues in his soul. They were what Marcel would call "mysteries" before they were "problems." Our heads recognize the objective truth of what he says in the *Summa* because our hearts first recognize in these words the truth that their own deepest, divinely designed desires cry out for in themselves, the "truth as subjectivity," as Kierkegaard rather dangerously phrased it.

In this book we meet not just a theology but a man: a sage and a saint. Words flow not just from a pen but from a man, and as the pen is mightier than the sword, the man is mightier than the pen.

—Peter Kreeft

INTRODUCTION

IN ABOUT fourth grade, I remember searching through the attic in our house (a favorite trick of mine in unsupervised moments) and running across old mementos from my mother's college years. In a dusty cardboard box were annuals, class notes, and old books. I picked up one, called *The Basic Writings of Thomas Aquinas*. Basic, I thought, I'll give it a read. Although each word on the page was perfectly understandable, the meaning of virtually every sentence was completely beyond me. I'd read books with big words that I could not understand, but a book with more manageable words that still remained a mystery—this was something new. I tried reading this book again in high school and again in college, without much more success. Perhaps there are some people who can immediately comprehend the great philosophical and theological achievement of Thomas Aquinas on their first read, but I was certainly not among them. This is the book I wish I had discovered.

Even if we run across this kind of book, one might wonder what a medieval Dominican friar could teach those living in a postmodern world? Indeed, what importance is any discussion of the theological virtues to a citizen of the twenty-first century? This introduction will address a number of topics including the sense in which theological virtues are *virtues*, the importance of St. Thomas Aquinas, and the contents and structure of his great work the *Summa theologiae*. But the question of happiness must be addressed first not only because it is the most important for living well but also because understanding more deeply the nature of happiness is foundational to seeing why we should care about the theological virtues or Thomas's treatment of them.

There is at least one thing shared by persons of every century from the very beginning of all human history. Whatever their religion, race, or nationality, all people want to be happy. At all stages of life, and in all periods of history, the search for happiness is the fundamental driving force of human motivation. However, although all people agree that they want to be happy, they sharply disagree about what, in fact, will make them happy. In order to make the importance of faith, hope, and love evident, some reflection on what will make human beings happy is in order, for the virtues derive their importance from their link to happiness. Indeed, it is only through a greater understanding of the nature of happiness that the importance of the theological virtues (and Thomas's explication of them) can be more fully appreciated.

The Nature of Happiness

In his book, *Healing the Culture,* the president of Gonzaga University, Robert Spitzer, S.J., distinguishes among four "levels" of happiness: level one consisting of bodily pleasure from food, drink, drugs, and sex; level two consisting of "winning" the competition for money, fame, power, and/or popularity; level three consisting of service to others; and the fourth level consisting of a relationship with Transcendent Good, Power, Love, and Beauty.

Level One Happiness

Happiness at level one is bodily pleasure, the most immediate and physically intense kind of happiness. Sexual activity, food, and drink give people level one happiness, a level that is easily attained and enjoyable to all. The life of the hedonist—"wine, women, and song"—attracts adherents from the young, and sometimes even the old. Its appeal is visceral, physical, and undeniable.

Although level one happiness rises quickly by eating, drinking, or having sex, once desire is sated, the pleasure quickly vanishes. Pleasures of the flesh embody the motto "easy come, easy go." Spitzer notes that level one happiness leads to a crisis because after some time bodily pleasure gives way to boredom and a deep sense of meaninglessness.

Hedonism is also subject to the law of diminishing returns. In the *Gorgias*, Plato compares the pursuit of bodily pleasure to filling a leaky jar. No matter how much water is poured into a leaky jar, it never remains full. Indeed, in the case of pleasure, the more "water" that is poured in, the more leaks seem to spring from the jar. The very first time a person drinks alcohol, the experience is often exhilarating. But after drinking becomes a habit, the drinker no longer feels any effect from one drink and requires two or three to achieve the exhilaration formerly attained through one. As the habit hardens, even more drinks will be needed to get the same "buzz." People quickly build a tolerance for alcohol or drugs that turns what once was a great thrill into a bore. Still more stimulation is needed to achieve the same effect. The more one abuses drugs or alcohol, the more one develops a tolerance. With bodily pleasures of all kinds, over time the same old stimulus can fail to stimulate.

In addition, the addicting nature of bodily pleasure leads its devotees to a kind of enslavement. Plato calls attention to this in the *Republic*. If human beings overly indulge the aspect of the human person that desires bodily pleasure, it will gain strength, eventually becoming like a many-headed beast that tyrannizes human freedom and allows no other goal but the unreachable one of continuous and ever-increasing levels of corporeal sensation. Happiness at level one does not satisfy, and those who devote themselves wholly to level one tend to end up addicted, sober, or dead. Long and sad human experience teaches that true happiness cannot be found at the bottom of a bottle or in a bed.

Level Two Happiness

Experiencing emptiness, many people are drawn to happiness at level two. Somewhat less immediate and intense than level one happiness, happiness at level two focuses on winning a chosen competition, for example, for power, popularity, fame, prestige, and/or money. Happiness consists in success in the comparison game of personal accomplishment and self-realization. It is commonly thought that the more money (fame, popularity, prestige, and/or power) a person has, the happier that person will be: "He who dies with the most toys wins." The "good life" as understood by many Americans emerges from this perspective. Happiness at level two is sought through becoming triumphant in a comparison game with others. Happiness is not only "keeping up with the Joneses," but utterly surpassing them in the acquisition of money, power, fame, popularity, and/or prestige.

Clearly, the losers or the mediocre are not happy in the comparison game, so it would seem that happiness goes to the winners. Unfortunately, even winners of the comparison game don't enjoy the elation of victory for long. After waiting 86 years for the Boston Red Sox to win a World Series, just days after the final inning of the final game, Red Sox fans found themselves, well, not as happy as they thought they would be. Summarizing the feelings of once-elated fans, a *New York Times* headline read: "Once a Championship Dream Is Realized, the Euphoria Is Fleeting."

Even more than a World Series victory, many people believe that more money will bring them greater life satisfaction. They think the richer they become, the happier they will be. Social scientist and psychologist David Myers, in his book *The Pursuit of Happiness: Who is Happy—and Why*, tackles this assumption using empirical data gathered over many years from all over the world, including surveys of CEOs of Fortune 500 companies. All the data point to the same conclusion. More money *does* make people happier if they cannot already provide for basic physical needs, such as food, shelter, and clothing. However, once these elementary needs are met, money does not increase human happiness. Myers concludes that "whether we base our conclusion on self-reported happiness, rates of depression, or teen problems, *our becoming much better off over the last thirty years has not been accompanied by one iota of increased happiness and life satisfaction.* It's shocking because it contradicts our society's materialistic assumptions, but how can we ignore the hard truth: *Once beyond poverty, further economic growth does not appreciably improve human morale.* Making more money—that aim of so many graduates and other American dreamers of the 1980s—does not breed bliss."[1] Reinforcing this finding, John Stossel's ABC special report, "The Mystery of Happiness: Who Has It? How to Get It," notes that lottery winners report that after the initial

---

[1] David G. Myers, *The Pursuit of Happiness: Who is Happy—and Why* (New York: William Morrow and Company, Inc., 1992), 44.

excitement wears off, they feel no happier than before their big win. In many cases, they are less happy. *People* magazine's February 2004 article "The High Cost of Winning" details the lives of six lottery winners who fell into family squabbles, divorce, drunk driving, financial ruin (as they outspent their winnings), attempted murder (as both murderer and target of murder), and suicide. Myers further observes, "Even the rich seldom feel rich. In a 1990 Gallup poll, Americans readily applied the label 'rich' to others. The average person judged that 21% of Americans were rich. But virtually none—less than 1 percent—perceived themselves as rich. To those earning $10,000 dollars a year, it takes a $50,000 income to be rich. To those making $500,000, rich may be a $1 million dollar income. When the Oakland Athletics signed outfielder José Canseco to a $4.7 million annual salary, his fellow outfielder Rickey Henderson became openly dissatisfied with his $3 million salary. Refusing to show up on time for spring training, he complained, 'I don't think my contract is fair.'"[2] As Aristotle points out, money is a means that simply cannot buy all that is needed for happiness.

Other "winners," feeling a sense of emptiness, seek new levels of competition for money, fame, power, popularity, or prestige. Level two winners sometimes turn to "upping the stakes," reasoning that an even greater level of achievement might bring them the lasting happiness that they lack. Myers puts it this way: "As we climb the success ladder we mostly look upward. Seldom do people compare themselves with those 'below' them in success. More often they compare themselves with those a rung or two above, those whose level of success they aspire to join. The philosopher Bertrand Russell saw no end to the upward comparison: 'Napoleon envied Caesar, Caesar envied Alexander, and Alexander, I daresay, envied Hercules, who never existed. One cannot, therefore get away from envy by means of success alone, for there will always be in history or legend some person even more successful than you are."[3] As an individual climbs the ladder of success, possibilities for victory grow fewer and more difficult. Myers writes that in the empirical research on happiness "we have exposed falsehoods, most notably the idea that more

---

[2] Ibid, 57.
[3] Ibid., 58.

money, and the pleasures and possessions it buys, will make middle-class people happier. . . . [M]aterialism has been our dominant ideology. But this American dream of prosperity achieved through individual initiative now seems at times like a nightmare, for never has a century known such abundance, or such massive genocide and environmental devastation. Never has a culture experienced such comfort and opportunity, or such widespread depression. Never has technology given people so many conveniences, or such terrible instruments of degradation and destruction. Never have we been so self-reliant, or so lonely. Never have we seemed so free, or our prisons so overstuffed. Never have we had so much education, or such high rates of teen delinquency, despair, and suicide. Never have we been so sophisticated about pleasure, or so likely to suffer broken or miserable marriages. These are the best of times materially, but not for the human spirit."[4]

Level Three Happiness

Robert Spitzer proposes a solution to free people from the difficulties of devotion to levels one and two living. Spitzer suggests removing the "only" from the pursuit of lower forms of happiness. People should not seek *only* pleasure or *only* winning. Competition is not bad, just *exclusive* focus on competition to the exclusion of all other realities. When comparison is made the ultimate goal of all human activity, people fail to get that which they really want beyond all else—happiness. Similarly, bodily pleasure is not bad in itself, but it can become destructive when it excludes or impedes worthwhile activity and becomes an all-consuming force. Human beings cannot "turn off" levels one or two desires but must add to them level three and level four perspectives. What are these perspectives?

A level three perspective focuses on serving others. It is less immediate and intense than either level one or level two, but it is more lasting. At level three, agents primarily and ultimately wish others well and do what is good for them. Since at this level people really care about the well-being of others, they want them to do well. Rejoicing in the success of others can replace jealousy and envy. Operating at level three are those who are driven to make a difference for the good in the world, whatever

---

[4] Ibid.

their occupation or station is in life. Success at level two, though important, is not all important, and so "winning" is not a matter of self-survival, and "losing" is not the end of all life's meaning. Instead of looking for the "bad news" in those around them in an effort to make themselves feel superior, people at level three look for the "good news" in others. Common cause replaces cutthroat competition. At level three, rather than view others as a means to their personal pleasure or competitive advantage, people view themselves and all other human beings as intrinsically valuable regardless of their place in a comparison game.

Although level three satisfies us much more effectively than level one or two, even level three does not satisfy the restless human heart. Friends disappoint. People cannot always help those whom they want to help. They long to have that which escapes their grasp. Their efforts at making the world a better place often fail. Sometimes those who are being helped do not sufficiently appreciate the efforts made on their behalf. Even when people are for the most part successful in helping others, they still want more.

Level Four Happiness

There is an even deeper level of happiness—level four. Level four does not reject what is good in level three but adds a deeper, transcendent dimension. It is the least immediate, but the most lasting form of happiness. It corresponds to the deepest desires in the human heart. Ultimately, human beings want a beauty that cannot fade, and a truth free from falsity. People want a life that does not end and a love that is totally unconditional. They want pure Beauty, pure Truth, pure Life, and pure Love. Augustine once prayed to the Almighty, "Our hearts are restless till they rest in Thee."[5] Ultimately, even when they don't fully realize it, people want a relationship with God.

The Importance of the Theological Virtues
for (Level Four) Happiness
As is made clear from Spitzer's discussion (which echoes Thomas Aquinas's discussion of happiness), people can find the deepest kind of

---

[5] Augustine, *Confessions,* trans. F. J. Sheed (Kansas City, MO: Sheed & Ward, 1970), 3.

happiness only in God. But how do human beings "connect" with God? Human beings cannot see God with their own eyes. They cannot relate to God as they relate to other human beings. How can human beings, so limited, so finite, and so fragile, have a relationship with the unlimited, infinite, and all-powerful God?

The answer, according to Thomas Aquinas, lies in the theological virtues of faith, hope, and love. Since they are imbued with divine power and given to us by God, these virtues are able to make up for what human beings lack in relating to the divine. People cannot "go up" to God, but the Almighty can "come down" to them. The theological virtues, three divine gifts, give people a share in the perfect truth of God's knowledge (faith), the life-giving power of God overcoming evil (hope), and the transcendent beauty of God's own good nature (love). In faith, God reveals himself as pure truth. In hope, God helps the faithful attain eternal enjoyment of the greatest good. In love, God communicates his happiness to us, a share in the joy of the eternal communion of Father, Son, and Holy Spirit.

Of course, a person's share in God's knowledge, power, and goodness is, in this life, incomplete, and so too, one's happiness while on this earth will always be imperfect. The fulfillment and perfection of their happiness, the fulfillment and perfection of a human being's sharing God's good nature, will take place only in heaven. Nevertheless, human beings can have a taste of heaven here below. For example, a great friend of God, the saint, already enjoys a deep participation in level four happiness despite perhaps suffering personal difficulties. The saints have the virtues of faith, hope, and love to a heroic degree, and therefore, even in persecution, they are deeply filled with joy. Leon Bloy once said, "there is only one tragedy—not to be a saint." People can endure every setback if they have the joy of a saint; but without joy even a palace can feel like a prison.

Although faith, hope, and love are gifts of God and a participation in divine life, these virtues perfect *human* nature. The theological virtues fit distinctly human questions and potentialities. A philosopher once suggested that humanity has from the beginning struggled with three fundamental questions: What can I know? What may I hope? What should I do? In God's great mercy, the theological virtues of faith, hope, and love answer these human queries in a way undreamt of by the philosophers. Each human person desires to know the most important and interesting of things, including the highest and most divine of things. It is this knowledge that is given in the virtue of faith, through which a person can come to an awareness of the mysteries of God. Similarly, despite fear of grave evils, including bodily and spiritual death, human beings have the potential to overcome these evils through hope in eternal life and the resurrection of the body. With God's help, in the virtue of hope, this potential is realized. Despite setbacks and human frailties on the one hand, and despite temptations to self-righteousness and pride on the other, hope enables us to be confident that with divine aid salvation can be attained. Finally, people have a capacity for a deep and true friendship with each other and with their Creator, and this possibility is made real through the virtue of love. Jesus said to his Apostles, "No longer do I call you servants . . . I have called you friends" (Jn 15:15). Through the virtue of love, all people can become friends of God. It would be hard to overestimate the importance of faith, hope, and love since, as the *Catechism of the Catholic Church* notes, they "are the foundation of Christian moral activity; they animate it and give it its special character" (1813). With these virtues, people can enjoy a foretaste of heaven on earth. Without them, however, earthly existence can be but a foretaste of the eternal separation from God, a separation called hell.

The theological virtues go together. People cannot enjoy communion with God, in time or in eternity, without love, for it is love that establishes us as friends of God. People cannot have love of God without hope and faith in God. As Thomas says in the first chapter of his *Compendium of Theology*: "Love cannot be rightly ordered unless the proper goal of our hope is established; nor can there be any hope if knowledge of the truth is lacking. Therefore the first thing necessary is faith, by which you may come to knowledge of the truth. Secondly, hope is necessary, that your intention may be fixed on the right end. Thirdly, love is necessary, that your affections may be perfectly put in order."[6] Without

---

6 Thomas Aquinas, *The Light of Faith* (Manchester, NH: Sophia Institute Press, 1993), 4.

love, people are not friends with God and have no share in his life. Without hope, people would despair of ever reaching their heavenly home. Without faith, they would not know in whom to hope and whom to love—Father, Son, and Holy Spirit. Faith, hope, and love each play a vital role in a person attaining true happiness, imperfectly here on earth and perfectly later in heaven.

Theological Virtues as Virtues

In what sense are these gifts of God (faith, hope, and love) called virtues? Derived from the Greek word for "excellence" (*areté*) and the Latin for "power" or "ability" (*virtus*), the virtues are for Aquinas the habits of a happy heart. As habits, virtues are enduring dispositions that remain in us, even when the acts connected with these habits are not present. Similarly, people have habitual knowledge of many things, even if they are not always thinking about those things. For example, I know (habitually or dispositionally) that triangles have three sides, even when I am focusing on something else and not thinking about geometry. It is because of dispositional knowledge that people do not have to wake up each day and relearn elementary facts about themselves and the universe. The virtues of faith, hope, and love remain even when people are asleep and even in those, like young children, who are unable to do the acts that arise from faith, hope, and love. Theological virtues are enduring characteristics. Indeed, no force in the world can take the theological virtues away from a person. A person can lose the infused virtues of faith, hope, and love, only if that person chooses deadly sin over remaining in communion with God.

A virtue is a *good* habit by which human acts are rendered good, that is, conducive to happiness. Without virtue, acts that otherwise would be conducive to happiness do not satisfy. Some people who have not yet become virtuous perform good acts but take no pleasure in them. By contrast, the person with a virtue is not only able to do what is right but is also able to enjoy doing it. As Aristotle wrote, and as Thomas often quotes, "the virtue of a thing is that which makes its subject good, and its work good" (*Nicomachean Ethics* II, 6). Virtue makes its subject good by realizing human potentialities, by perfecting human nature. "Be all that you can be" reflects, in a popular way, Thomistic ethics. With God's help, people have the capacity to understand the very best (faith), to seek the very best (hope), and to be united to the very best (love). When people are able to become perfect in this way, the actions that they perform will be good, both for themselves and for others.

On the Importance of St. Thomas Aquinas

If history is any guide, the teaching of Thomas should be taken very seriously. Throughout the centuries, Thomas has been a teacher, sometimes the most important teacher, of subsequent philosophers of tremendous import (Scotus, Ockham, Descartes, Heidegger, Edith Stein, Maritain, Pieper, Gilson, MacIntyre). Thomas's influence on Catholic theology is even greater. If there is some truth in the words of Alfred North Whitehead that all Western philosophy is a footnote to Plato, one could also say that after the thirteenth century all Catholic theology is a footnote to Aquinas. Thomas's *Summa theologiae* stood open with the Bible during the Council of Trent. Vatican I made many of Thomas's views official Catholic dogmas—including his teaching on the relationship of faith and reason and the natural ability to come to knowledge of God. Vatican II's decree on priestly formation recommended that "by way of making the mysteries of salvation known as thoroughly as they can be, students should learn to penetrate them more deeply with the help of the speculative reason exercised under the tutelage of St. Thomas" (*Optatam totius* 16).

A generation after the Second Vatican Council, Pope John Paul II in *Fides et Ratio* (*Faith and Reason*) emphasized "the incomparable value of the philosophy of Saint Thomas" and taught that "the Church has been justified in consistently proposing Saint Thomas as a master of thought and a model of the right way to do theology" (*Fides et Ratio* 57, 43). Why did Pope John Paul II see such value in the study of St. Thomas? Such a question invites a "taste and see" answer, for I have never known a single person who has read Thomas seriously without being impressed with the brilliant clarity and profound depth of his thought. Indeed, on virtually any list of the most outstanding philosophers or theologians of all time, Thomas ranks among the best. He is especially relevant in the twenty-first century.

Thomas was a thinker who sought truth wherever it might be found. In the contemporary world, filled as it is with so many diverse and conflicting voices, Thomas provides a model for a discerning synthesis of a diversity of views. Thomas might be compared to the conductor of an orchestra who harmonizes many different kinds of instruments—brass, strings, winds, and percussion—into a harmonious and compelling whole. If one is counting quotations, one can find in Thomas numerous Greek, Roman, Hebrew, biblical, Patristic, and Arabic sources including Socrates, Aristotle, Plotinus, Proclus, Cicero, Justin, Clement, Gregory the Great, Augustine, Dionysius, Boethius, Anselm, Abelard, Albert, Maimonides, and Avicenna. In the contemporary world, with its wide diversity of points of view, there is no better model for intellectual inquiry than Thomas Aquinas, who at once held fast to the best of the Augustinian theological tradition and integrated new insights from Arab, Jewish, Stoic, and Greek thinkers. Wisdom consists not in embracing everything new because of its novelty or everything old because of its antiquity but in bringing into harmony and synthesis the best of the new and the old.

In addition, Thomas demonstrated the compatibility of faith and reason. Thomas proposed an alternative between fideism (a kind of religious fundamentalism closed to the insights of reason) and rationalism (a kind of secular humanism closed to the insights of revelation). Just as modern technology has revolutionized human life over the last 100 years, the arrival of Aristotle's works in the thirteenth century was an intellectual earthquake for the established Augustinian theology of the day. For centuries, most of Aristotle's works were inaccessible to Latin readers, but when the works were translated into Latin from their original Greek via Arabic intermediaries, such as Averroes and Avicenna, the effect was immediate. For example, the Genesis story indicates that the world has a beginning point in time; Aristotle is understood to teach the eternity of the world. Christians believe in the individual immortality of the soul; Aristotle is understood to teach the impossibility of individual immortality. For believers, God is personal, knowing even the number of hairs on their heads; for Aristotle, God knows only the noblest and highest object, ultimately Himself. Because Aristotle seemed to contradict several fundamental tenets of the Christian faith, the reading of Aristotle was in many places completely banned. Aristotle seemed to be a most formidable and dangerous alternative to Christian belief. Others reading Aristotle, called Latin Averroists or Heterodox Aristotelians, found profound wisdom in Aristotle's writings but seemed to believe that the very same statement could be false in theology but true in philosophy. A kind of schizophrenia threatened to develop between reason and revelation, philosophical wisdom and religious tradition. What one professed at Church on Sunday and what one believed the rest of the week appeared to be irreconcilably at odds.

Today, contemporary thinkers find themselves in a situation that is not entirely different. On the one hand, some religious fundamentalists see nothing but danger in contemporary ways of life, technology, and critical thinking. In this view, the life of the mind is nothing but a danger to belief. On the other hand, secular humanists consider faith in God as akin to belief "in ghosts or elves or the Easter Bunny."[7] Religious belief is, in their view, an irrational and dangerous delusion fit only for intellectual lightweights. Rejecting both extremes, the perspective of St. Thomas is that knowledge never poses a threat to faith, and faith strengthens the search for knowledge.

Aquinas taught that faith and reason cannot be opposed because they both approach the truth that comes ultimately from God: faith in a complete and perfect way, natural reasoning in an incomplete and imperfect way. In the spirit of Thomas, one could speak of two books, the book of nature (creation) and the book of grace (revelation). In Thomas, secular reason and sacred revelation come together for the benefit of both. Both books are written by God, and there are no contradictions between the two (though contradictions may arise from a *misinterpretation* of either or both books). Since God is the origin of all truth, alleged conflicts between faith and reason are just that, *alleged* conflicts. The life of the mind and the life of faith are not incompatible, but rather mutually enriching.

---

7 Daniel C. Dennett, "The Bright Stuff," *New York Times*, July 12, 2003.

The *Summa theologiae* and the Place
of the Theological Virtues

The structure of Thomas's most famous and influential work, the *Summa theologiae*, may be unfamiliar to the contemporary reader. Arising from disputes about how to interpret Scripture and the Fathers of the Church, Thomas's *Summa* has an intricate organization that takes the form of a mini-debate. The basic unit is called an "article," which begins with a query that can be answered either positively or negatively, such as: "Does God exist?" or "Is it always wrong to wage war?" In its original form, Thomas first outlines arguments against his view in various "objections" of various lengths and number. Next, Thomas brings forward an authority to indicate whether the question will be answered positively or negatively. After the authoritative *"sed contra"* or "to the contrary," Thomas introduces his reasons for answering the question the way he does beginning with "I answer that," sometimes also known by the Latin as a *respondeo* or in English as the "response" or "body of the article." He concludes by answering each of the previous objections. Each article may be compared to a trial in which the truth or falsity of a declaratory statement is at issue. First, the prosecuting attorney brings forward evidence and arguments against the accused. The judge intervenes to clarify the law and apply it to the situation in question. Finally, the defense attorney shows why each argument brought forward by the prosecutor fails. The side of the prosecuting attorney is represented by the various numbered objections: "Objection 1, Objection 2," and so on. An authoritative judgment is cited with the "On the contrary," and then in the "I answer that" Thomas responds with his own account of the issue at hand. Finally, in the replies, each objection is treated. Each article, therefore, has five steps:

1. the formulation of the question at issue,

2. a consideration of opposing views,

3. investigation into previous answers to the question,

4. answering the question by proving (providing reasons) for the thesis, and

5. a response to the opposing views.

As Peter Kreeft notes:

> No one of these five steps can be omitted if we want to have good
> grounds for settling a controverted question. If our question is vaguely
> or confusedly formulated, our answer will be, too. If we do not con-
> sider opposing views, we spar without a partner and paw the air. If
> we do not do our homework, we only skim the shallows of our-
> selves. If we do not prove our thesis, we are dogmatic, not critical.
> And if we do not understand and refute our opponents, we are left
> with nagging uncertainty that we have missed something and not
> really ended the contest.[8]

Although Thomas's original arrangement of an article makes use of
the structure just described, in this present work the articles have been
recast to make them easier for someone unfamiliar with Thomas to
read and follow. So instead of beginning with the objections, each article begins with Thomas's answers to the query at hand and then goes to
the first objection, followed by the reply to the first objection and so
on. I hope that a greater accessibility and ease in following the argument of Thomas justifies taking liberties with the original structure.

A number of articles are grouped together by Thomas to address a
given topic, such as "the cause of faith" or "the nature of heresy," to make
up what is known as a "question." These questions are gathered together
to make up the various parts of the *Summa*. The *Summa theologiae* is a
massive work made up of four major parts, the *prima pars* or first part (I)
consisting of 119 questions, the *prima secundae* or first part of the second
part (I–II) consisting of 114 questions, the *secunda secundae* or second
part of the second part (II–II) consisting of 189 questions, and the *tertia
pars* or third part (III) consisting of 90 questions. Following Thomas's
death, by using articles Thomas had written as a young man commenting on Peter Lombard's *Sentences*, editors added a *tertiae partiae supple-
mentum* or Supplement (III–S) of some 99 questions to complete the
original plan of writing that Thomas had envisioned for the *Summa*.

In the first part (I), Thomas begins with God and then considers
that which comes from God in creation. Aquinas briefly considers issues

---

[8] Peter Kreeft, *Summa of the Summa* (San Francisco: Ignatius Press, 1990), 18.

of theology and philosophy but spends most of his time talking about God's existence, nature, powers, the Blessed Trinity, the angels, the six days of creation, the nature of human beings, and the government of creatures. In the first part of the second part (I–II), Thomas treats how creatures return to God via their action. He writes,

> [M]an is said to be made to God's image, insofar as the image implies *an intelligent being endowed with free-will and self-movement*: now that we have treated of the exemplar, i.e., God, and of those things which came forth from the power of God in accordance with His will, it remains for us to treat of His image, i.e., man, inasmuch as he too is the principle of his actions, as having free-will and control of his actions.

In this section (I–II), Thomas addresses human happiness, voluntary human action, human emotions or "passions," habits (both good habits, called virtues, and evil habits, called vices), natural law, human law, and divine law, as well as grace. In the second part of the second part (II–II), Thomas considers specific virtues as well as specific vocations to which a person may be called. In this section, Thomas addresses the theological virtues of faith, hope, and love, the cardinal virtues of prudence, justice, courage, and temperance, as well as acts pertaining to certain vocations such as priesthood, monastic life, and the office of bishop. In the third part (III), Thomas addresses the way people return to God, namely through Christ via the Sacraments. Aquinas treats the return of human beings to God via the Incarnation of Christ, the life of Christ, and the Sacraments of Baptism, Confirmation, the Holy Eucharist, and Confession. The *Supplement* (III–S) finishes the treatment of Penance along with Anointing of the Sick, Holy Orders, and Matrimony, and it concludes with a treatment of the General Resurrection of all believers. Considered at the "macro level," the *Summa* has a neo-Platonic "exitus-reditus" (exit and return) scheme, beginning with God, proceeding from God and returning to God.[9] The very purpose

---

[9] Within various articles and in various footnotes, the reader will also find references to other places within the *Summa*, such as II–II, q. 64, a. 7 ad 1 or III, q. 5, a. 2, ad 3. This standard form of abbreviation refers to the second part of the second part, question 64, article 7, response to the first objection

of Thomas's life and all his writings was to aid human beings in their return to God. At the center of his greatest work, the *Summa theologiae*, is Thomas's treatment of the theological virtues: faith, hope, and love. *Aquinas on Faith, Hope, and Love* is a selection of articles coming from the beginning of the second part of the second part (II–II).

Although it is always ideal to read a work as a whole, in its original language, few people have the time and background to read the multivolume *Summa theologiae* in the Latin of the critical Leonine edition. Similarly, it would be wonderful if students of art could all visit the Vatican and take in Michelangelo's Sistine Chapel in its entirety with their own eyes rather than rely on a series of photographs that inevitably fail to convey the "big picture." However, these limitations should not deter people from doing what they can. As with both the Sistine Chapel and the *Summa*, it is better to become familiar with a replication of sections of a masterpiece than not to consider it at all. Indeed, it is usually in this way that a great love for art or wisdom begins.

In order to make Thomas's treatment more accessible to the general reader, *Aquinas on Faith, Hope and Love* uses the time-honored Dominican Father's English translation, edited and amended, and provides footnotes to guide the reader at various points, including suggested further reading on a range of topics. This book contains selections from Thomas's treatment of faith, hope, and love that are most influential, important, or likely to be most interesting to the contemporary reader.

Cardinal Bessarion (d. 1472) once said: "Thomas is among all the saints the most learned; and among all the learned the most saintly." Aquinas lived out faith, hope, and love and so better understood these virtues. It is my hope that *Aquinas on Faith, Hope, and Love* will help readers to better understand the theological virtues so as to better live them.

---

or in the second example to the third part, question 5, article 2, the response to the third objection.

ON FAITH

INTRODUCTION
TO FAITH

~~~~~~~~~~~~~~~~~~~~~

IN A SENSE, the Christian faith began with a young woman named Mary who trusted the words of an angel and brought God into the world. The apostles came to have faith in Jesus as the only Son of God, and proclaimed this faith to everyone who would listen even at the risk of their lives. Through the centuries, the faith was enkindled in the hearts of believers through baptism of water, blood, or desire. This faith was refined not just by the blood of martyrs but also by the prayerful interpretation of Scripture by holy saints, ecumenical councils, and popes. When heretical views arose, like the belief that Jesus was not really a human being or the belief that Jesus was merely a human being, these erroneous interpretations of the faith proclaimed in the Scriptures were countered by confessions of faith less open to misunderstanding.

Although the word 'faith' appears in each of the previous sentences, it is used in slightly different senses in each one. Faith, like love, is "a many splendored thing". In this introduction, I will say a bit about the different ways Aquinas talks about faith: the compatibility of reason and faith, including the mysteries of faith; faith in an objective sense vs. faith in the subjective sense; faith as a theological virtue and "degrees" of faith; vices contrary to the virtue of faith and the possibility of overcoming vice and weak faith.

Thomas Aquinas explores the various splendors of faith in the beginning of the second part of the second part of the *Summa theologiae*.

He examines the object of faith, namely God and by extension that which God reveals to us. He considers the act of faith, namely that with the help of grace, a person believes in God and what God reveals. This revelation goes beyond what reason alone can show to be true but is nevertheless not contrary to reason. This faith is living, saving faith when coupled with charity. He writes of the outward manifestations of faith, such as a public confession and manifest living of faith.

For Thomas, faith and reason are always compatible, harmonious, and mutually enriching. It is possible, indeed it happens regularly, that someone misinterprets either faith or reason (or both) and thereby arrives at a contradiction. But such apparent contradictions arise because of some sort of misunderstanding. Faith and reason cannot ever truly conflict because God is the author both of the truths of revelation found in the book of grace and of the truths found by reason in the book of nature. Indeed, some truths revealed by faith (such as the existence of God and certain basic moral truths) are also able in principle to be known through natural reason. Nevertheless, God reveals these truths to us so that we can have a greater certainty about them and so that various errors do not become mixed up with the truth. Even though some truths of faith can be known through the powers of the human mind unaided by the supernatural revelation of grace, other truths of faith can only be known by revelation and not intuited from the created order. These truths of faith, the "mysteries of faith," pertain to God's actions in history and God's own triune nature. Although the created order led pre-Christian philosophers such as Plato and Aristotle to know something of the power and existence of a Supreme Being, only through revelation could human beings come to believe that God became a man in Jesus or that God is a Trinity of Divine Persons, Father, Son, and Holy Spirit. Such truths do not contradict reason, they are not irrational or unreasonable, but they surpass reason in so far as by God's supernatural action alone (and not through reasoning from the created order) are they revealed to us.

Faith for Thomas has both an objective and a subjective sense. In an objective sense, "the faith" is that which is revealed by God, the beliefs spelled out, for example, in the Apostle's creed, that ancient summary of the essential elements of the revelation culminating in the life, suffering, death, and resurrection of Jesus. Subjectively considered, "faith" is something within each believer, a gift from God that can be accepted and nurtured or neglected and rejected.

For Thomas, faith is a virtue, a habit of the mind making the intellect assent to the Truth who is God. Among those who have this virtue, faith, a gift given by God and not earned by human merit or insight, all share the same faith insofar as they believe and entrust themselves to the same God who enlightens their minds, but not all people have the same understanding or devotion in their faith. For some people, faith has become lifeless because it is lacking charity. They still believe that God exists, but they no longer cling to God with love, nor do they properly love their neighbor. Such lifeless faith even devils can have, and this lifeless faith—a matter merely of the intellect and not the heart—does not lead to salvation. Those who have been given and have accepted the gift of faith purify their hearts with a holy fear, not the fear of a slave who is motivated simply by punishment, but rather the fear of a good son who wants to please his father and fears doing anything that would damage their wonderful relationship.

Faith is a virtue given by God, but like every virtue or strength, faith has certain vices opposed to it. The first among these is unbelief in the sense of a willful rejection of faith through pride. Another motivation for unbelief is fear of religion. Likewise, heresy is a sin against faith, a picking and choosing from what God has revealed of what we will believe and what we will reject. Apostasy, another sin against faith, is the rejection of the faith previously held.

But these sins, like any other sin, need not be fatal to one's relationship with God. A dead faith, a faith made lifeless by a lack of charity, can be resurrected through God's forgiveness of sins and restoration of charity. Likewise, a weak faith can be strengthened. Many difficulties in belief are moral difficulties: we don't want to believe because if we did we'd have to change our behavior. Other difficulties are intellectual, and books like Thomas's *Summa theologiae* can help remove such obstacles and enkindle a vibrant faith. For example, a person might have come to believe in "scientism", namely that it is unreasonable to believe anything that cannot be proved through the scientific method. This belief would lead a person to reject faith, since the truths of faith—such as the divinity of Christ—cannot be proved through the scientific method. However, this intellectual difficulty can be eased through noting that the statement, "it is unreasonable to believe anything that cannot be proved through the scientific method" cannot itself be proved through the scientific method. There is no empirical test that leads to the conclusion that only empirical tests are reliable. Like a snake that eats its own tale, scientism is self-contradictory. By contrast, "[f]aith and reason are like two wings on which the human person rises to the contemplation of truth."[1]

---

[1] Pope John Paul II, *Fides et Ratio,* 1998.

QUESTION **1**

THE OBJECT OF FAITH

ARTICLE 1 ∾ **Is the object of faith the First Truth?**

Yes, despite objections to the contrary, Dionysius says (*Div. Nom.* vii)[1] that "faith is about the simple and everlasting truth." Now this is the First Truth.[2] Therefore the object[3] of faith is the First Truth.

---

1 Dionysius the Pseudo-Areopagite was mistakenly believed to be the Dionysius converted by St. Paul in Acts 17:34. In part because of his supposed antiquity, Dionysius's works, including *Celestial Hierarchies* and *De divinis nominibus* (*On the Divine Names*) cited here by Thomas, had a tremendous influence in the Middle Ages and on Thomas himself.

2 Pontius Pilate famously asked, "What is truth?" (Jn 18:37). Thomas's question presupposes that there is such a thing as truth, which he defines as a correspondence of mind and reality. (*ST* I, q. 16, art. 1) Although truth has deep metaphysical roots, a basic understanding of what Thomas means is not difficult to grasp. For example, if I think that I have a key in my pocket, and indeed in reality I do have a key in my pocket, then it is "true" that there is a key in my pocket. That is, there is a correspondence between my mind and the reality. On the other hand, if there is no key in my pocket, but I think that there is a key, my belief that there is a key is not true (but rather false). For more on truth, see Thomas's *Disputed Questions on Truth*.

3 The term "object" is an important technical term for Thomas. T. C. O'Brien notes: "The very use of the term 'object' denominates things, realities, persons, in view of man's distinctive engagement with them. Apart from their perspective, objects are not objects, they are just themselves. There are no material objects or formal object(s) lying around 'out there'; there are things, there are persons. These are denominated objects in the sense that man has a receptivity towards them, that his actions are a reaching (and a needful reaching) towards them. . . . That God is object means that the acts of faith, hope, and love exist and are what they are because God communicates himself as

I answer that, The object of every cognitive habit includes two things: first, that which is known materially, and is the material object, so to speak, and, secondly, that whereby it is known, which is the formal aspect of the object.[4] Thus in the science of geometry, the conclusions are what is known materially, while the formal aspect of the science is the mean of demonstration, through which the conclusions are known.

Accordingly, if we consider, in faith, the formal aspect of the object, it is nothing else than the First Truth.[5] For the faith of which we are speaking does not assent to anything except because it is revealed by God.[6] Hence the mean on which faith is based is the

---

the one to be believed, to be hoped in and to be loved in return." Thus, to speak of God as the "formal object of faith" is not to reduce God to a mere "thing" or impersonal "entity." Rather, it is to speak about how a human being can relate to the Creator, namely qua a personal being to be believed. Again, as O'Brien puts it: "The language of object in this use is meant to describe God's giving himself. The theological force, so far from being impersonal or from managing God, means that the acts of the theological virtues are pure reciprocity, and are freely given responses to God, lovingly communicating himself to man." T. C. O'Brien in St. Thomas Aquinas, *Summa theologiae,* vol. 31 (New York: Blackfriars, 1966), 182, 184.

[4] In *ST* II–II, question 9, article 2 ad 3, Thomas writes, "every cognitive habit regards formally the mean through which things are known, and materially, the things that are known through the mean." In other words, we can distinguish between how we come to accept certain truths (the 'form') and the truths that are accepted (the 'material'). Formally, we believe *because* God reveals. Materially, we believe *what it is* that God reveals. We are informed by God who forms our mind in accord with himself, the First Truth.

[5] The "First Truth" is God. As mentioned earlier, truth is the correspondence of mind and reality. Since all reality comes from God, and therefore corresponds to his divine mind, reality is said to be true to the extent that it corresponds to God's mind. God therefore is the *First Truth* against which all other truths are measured. God's truth is, in addition, first in the order of being, since everything created depends on God for its existence. God's truth is also first in the order of time, since God existed before all things. Finally, God's truth is first in the order of importance, for God's truth is more essential for right living, deep wisdom, and enduring happiness than any created truth.

[6] One's conception of God greatly influences whether one can accept even the possibility of revelation. As C. S. Lewis remarks: "An 'impersonal God'— well and good. A subjective God of beauty, truth and goodness, inside our own heads—better still. A formless life-force surging through us, a vast power which we can tap—best of all. But God Himself, alive, pulling at the other end of the cord, perhaps approaching at an infinite speed, the hunter,

Divine Truth.7 If, however, we consider materially the things to which faith assents, they include not only God, but also many other things, which, nevertheless, do not come under the assent of faith, except as bearing some relation to God, in as much as, to wit, through certain

king, husband—that is quite another matter. . . . There comes a moment when people who have been dabbling in religion ('Man's search for God'!) suddenly draw back. Supposing we really found Him? . . . Worse still, supposing He found us? So it is a sort of Rubicon. One goes across; or not. But if one does, there is no manner of security against miracles (or revelation). One may be in for *anything*." C. S. Lewis, *Miracles* (New York: Macmillan Company, 1947), 113–14.

7 The idea of "Divine Truth" is for the postmodern atheist a double absurdity. Such thinkers claim that (1) there is no truth (NT) and that (2) there are no (unambiguous) true statements (NTS). These "universal negative propositions," as logicians call them, are sometimes put forward as if they were indications of intellectual modesty. Another example of a universal negative proposition is "there is no God," a characteristic belief of the postmodern deconstructionists themselves. However, in order to *know* that there is no God, one must have knowledge of the entire universe in every level of reality, and knowing all this, then conclude that there is no God. Indeed, a being with knowledge of the entire universe sounds a lot like what Christians call God. Hence, the only being in a position to know that there is no God would be God. To claim to know that there is no God is not a statement of intellectual modesty but a bold statement that presupposes knowledge that surpasses what any human being could ever know. Aside from the difficulty connected with negative propositions in general, negative propositions about the existence of truth and the ambiguity of statements run into particular problems. They presuppose that about which one could never have knowledge. It can be humble acceptance of personal limitations to say, "*I myself* do not know the truth" about this or that matter, but it is proud presumption to say, "*No one* can know the truth." Thus, though denying the existence of truth is sometimes portrayed as an act of modesty, it can be an act of pride. In addition, the statement "There is no truth" (NT) is self-referentially incoherent. Another example of a self-referentially incoherent statement, a statement that refutes itself in its very assertion, is: "This sentence is not written in English." Of course, the previous sentence is written in English rather than Latin or German, so the sentence is self-referentially false. Likewise, if there is no truth, then it must be true that "there is no truth." But if this single statement is true, then it is false to say there is no truth, for at least one thing is true, namely that "there is no truth." Hence, the statement "there is no truth" is a self-referentially incoherent statement. Finally, even if it were not self-referentially incoherent, believing NT or NTS could only be a matter of "faith" and cannot be arrived at through any rational argument. If the

effects of the Divine operation, man is helped on his journey towards the enjoyment of God.[8] Consequently from this point of view also the object of faith is, in a way, the First Truth,[9] in as much as nothing comes under faith except in relation to God,[10] even as the object of the medical art is health, for it considers nothing save in relation to health.

Objection 1. It would seem that the object of faith is not the First Truth. For it seems that the object of faith is that which is proposed to us to be believed. Now not only things pertaining to the Godhead, i.e. the First Truth, are proposed to us to be believed, but also things concerning Christ's human nature, and the sacraments of the Church, and the condition of creatures. Therefore, the object of faith is not only the First Truth.

Reply to Objection 1. Things concerning Christ's human nature, and the sacraments of the Church, or any creatures whatever, come

---

premises of an argument are untrue, the argument is unsound. If the words of the premises are ambiguous, the syllogism is invalid, and the conclusion does not follow. If indeed NTS is true, then the premises leading to the conclusion NTS are ambiguous. If the premises are ambiguous, the argument leading to the conclusion NTS is invalid and one has no reason to hold the conclusion. Likewise, if indeed NT is true, then the premises leading to NT are not true. If these premises are untrue and hence the argument unsound, then the premises offer no warrant for the conclusion, and one has no reason to believe NT is true.

[8] The *formal aspect* of faith is *why* one believes, namely because God revealed it. The *material aspect* is *what* one believes, for example, that Jesus died under Pontius Pilate. A Christian believes that Jesus died under Pontius Pilate because God revealed this through the teaching of the apostles as recorded in Scripture. A non-Christian historian may also believe that Jesus died under Pontius Pilate but perhaps because of the historical evidence alone. The formal aspect of faith is the most important because it is in this respect that the person of faith accepts and clings to God in the most direct and immediate way.

[9] God is the most pure truth for Aquinas. The divine intellect is perfect, and a perfect intellect has no falsity but only truth; thus the divine intellect is purest truth. There is a perfect correspondence between the mind of God and the being of God (since God's Mind/Understanding *is* God's Being/Essence) and when there is a correspondence between mind and being there is truth, and with a perfect correspondence, perfect truth.

[10] Faith involves both *believing someone* (formal aspect of faith) and *believing something* (material aspect of faith).

under faith insofar as by them we are directed to God and in as much as we assent to them on account of the Divine Truth. The same answer applies to the Second Objection, as regards all things contained in Holy Scripture.

ARTICLE 2 ⁘ **Is the object of faith something complex, by way of a proposition?**[11]

Yes, despite objections to the contrary, Faith is a mean between science and opinion.[12] Now the mean is in the same genus[13] as the extremes. Since, then, science and opinion are about propositions, it seems that faith is likewise about propositions; so that its object is something complex.[14]

---

[11] This query seeks to better understand the relationship between God (who is perfectly simple and without composition) and faithful human understanding of God (which is not simple and does have composition).

[12] The editors of the Dominican Fathers' translation note that Thomas uses the word "science" in its medieval, Aristotelian sense: "[S]cience is a certain knowledge of a demonstrated conclusion through its demonstration." (www.op.org/summa/a4/summa-II-IIq2a9.pdf) Faith is like "science" (in Thomas's medieval sense of the word) in that it comes to an unconditional assent to the truth of what is believed. Faith is like opinion, and unlike science, in that it does not have demonstration of that which is believed. For both faith and science, the conclusion is assented to unconditionally. For both faith and opinion, there is no demonstration of what is held. Faith, sharing characteristics of both science and opinion but identical with neither, is a mean between science and opinion.

[13] Aristotle, in Book one, part 5 of his *Topics*, defines genus as what is said in the category of essence of a number of things exhibiting differences in kind. More simply, Porphyry in chapter two of his *Isagogue*, holds that genus is that which is predicated of many things differing in species in answer to the question what a thing is. For example, the genus Socrates is animal; the species of Socrates is man.

[14] Stephen Brown notes: "The creed or symbol is a 'collection of truths of the faith' expressed in set words. The truths are expressed in statements or propositions. *The true believer, however, does not stop at the words; he believes in the realities expressed in the words.* Believers live their lives in accord with these realities. . . . They receive from God an invitation to a new way of seeing and a new way of living." Stephen Brown, "The Theological Virtue of Faith" in *The Ethics of Aquinas*, ed. Stephen Pope (Washington DC: Georgetown University Press, 2002), 228 [emphasis added].

I answer that, The thing known is in the knower according to the mode of the knower. Now the mode proper to the human intellect is to know the truth by synthesis and analysis,[15] as stated in I, q. 85, a. 5. Hence things that are simple in themselves are known by the intellect with a certain amount of complexity, just as on the other hand, the Divine intellect knows, without any complexity, things that are complex in themselves.[16]

Accordingly the object of faith may be considered in two ways. First, as regards the thing itself which is believed, and thus the object of faith is

---

[15] Synthesis (*componere*) and analysis (*dividere*), also sometimes called composition and division, are characteristic of human understanding. Unlike angels or God, human beings know in piecemeal fashion rather than through one act of understanding according to Thomas. We apprehend something, say for instance a dog, and then move to make judgments about it by connecting or dividing it with another thing apprehended, for instance the color brown. "The dog is brown" would be an example of composition, an affirmative judgment, uniting the subject and predicate. "The dog is not brown" would be an example of division, a negative judgment, separating subject and predicate. We may then move to reasoning where various judgments are combined to move to new conclusions. "The dog is brown, my cat is scared of brown dogs, therefore. . . ." The difference between the human and the angelic intellect might be compared to the difference between a child just learning to read and an adult reader. Little children sound out each letter, piece together syllables, and then go back and run the syllables together hoping to make a word they recognize. By contrast, adults can read entire words at once. At times, they can understand an entire sentence in one glance. They read. They don't sound out. Like the child learning to read, the human intellect works discursively apprehending things, putting together or dividing things apprehended in a judgment, and finally reasoning from one judgment to the next. Like the adult reader (at least in cases of very short sentences), the angelic intellect immediately understands in one act of immediate intuition what it takes human beings many acts and a long time to piece together.

[16] The first part of the *Summa* treats the question of God's knowledge (Q.14, especially articles 11–15). God knows in a way that does not compromise the divine perfection of simplicity and immutability. Human beings know by means of synthesis and analysis, by composition "This man is a good baseball player" and by division "this man is not a good baseball player." Human knowing compares things to one another, noting similarities and differences. Divine knowing need not compare one thing to another since in one act of understanding God knows everything in its exact specificity—including its relationship to other things.

something simple, namely the thing itself about which we have faith.[17] Secondly, on the part of the believer, and in this respect the object of faith is something complex by way of a proposition.[18] Hence in the past both opinions have been held with a certain amount of truth.

Objection 1. It would seem that the object of faith is not something complex by way of a proposition. For the object of faith is the First Truth, as stated above (1). Now the First Truth is something simple. Therefore the object of faith is not something complex.

Reply to Objection 1. This argument considers the object of faith on the part of the thing believed.

Objection 2. Further, the exposition of faith is contained in the creed. Now the creed does not contain propositions, but things: for it is not stated therein that God is almighty, but: "I believe in God . . . almighty." Therefore the object of faith is not a proposition but a thing.

Reply to Objection 2. The creed mentions the things about which faith is, insofar as the act of the believer is terminated in them, as is evident from the manner of speaking about them. Now the act of the believer does not terminate in a proposition, but in a thing. For as in science we do not form propositions, except in order to have knowledge about things through their means, so is it in faith.[19]

---

[17] God is the object of faith, and as Thomas noted earlier in the *Summa*, God is simple (I, Q.3). By God's simplicity, Aquinas means that there is no composition in God, no parts, and no aspect that potentially could be better than it presently is. God, for all eternity, enjoys all perfections perfectly.

[18] Since human knowing makes use of composition and division in making judgments, the object of faith in relation to human knowing is something complex, propositions such as "I believe in God" or "God is a loving communion of Divine Persons." These statements about God have syllables, individual words, and related concepts, but God himself, unlike sentences about God, is utterly simple, possessing all perfection.

[19] Here Thomas clarifies that the person of faith has faith *in God himself*, not faith *in a proposition* about God such as "There is a God." We use propositions to express what we believe, but what we believe in is *God*, not *words* about God. The person of faith is in communion with God via this faith. The person of faith has a participation in the very knowledge of God that utterly transcends simply knowing words about God.

Objection 3. Further, faith is succeeded by vision, according to 1 Corinthians 13:12: "We see now through a glass in a dark manner; but then face to face. Now I know in part; but then I shall know even as I am known." But the object of the heavenly vision is something simple, for it is the Divine Essence. Therefore the faith of the wayfarer is also.

Reply to Objection 3. The object of the heavenly vision will be the First Truth seen in itself, according to 1 John 3:2: "We know that when He shall appear, we shall be like to Him: because we shall see Him as He is": hence that vision will not be by way of a proposition but by way of a simple understanding. On the other hand, by faith, we do not apprehend the First Truth as it is in itself. Hence the comparison fails.

ARTICLE 3 ⁓ Can anything false come under faith?

No, despite objections to the contrary, No virtue that perfects the intellect is related to the false, considered as the evil of the intellect, as the Philosopher[20] declares (*Ethic.* vi, 2). Now faith is a virtue that perfects the intellect, as we shall show further on (q. 4, aa 2 and 5). Therefore nothing false can come under it.

I answer that, Nothing comes under any power, habit or act, except by means of the formal aspect of the object: thus color cannot be seen except by means of light, and a conclusion cannot be known save through the mean of demonstration. Now it has been stated (a. 1) that

---

[20] "The Philosopher" is a way that Thomas speaks of Aristotle (384–322 B.C.), the ancient Greek student of Plato. In the *Summa*, Aristotle is one of his most frequently cited sources, along with Scripture and Augustine. In fact, Thomas thought so highly of Aristotle that he wrote commentaries on many of Aristotle's most important works, including the *Nicomachean Ethics* and the *Metaphysics*. Amazingly, although Thomas's duties as master of theology necessitated commenting on Scripture and did not require commenting on Aristotle, more than 13 percent of Thomas's entire literary corpus is devoted to commentaries on Aristotle, roughly the same percentage as Thomas devoted to commentaries on Scripture. These commentaries were so well received that within fifty years after his death Thomas was called "the Expositor" mirroring the celebrated title of Avicenna, "the Commentator." Even today, many contemporary scholars believe that Thomas's commentaries on Aristotle are the best ever written. Using Aristotle, Thomas was able to demonstrate the compatibility of faith and reason. Nothing true known by reason is lost through acceptance of faith.

the formal aspect of the object of faith is the First Truth, so that nothing can come under faith save insofar as it stands under the First Truth, under which nothing false can stand, as neither can non-being stand under being, nor evil under goodness. It follows therefore that nothing false can come under faith.[21]

Objection 1. It would seem that something false can come under faith. For faith is divided with hope and charity. Now something false can come under hope, since many hope to have eternal life, who will not obtain it. The same may be said of charity, for many are loved as being good, who, nevertheless, are not good. Therefore something false can be the object of faith.

Reply to Objection 1. Since the true is the good of the intellect, but not of the appetitive power, it follows that all virtues which perfect the intellect exclude the false altogether because it belongs to the nature of a virtue to bear relation to the good alone. On the other hand, those virtues that perfect the appetitive faculty do not entirely exclude the false, for it is possible to act in accordance with justice or temperance, while having a false opinion about what one is doing. Therefore, as faith perfects the intellect, whereas hope and charity perfect the appetitive part, the comparison between them fails. Nevertheless, neither can anything false come under hope, for a man hopes to obtain eternal life, not by his own power (since this would be an act of presumption), but with the help of grace, and if he perseveres therein he will obtain eternal life surely and infallibly.

In like manner it belongs to charity to love God, wherever He may be, so that it matters not to charity whether God be in the individual whom we love for God's sake.

---

[21] Since God is perfectly good, God would not lie. Since God is all-knowing, God could never be mistaken. Therefore, anything revealed by God cannot be false. Any contradiction between faith and reason must be impossible. Alleged conflicts arise only from a misunderstanding of revelation or reason or both. God is the author of two "books," the book of nature (creation, science, and history) and the book of grace (revelation). Although the books are not the same, neither do they contradict one another. A wonderful, profound meditation on this theme of faith and reason is provided by John Paul II in *Fides et Ratio*, which echoes many of Thomas's insights.

Objection 2. Further, Abraham believed that Christ would be born, according to John 8:56: "Abraham your father rejoiced that he might see My day: he saw it, and was glad." But after the time of Abraham, God might not have taken flesh, for it was merely because He willed that He did, so that what Abraham believed about Christ would have been false. Therefore the object of faith can be something false.

Reply to Objection 2. That "God would not take flesh," considered in itself, was possible even after Abraham's time, but insofar as it stands in God's foreknowledge, it has a certain necessity of infallibility, as explained in I, q. 14, aa 13 and 15: and it is thus that it comes under faith. Hence insofar as it comes under faith, it cannot be false.[22]

Objection 3. Further, the ancients believed in the future birth of Christ, and many continued so to believe, until they heard the preaching of the Gospel. Now, when once Christ was born, even before He began to preach, it was false that Christ was yet to be born. Therefore something false can come under faith.

Reply to Objection 3. After Christ's birth, to believe in Him was to believe in Christ's birth at some time or other. The fixing of the time, wherein some were deceived was not due to their faith, but to a human conjecture. For it is possible for a believer to have a false opinion through a human conjecture, but it is quite impossible for a false opinion to be the outcome of faith.[23]

---

[22] Walter Farrell called faith a "freedom for the mind," which enables us to move beyond what can be known by our own power. In a human way, we have faith in a doctor or scientist who tells us about the lab results. Our own awareness is increased, though we ourselves did not do the testing that brought about the results. Similarly, out of love for us God tells us more about himself than could ever be known through philosophical or scientific endeavor, so that we will know him better and love him more. Faith might be compared to laser eye surgery: a gift from a power outside ourselves that perfects and transcends that which we could accomplish through our own power, giving us a clearer, fuller, and more truthful vision of reality.

[23] It is important to distinguish what is truly revealed by God from what is closely connected or even thought to be revealed by God, but in fact is not part of revelation. The infallibility of faith does not extend to matters outside of faith, nor does it extend to every interpretation that may be proposed of

ARTICLE 7 ⤳ Have the articles of faith increased in the course of time?

Yes, despite objections to the contrary, Gregory says (*Hom.* xvi *in Ezech.*) that "the knowledge of the holy fathers increased as time went on . . . and the nearer they were to Our Savior's coming, the more fully did they receive the mysteries of salvation."[24]

I answer that, The articles of faith[25] stand in the same relation to the doctrine of faith, as self-evident principles to a teaching based on natural reason.[26] Among these principles there is a certain order, so that some are contained implicitly in others; thus all principles are reduced, as to their first principle, to this one: "The same thing cannot be affirmed and denied at the same time," as the Philosopher states (*Metaph.* iv, text.

matters of faith. The Church aids the faithful in distinguishing between that which is infallible and revealed by God and that which is not, by means of dogmas promulgated by Church councils or by the authority of the pope alone. Dogmas are those propositions, statements about reality, which the Church explicitly propounds as revealed by God. Needless to say, many matters remain "open questions" among those who fully accept the dogmas proclaimed by the church to be revealed by God.

24 Pope St. Gregory the Great reigned from 590 to 604 and had a tremendous influence throughout the Middle Ages through shaping the liturgy and through his writing, especially his book *Moralia in Job*. Indeed, his reign is sometimes marked as the end of antiquity and the beginning of the Middle Ages. For a fascinating introduction, read Carol Straw, *Gregory the Great: Perfection in Imperfection* (Berkeley: University of California Press, 1991).

25 The articles of faith are the truths expressed in the creed.

26 One cannot demonstrate through deductive argument the principle of non-contradition (that a thing cannot both exist and not exist at the same time and in the same respect), since nothing could be prior to this first principle. Philosophy must presuppose this in order to operate, and although this principle can be defended against criticism (cf. Aristotle, *Metaphysics,* book 4), there is no prior principle that can be adduced to show that the principle of non-contradiction is true. Similarly, mysteries of faith are presupposed by theology. God reveals them and the faithful believe them. These principles, these revealed truths, can be defended against criticism but not all these truths can be shown to be true on the basis of natural reason. For example, only faith (not natural reason) can establish as true that God is three Divine Persons, or that Jesus is true God and true man. On the other hand, other truths revealed by God (such as "you shall not steal") can be shown to be true through natural reason.

9). On like manner all the articles are contained implicitly in certain primary matters of faith, such as God's existence, and His providence over the salvation of man, according to Hebrews 11: "He that comes to God, must believe that He is, and is a rewarder to them that seek Him." For the existence of God includes all that we believe to exist in God eternally, and in these our happiness consists; while belief in His providence includes all those things which God dispenses in time, for man's salvation, and which are the way to that happiness: and in this way, again, some of those articles which follow from these are contained in others: thus faith in the Redemption of mankind includes belief in the Incarnation of Christ, His Passion and so forth.

Accordingly we must conclude that, as regards the substance of the articles of faith, they have not received any increase as time went on: since whatever those who lived later have believed, was contained, albeit implicitly, in the faith of those Fathers who preceded them.[27] But there was an increase in the number of articles believed explicitly, since to those who lived in later times some were known explicitly which were not known explicitly by those who lived before them. Hence the Lord said to Moses (Ex 6:2, 3): "I am the God of Abraham, the God of Isaac, the God of Jacob (Vulg.: 'I am the Lord that appeared to Abraham, to Isaac, and to Jacob') . . . and My name Adonai I did not show them": David also said (Ps 118:100): "I have had understanding above ancients": and the Apostle says (Eph 3:5) that the mystery of Christ, "in other generations was not known, as it is now revealed to His holy apostles and prophets."[28]

---

[27] By "Fathers" Thomas means Old Testament patriarchs such as Moses or Abraham, not patristic authors writing after Christ like Augustine or Jerome.

[28] In contemporary terms, Thomas's discussion here can be linked to what is called the "development of doctrine," though here Thomas is really talking about the unfolding of knowledge about God through Old Testament times culminating in Jesus. Aquinas in some sense had an account of the development of doctrine, for him understood as the unfolding of implicit to a more explicit teaching. *Prima facie,* there is a difficulty reconciling Aquinas's belief that the apostles have the fullest knowledge of the mysteries of faith and that earlier fathers have a more implicit faith than later fathers of the Church. Aquinas acknowledged both truths. The apostles, having intimate association with the Risen Christ as well as special graces allowing them to fulfill

Objection 1. It would seem that the articles of faith[29] have not increased in the course of time, because, as the Apostle says (Heb 11:1), "faith is the substance of things to be hoped for." Now the same things are to be hoped for at all times. Therefore, at all times, the same things are to be believed.

Reply to Objection 1. Among men the same things were always to be hoped for from Christ. But as they did not acquire this hope save through Christ, the further they were removed from Christ in point of time, the further they were from obtaining what they hoped for. Hence the Apostle says (Heb 11:13): "All these died according to faith, not having received the promises, but beholding them afar off." Now the further off a thing is the less distinctly is it seen; wherefore those who were nigh to Christ's advent had a more distinct knowledge of the good things to be hoped for.

---

their vocation, knew Jesus in a privileged way. But reflection on the revelation recorded in Scripture is ongoing. For Aquinas, the first principles of theology are the articles of the creed, and the creed in turn summarizes what is found in Scripture. The divine authorship of Scripture gives the text a profound depth of meaning unlike any other. Since no human being can comprehend God's essence, it follows that a complete understanding of the many true meanings of Scripture is and will always remain elusive. God's incomprehensible essence is one with God's understanding, will, and intention. Just as God himself is beyond perfect human comprehension, so the Word of God is beyond perfect human comprehension. Scripture therefore must always remain mysterious and pregnant with meaning in a way no other text is. St. Thomas says as much explicitly: "[T]he authority of Sacred Scripture is not derogated when it is differently explained, the faith being saved, because the Holy Spirit made it fruitful with a greater truth than any man can discover." *Commentary on the Sentences of Peter Lombard,* book 2, *Dist.* XII, q. 1, art. 2; *Aquinas Selected Works,* ed. and trans. Ralph McInerny (London: Penguin Books, 1998), 92. For more, see Christopher Kaczor, "Thomas Aquinas on the Development of Doctrine," *Theological Studies* 62 (June 2001): 283–302.

29 The previous article asked "Whether the matters of faith should be distinguished into articles." Yes, answers Thomas, since human knowing understands things in a multiplicity. The "articles of faith" are the various statements of basic Christian belief such as "God, the Father Almighty is maker of heaven and earth," "Jesus Christ is true God and true man," and "Jesus suffered, died, and rose."

Objection 2. Further, development has taken place, in sciences devised by man, on account of the lack of knowledge in those who discovered them, as the Philosopher observes (*Metaph.* ii). Now the doctrine of faith was not devised by man, but was delivered to us by God, as stated in Ephesians 2:8: "It is the gift of God." Since, then, there can be no lack of knowledge in God, it seems that knowledge of matters of faith was perfect from the beginning and did not increase as time went on.

Reply to Objection 2. Progress in knowledge occurs in two ways: first, on the part of the teacher, be he one or many, who makes progress in knowledge as time goes on: and this is the kind of progress that takes place in sciences devised by man; second, on the part of the learner; thus the master, who has perfect knowledge of the art, does not deliver it all at once to his disciple from the very outset, for he would not be able to take it all in, but he condescends to the disciple's capacity and instructs him little by little. It is in this way that men made progress in the knowledge of faith as time went on.[30] Hence the Apostle (Gal 3:24) compares the state of the Old Testament to childhood.

ARTICLE 9 ⁓ **Is it suitable for the articles of faith to be embodied in a creed?**[31]

Yes, despite objections to the contrary, The universal Church cannot err, since she is governed by the Holy Spirit, Who is the Spirit of truth: for such was Our Lord's promise to His disciples (Jn 16:13): "When He, the Spirit of truth, is come, He will teach you all truth." Now the creed is published by the authority of the universal Church. Therefore it contains nothing defective.[32]

---

[30] Since the ultimate "teacher" of faith is God himself, and since God already enjoys all possible perfections thereby excluding the possibility of further development on the part of the teacher, development can take place only on the part of the learners, the human family.

[31] For a remarkable exploration of the origins, functions, and importance of creeds, see Jaroslav Pelikan, *Credo: Historical and Theological Guide to Creeds and Confessions of Faith in the Christian Tradition* (New Haven: Yale University Press, 2003).

[32] Thomas firmly believes in Jesus' promise to protect and guide the Church. Even though there is no guarantee of impeccability (inability to sin), the Church is protected by the Holy Spirit from ever proclaiming a falsehood as

I answer that, As the Apostle says (Heb 11:6), "he that comes to God, must believe that He is." Now a man cannot believe, unless the truth be proposed to him that he may believe it. Hence the need for the truth of faith to be collected together, so that it might the more easily be proposed to all, lest anyone might stray from the truth through ignorance of the faith. It is from its being a collection of maxims of faith that the creed or symbol (Greek *symballein*) takes its name.[33]

Objection 1. It would seem that it is unsuitable for the articles of faith to be embodied in a creed, because Holy Writ is the rule of faith, to which no addition or subtraction can lawfully be made, since it is written (Dt 4:2): "You shall not add to the word that I speak to you, neither shall you take away from it." Therefore it was unlawful to make a creed as a rule of faith, after the Holy Writ had once been published.

Reply to Objection 1. The truth of faith is contained in Holy Writ, diffusely, under various modes of expression, and sometimes obscurely, so that, in order to gather the truth of faith from Holy Writ, one needs long study and practice, which are unattainable by all those who require to know the truth of faith, many of whom have no time for study, being busy with other affairs. And so it was necessary to gather together a clear

_____

true and binding on all the faithful. Without this protection, the very mission of Jesus as communicating a saving Gospel truth would have failed because there would be no reliable way for his message of salvation to be communicated through the centuries.

33 To be called "dogmatic" or "doctrinaire" is not a compliment, and yet dogmas and doctrines are essential aspects of Christianity. To be Christian in even the most minimal sense is to be a follower and believer in Christ. But in order to follow and believe in Christ it is necessary to know *who* Jesus is, *what* Jesus did and continues to do, and *how* to live a life in imitation of his. Doctrines and dogmas are nothing other than particular answers to these kinds of questions. To be Christian is to provide some answers, explicit or implicit, to these questions. Indeed, Christian or not, one cannot help but have some kind of "dogmas" and "doctrines" in human life. Indeed, to be human is to live out answers, explicit or implicit, to fundamental questions about whether there is a God, the meaning of the human journey, and the possibility of life after death. For more on the importance of dogmas and doctrines, see Pelikan's *Credo: Historical and Theological Guide to Creeds and Confessions of Faith in the Christian Tradition,* as well as Charles C. Hefling, Jr., *Why Doctrines?* (Cambridge, MA: Cowley Publications, 1984).

summary from the sayings of Holy Writ, to be proposed to the belief of all. This indeed was no addition to Holy Writ, but something taken from it.[34]

Objection 2. Further, according to the Apostle (Eph 4:5) there is but "one faith." Now the creed is a profession of faith. Therefore it is not fitting that there should be more than one creed.

Reply to Objection 2. The same doctrine of faith is taught in all the creeds. Nevertheless, the people need more careful instruction about the truth of faith, when errors arise, lest the faith of simple-minded persons be corrupted by heretics. It was this that gave rise to the necessity of formulating several creeds, which nowise differ from one another, save that on account of the obstinacy of heretics, one contains more explicitly what another contains implicitly.[35]

---

[34] Scripture and Tradition, such as creedal statements, are complementary and not opposed. A similar view is expressed later in Vatican II: "Sacred tradition and Sacred Scripture form one sacred deposit of the word of God, committed to the Church. Holding fast to this deposit the entire holy people united with their shepherds remain always steadfast in the teaching of the Apostles, in the common life, in the breaking of the bread and in prayers (see Acts 2, 42), so that holding to, practicing and professing the heritage of the faith, it becomes on the part of the bishops and faithful a single common effort. But the task of authentically interpreting the word of God, whether written or handed on, has been entrusted exclusively to the living teaching office of the Church, whose authority is exercised in the name of Jesus Christ. This teaching office is not above the word of God, but serves it, teaching only what has been handed on, listening to it devoutly, guarding it scrupulously and explaining it faithfully in accord with a divine commission and with the help of the Holy Spirit, it draws from this one deposit of faith everything which it presents for belief as divinely revealed. It is clear, therefore, that sacred tradition, Sacred Scripture and the teaching authority of the Church, in accord with God's most wise design, are so linked and joined together that one cannot stand without the others, and that all together and each in its own way under the action of the one Holy Spirit contribute effectively to the salvation of souls." Vatican II, *Dei Verbum,* 10.

[35] Here again Thomas alludes to the development of doctrine. Christ is the fullness of revelation, and public revelation ends with the death of the last apostle. However, the Church's understanding of the full implications of revelation can and does develop guided by the Holy Spirit. The classic work on the development of doctrine is John Henry Cardinal Newman's *Essay on the Development of Christian Doctrine* (Notre Dame: University of Notre Dame Press, 1989).

Objection 3. Further, the confession of faith, which is contained in the creed, concerns all the faithful. Now the faithful are not all competent to believe in God, but only those who have living faith. Therefore it is unfitting for the creed of faith to be expressed in the words: "I believe in one God."

Reply to Objection 3. The confession of faith is drawn up in a creed in the person, as it were, of the whole Church, which is united together by faith. Now the faith of the Church is living faith,[36] since such is the faith to be found in all those who are of the Church not only outwardly but also by merit. Hence the confession of faith is expressed in a creed, in a manner that is in keeping with living faith, so that even if some of the faithful lack living faith, they should endeavor to acquire it.

Objection 4. Further, the descent into hell is one of the articles of faith, as stated above (a. 8). But the descent into hell is not mentioned in the creed of the Fathers.[37] Therefore the latter is expressed inadequately.

---

[36] "Living faith" is a faith animated by charity, friendship with God. "Dead faith" lacks charity, and in this sense Thomas believes that even the demons have faith (*ST* II–II, q. 5, a. 2).

[37] Thomas refers here to the Nicene Creed, said each Sunday at Catholic Mass and accepted also by the Eastern Orthodox and most Protestants. This creed is usually attributed to the bishops (Fathers) assembled at the Council of Constantinople (381). The Nicene Creed is as follows: "I believe in one God, the Father, Almighty, maker of heaven and earth, of all that is, seen and unseen. I believe in one Lord, Jesus Christ, the only Son of God, eternally begotten of the Father, God from God, Light from Light, true God from true God, begotten, not made, of one being with the Father. Through him all things were made. For us men and for our salvation, he came down from heaven: by the power of the Holy Spirit he became incarnate of the Virgin Mary, and became man. For our sake he was crucified under Pontius Pilate; he suffered death and was buried. On the third day he rose again in accordance with the Scriptures; he ascended into heaven and is seated at the right hand of the Father. He will come again in glory to judge the living and the dead, and his kingdom will have no end. I believe in the Holy Spirit, the Lord, the giver of life, who proceeds from the Father (and the Son). With the Father and the Son he is worshipped and glorified. He has spoken through the prophets. I believe in one, holy, catholic, and apostolic Church. I acknowledge one baptism for the forgiveness of sins. I look for the resurrection of the dead, and the life of the world to come. Amen."

Reply to Objection 4. No error about the descent into hell had arisen among heretics, so that there was no need to be more explicit on that point. For this reason it is not repeated in the creed of the Fathers, but is supposed as already settled in the creed of the Apostles. For a subsequent creed does not cancel a preceding one; rather does it expound it, as stated above (ad 2).

Objection 5. Further, Augustine (*Tract. xxix in Joan.*) expounding the passage, "You believe in God, believe also in Me" (Jn 14:1), says: "We believe Peter or Paul, but we speak only of believing 'in' God." Since then the Catholic Church is merely a created being, it seems unfitting to say: "In the One, Holy, Catholic and Apostolic Church."

Reply to Objection 5. If we say: " 'In' the holy Catholic Church," this must be taken as verified insofar as our faith is directed to the Holy Spirit, Who sanctifies the Church; so that the sense is, "I believe in the Holy Spirit sanctifying the Church." But it is better and more in keeping with the common use, to omit the 'in,' and say simply, "the holy Catholic Church," as Pope Leo (Rufinus, *Comm. in Sym. Apost.*) observes.

ARTICLE 10 ⁓ Does it belong to the pope to draw up a creed of faith?

Yes, despite objections to the contrary, The publication of the Creed was made by a general council. Now such a council cannot be convoked otherwise than by the authority of the pope, as stated in the Decretals[38] (*Dist.* xvii, Can. 4, 5). Therefore it belongs to the authority of the Pope to draw up a creed.[39]

---

[38] The Decretals, properly called the Concord of Discordant Canons, was composed by Gratian and completed around 1141, more than a century before Thomas wrote the *Summa*. The Decretals systematized various Church decrees, laws, and pronouncements, and was a handy and authoritative reference in the Middle Ages.

[39] Christ came to reconcile us to the Father and to speak the truth to us in love. He did not leave us orphans but gave us a living Spirit, a Spirit of unity. Church disunity then is a sign of a lack of the Spirit, often traceable to the personal failures of Church members, usually on both sides of the dispute. But such disunity, and, sadly often, such lack of charity, cannot be compatible

I answer that, As stated in Objection 1, a new edition of the creed becomes necessary in order to set aside the errors that may arise. Consequently to publish a new edition of the creed belongs to that authority which is empowered to decide matters of faith finally, so that they may be held by all with unshaken faith. Now this belongs to the authority of the Sovereign Pontiff, "to whom the more important and more difficult questions that arise in the Church are referred," as stated in the Decretals (*Dist.* xvii, Can. 5). Hence our Lord said to Peter whom he made Sovereign Pontiff (Lk 22:32): "I have prayed for you," Peter, "that your faith fail not, and thou, being once converted, confirm your brethren." The reason of this is that there should be but one faith of the whole Church, according to 1 Corinthians 1:10: "That you all speak the same thing, and that there be no schisms among you": and this could not be secured unless any question of faith that may arise be decided by him who presides over the whole Church, so that the whole Church may hold firmly to his decision. Consequently it belongs to the sole authority of the Sovereign Pontiff to publish a new

---

with the plan of the one true God who is the Father of one family, with one faith and one baptism. The Holy Father, the Bishop of Rome, speaks with a living voice, responding to the signs of the times, and interpreting human experience, the Scripture, Church councils, and his forefathers on the Petrine chair in light of present questions, needs, and concerns. Christ's vicar on earth, sinful and ignorant though he may be in some respects, safeguards the unity of the Church, and guided by the Holy Spirit, has as a mission the continuing fathering of the Church here on earth. Since neither Scripture nor Church councils can interpret themselves, some living, unified, singular representative of Christ is needed to ensure that his message is transmitted. In this, every Vicar of Christ is like Peter before him who, although he denied the Lord three times, was still called to confirm his brethren and feed Christ's sheep. As T. C. O'Brien notes, St. Thomas was a strong defender of the pope's primacy: "He describes the Pope as the 'vicar of Christ' (II–II, q. 39, a. 1), the 'visible head of the Church' (III, q. 8, a. 7), 'who has the care of the whole Church (II–II, q. 89, a. 9 ad 3, see Quodlibetal Question IV, 13). The clearest statement of infallibility, grounded on the providential promise of the Spirit (Jn 10:26) is in Quodlibetal Question IX, 16)." T. C. O'Brien in St. Thomas Aquinas, *Summa theologiae,* vol. 31 (New York: Blackfriars, 1966), 55. For more on this topic, see Y. Congar, "St. Thomas and the Infallibility of the Papal Magisterium," *The Thomist* 38 (1974): 81–105.

edition of the creed, as do all other matters which concern the whole Church, such as to convoke a general council and so forth.[40]

Objection 1. It would seem that it does not belong to the Sovereign Pontiff to draw up a creed of faith. For a new edition of the creed becomes necessary in order to explain the articles of faith, as stated above (a. 9). Now, in the Old Testament, the articles of faith were more and more explained as time went on, by reason of the truth of faith becoming clearer through greater nearness to Christ, as stated above (a. 7). Since, then, this reason ceased with the advent of the New Law, there is no need for the articles of faith to be more and more explicit. Therefore it does not seem to belong to the authority of the Sovereign Pontiff to draw up a new edition of the creed.

---

[40] Again, the Second Vatican Council recognizes the unique responsibility of the pope in securing Christian unity and as being Christ's vicar on earth: "[T]he college or body of bishops has no authority unless it is understood together with the Roman Pontiff, the successor of Peter as its head. The pope's power of primacy over all, both pastors and faithful, remains whole and intact. In virtue of his office, that is as Vicar of Christ and pastor of the whole Church, the Roman Pontiff has full, supreme and universal power over the Church. And he is always free to exercise this power. The order of bishops, which succeeds to the college of apostles and gives this apostolic body continued existence, is also the subject of supreme and full power over the universal Church, provided we understand this body together with its head the Roman Pontiff and never without this head. This power can be exercised only with the consent of the Roman Pontiff. Our Lord placed Simon alone as the rock and the bearer of the keys of the Church, and made him shepherd of the whole flock; it is evident, however, that the power of binding and loosing, which was given to Peter, was granted also to the college of apostles, joined with their head. This college, insofar as it is composed of many, expresses the variety and universality of the People of God, but insofar as it is assembled under one head, it expresses the unity of the flock of Christ. In it, the bishops, faithfully recognizing the primacy and preeminence of their head, exercise their own authority for the good of their own faithful, and indeed of the whole Church, the Holy Spirit supporting its organic structure and harmony with moderation. The supreme power in the universal Church, which this college enjoys, is exercised in a solemn way in an ecumenical council. A council is never ecumenical unless it is confirmed or at least accepted as such by the successor of Peter; and it is prerogative of the Roman Pontiff to convoke these councils, to preside over them and to confirm them." *Lumen Gentium,* 22, Second Vatican Council.

Reply to Objection 1. The truth of faith is sufficiently explicit in the teaching of Christ and the apostles. But since, according to 2 Peter 3:16, some men are so evil-minded as to pervert the apostolic teaching and other doctrines and Scriptures to their own destruction, it was necessary as time went on to express the faith more explicitly against the errors which arose.

Objection 2. Further, no man has the power to do what is forbidden under pain of anathema by the universal Church. Now it was forbidden under pain of anathema by the universal Church, to make a new edition of the creed. For it is stated in the acts of the first council of Ephesus (P. ii, Act. 6) that "after the creed of the Nicene council had been read through, the holy synod decreed that it was unlawful to utter, write or draw up any other creed, than that which was defined by the Fathers assembled at Nicaea together with the Holy Spirit," and this under pain of anathema. The same was repeated in the acts of the council of Chalcedon (P. ii, Act. 5). Therefore it seems that the Sovereign Pontiff has no authority to publish a new edition of the creed.

Reply to Objection 2. This prohibition and sentence of the council was intended for private individuals, who have no business to decide matters of faith: for this decision of the general council did not take away from a subsequent council the power of drawing up a new edition of the creed, containing not indeed a new faith, but the same faith with greater explicitness. For every council has taken into account that a subsequent council would expound matters more fully than the preceding council, if this became necessary through some heresy arising. Consequently this belongs to the Sovereign Pontiff, by whose authority the council is convoked, and its decision confirmed.

Objection 3. Further, Athanasius was not the Sovereign Pontiff, but patriarch of Alexandria, and yet he published a creed which is sung in the Church. Therefore it does not seem to belong to the Sovereign Pontiff any more than to other bishops, to publish a new edition of the creed.

Reply to Objection 3. Athanasius drew up a declaration of faith,[41] not under the form of a creed, but rather by way of an exposition of

---

[41] The "Athanasian creed" was probably written after the time of the Bishop of Alexandria, St. Athanasius (296–373), yet expresses the beliefs he defended: "Whosoever will be saved, before all things it is necessary that he hold the Catholic Faith. Which Faith except everyone do keep whole and undefiled, without doubt he shall perish everlastingly. And the Catholic Faith is this, that we worship one God in Trinity and Trinity in Unity. Neither confounding the Persons, nor dividing the Substance. For there is one Person of the Father, another of the Son, and another of the Holy Spirit. But the Godhead of the Father, of the Son and of the Holy Spirit is all One, the Glory Equal, the Majesty Co-Eternal. Such as the Father is, such is the Son, and such is the Holy Spirit. The Father Uncreated, the Son Uncreated, and the Holy Spirit Uncreated. The Father Incomprehensible, the Son Incomprehensible, and the Holy Spirit Incomprehensible. The Father Eternal, the Son Eternal, and the Holy Spirit Eternal, and yet they are not Three Eternals but One Eternal. As also there are not Three Uncreated, nor Three Incomprehensibles, but One Uncreated, and One Incomprehensible. So likewise the Father is Almighty, the Son Almighty, and the Holy Spirit Almighty. And yet they are not Three Almighties but One Almighty.

"So the Father is God, the Son is God, and the Holy Spirit is God. And yet they are not Three Gods, but One God. So likewise the Father is Lord, the Son Lord, and the Holy Spirit Lord. And yet not Three Lords but One Lord. For, as we are compelled by the Christian verity to acknowledge every Person by Himself to be God and Lord, so are we forbidden by the Catholic Religion to say, there be Three Gods or Three Lords. The Father is made of none, neither created, nor begotten. The Son is of the Father alone; not made, nor created, but begotten. The Holy Spirit is of the Father, and of the Son, neither made, nor created, nor begotten, but proceeding.

"So there is One Father, not Three Fathers; one Son, not Three Sons; One Holy Spirit, not Three Holy Spirits. And in this Trinity none is afore or after Other, None is greater or less than Another, but the whole Three Persons are Co-Eternal together, and Co-Equal. So that in all things, as is aforesaid, the Unity in Trinity, and the Trinity in Unity is to be worshipped. He therefore that will be saved, must thus think of the Trinity.

"Furthermore, it is necessary to everlasting Salvation, that he also believe rightly the Incarnation of our Lord Jesus Christ. For the right Faith is, that we believe and confess, that our Lord Jesus Christ, the Son of God, is God and Man.

"God, of the substance of the Father, begotten before the worlds; and Man, of the substance of His mother, born into the world. Perfect God and Perfect Man, of a reasonable Soul and human Flesh subsisting. Equal to the Father as touching His Godhead, and inferior to the Father as touching His Manhood. Who, although He be God and Man, yet He is not two, but One

doctrine, as appears from his way of speaking. But since it contained briefly the whole truth of faith, it was accepted by the authority of the Sovereign Pontiff,[42] so as to be considered as a rule of faith.

Christ. One, not by conversion of the Godhead into Flesh, but by taking of the Manhood into God. One altogether, not by confusion of substance, but by Unity of Person. For as the reasonable soul and flesh is one Man, so God and Man is one Christ. Who suffered for our salvation, descended into Hell, rose again the third day from the dead. He ascended into Heaven, He sitteth on the right hand of the Father, God Almighty, from whence he shall come to judge the quick and the dead. At whose coming all men shall rise again with their bodies, and shall give account for their own works. And they that have done good shall go into life everlasting, and they that have done evil into everlasting fire. This is the Catholic Faith, which except a man believe faithfully and firmly, he cannot be saved."

42 Thomas affirms elsewhere (II–II, q. 100, a. 1) the peccability of popes, that is to say, that they can sin like anyone else; indeed, other things being equal, their sin is greater because of their office. Nevertheless, even the most sinful pope is still protected by the Holy Spirit from proclaiming something true that is false as a belief to be held by all Christians. Infallibility (protection from error in teaching) is not the same thing as impeccability (protection from personal sin).

FAITH ITSELF

QUESTION 2

THE ACT OF FAITH

ARTICLE 2 ⟶ **Is the act of faith suitably distinguished as believing God (*credere Deo*), believing in a God (*credere Deum*), and believing in God (*credere in Deum*)?**

Yes, despite objections to the contrary, It is the authority of Augustine who makes this distinction (*De Verb. Dom.*, Serm. lxi—*Tract. xxix in Joan.*).[1]

I answer that, The act of any power or habit depends on the relation of that power or habit to its object. Now the object of faith can be considered in three ways. For, since "to believe" is an act of the intellect, insofar as the will moves it to assent, as stated above (a. 1, ad 3), the object of faith can be considered either on the part of the intellect, or on the part of the will that moves the intellect.

If it be considered on the part of the intellect, then two things can be observed in the object of faith, as stated above (q. 1, a. 1). One of these is the material object of faith, and in this way an act of faith is

---

[1] After Sacred Scripture, St. Augustine of Hippo (d. 430) is probably the most important authority for Thomas. The author of numerous famous works including the *Confessions*, the *City of God, On Christian Doctrine*, and commentaries on various books of the Bible, Augustine's influence throughout the Middle Ages can hardly be exaggerated. For an introduction to Augustine's beliefs and life, read Peter Brown, *Augustine of Hippo: A Biography* (Berkeley: University of California Press, 2000). Or, better still, read Augustine's own autobiography—the *Confessions*.

31

"to believe in a God *(credere Deum),*"[2] because, as stated above (q. 1, a. 1) nothing is proposed to our belief, except inasmuch as it is referred to God. The other is the formal aspect of the object, for it is the medium on account of which we assent to such and such a point of faith, and thus an act of faith is "to believe God *(credere Deo),*"[3] since, as stated above (q. 1, a. 1) the formal object of faith is the First Truth, to Which man gives his adhesion, so as to assent for its sake to whatever he believes.

Thirdly, if the object of faith be considered insofar as the intellect is moved by the will, an act of faith is "to believe in God." For the First Truth is referred to the will, through having the aspect of an end.[4]

---

[2] The threefold distinction drawn from Augustine is (1) believing in a God or believing about God *(credere Deum)*, (2) believing God *(credere Deo)*, and (3) believing in God *(credere in Deum)*. Believing in a God or believing about God *(credere Deum)* (1) refers to the affirmation of propositions concerning God, for example that there is a God or that God has this characteristic or that property. *Credere Deum* is to believe that there is some Supreme Being. *Credere Deum* is the material object of faith.

[3] Believing God *(credere Deo)* (2) designates a trust that God is reliable, just as a mother might say to a daughter scared of being lost: "Believe in me; trust my experience. Let's head this way." Obviously, the mother isn't imploring the daughter to affirm that the mother exists in the world, rather she is urging her daughter to trust her. Similarly, some people might believe that God exists, but not really trust Him or rely on Him. They believe that there is a God *(credere Deum)*, but they do not place their trust in God *(credere Deo)*. *Credere Deo* is the formal object of faith.

[4] The final sense of belief, (3) believing in God, believing unto God, or believing for the sake of God *(credere in Deum)*, refers to believing motivated by an act of the will seeking to adhere to God. The creed begins "credo in Deum" (I believe in God) indicating this third kind of belief. So the creed is not merely affirming that there is a God *(credere Deum)* and not merely affirming a trust in God *(credere Deo)* but a seeking to become more united to God. This third sense of belief is the deepest because it presupposes the first sense of belief (that there is a God) and the second sense of belief (trusting in this God) and moves to a deeper sense in which not only the intellect (first two senses of belief), but also the will of the acting person is involved. It is a more complete sense of belief than the other two and builds upon them. As Augustine notes, in the passage Thomas is citing in the response, the devils believe that there is a God (1), but they do not believe in God (3) in the sense of adhering their wills to God. To believe in God (3) is for Augustine to "love him, by believing to esteem highly, by believing to go into Him and to be incorporated in His members" (Augustine's *Sermons on John*, tractate xxix). The contrast between

Objection 1. It would seem that the act of faith is unsuitably distinguished as believing God, believing in a God, and believing in God. For one habit has but one act. Now faith is one habit since it is one virtue. Therefore it is unreasonable to say that there are three acts of faith.

Reply to Objection 1. These three do not denote different acts of faith, but one and the same act having different relations to the object of faith.

Objection 3. Further, that which can be said of unbelievers, cannot be called an act of faith. Now unbelievers can be said to believe in a God. Therefore it should not be reckoned an act of faith.

Reply to Objection 3. Unbelievers cannot be said "to believe in a God" as we understand it in relation to the act of faith. For they do not believe that God exists under the conditions that faith determines; hence they do not truly believe in a God, since, as the Philosopher observes (*Metaph.* ix, text. 22) "to know simple things defectively is not to know them at all."

Objection 4. Further, movement towards the end belongs to the will, whose object is the good and the end. Now to believe is an act, not of the will, but of the intellect. Therefore "to believe in God," which implies movement towards an end, should not be reckoned as a species of that act.

Reply to Objection 4. As stated above (I–II, q. 9, a. 1) the will moves the intellect and the other powers of the soul to the end: and in this respect an act of faith is "to believe in God."

Article 3 ⤙ **Is it necessary for salvation to believe anything beyond natural reason?**[5]

Yes, despite objections to the contrary, It is written (Heb 11:6): "Without faith it is impossible to please God."

---

believing (2) and believing (3) is explored further in question 2, article 3: "Whether charity is the form of faith?" Believing (2) amounts to unformed, dead, unsaving faith. Believing (3) is formed, living, saving faith.

[5] In this article, Thomas takes up and critiques a "rationalist" position that one should only believe that which can be proven through unaided reason. For

I answer that, Wherever one nature is subordinate to another, we find that two things concur towards the perfection of the lower nature, one of which is in respect of that nature's proper movement, while the other is in respect of the movement of the higher nature. Thus water by its proper movement moves towards the center (of the earth), while according to the movement of the moon, it moves around the center by ebb and flow. In like manner the planets have their proper movements from west to east, while in accordance with the movement of the first heaven, they have a movement from east to west. Now the created rational nature alone is immediately subordinate to God, since other creatures do not attain to the universal, but only to something particular, while they partake of the Divine goodness either in "being" only, as inanimate things, or also in "living," and in "knowing singulars," as plants and animals; whereas the rational nature, in as much as it apprehends the universal notion of good and being, is immediately related to the universal principle of being.[6]

---

example, since the Trinity cannot be shown to exist by philosophical argumentation, the rationalists' position is that one ought not believe in it. Rationalism misconstrues the power of the human intellect in relation to divine things, supposing that autonomous human reason is the measure of all things. To understand something the mind must be equal to it, and only God's mind is equal to his Infinite Being. Therefore, only God can fully understand God. We have trouble understanding fully even lesser things, so it is no surprise that we do not fully understand greater things like God. Since even our understanding of human persons is incomplete without the person's "self-revelation," it is reasonable to believe that our understanding of God is incomplete and in need of further aid from God himself. A key difficulty with rationalism would seem to be that there is no sound rational argument that we should *only* accept that which can be shown to be true as the result of apodictic, deductive demonstrations. After all, the first principle of reasoning itself—a thing cannot be and not be at the same time and in the same respect—cannot be shown to be true as a result of deductive demonstrations. Hence, rationalism appears to be self-referentially incoherent, self-contradictory.

6 Human beings, in other words, can know the good as such or the true as such, rather than simply knowing various instances of good or true things. Since God is perfect goodness and truth, and human beings are ordered to the good and the true by their will and reason, human beings are ordered to God and can only be ultimately fulfilled by God.

Consequently the perfection of the rational creature consists not only in what belongs to it in respect of its nature, but also in that which it acquires through a supernatural participation of Divine goodness.[7] Hence it was said above (I–II, q. 3, a. 8) that man's ultimate happiness consists in a supernatural vision of God: to which vision man cannot attain unless he be taught by God, according to John 6:45: "Every one that has heard of the Father and has learned comes to Me."[8] Now man acquires a share of this learning, not indeed all at once, but by little and little, according to the mode of his nature: and every one who learns thus must needs believe, in order that he may acquire science in a perfect degree; thus also the Philosopher remarks (*De Soph. Elench.* i, 2) that "it behooves a learner to believe."

Hence in order that a man arrive at the perfect vision of heavenly happiness, he must first of all believe God, as a disciple believes the master who is teaching him.[9]

---

[7] God reveals truths that we could not come to know through our own rational investigation for several reasons. One point of teaching Christian wisdom is to know what it is that we truly desire so that we can have a still greater desire. If the object of our love is worthy, the more we get to know the object of our love, the greater our love becomes. The revelation of "mysteries of faith" transcending human reason also curbs the presumption of those who would be proud of their superior knowledge of the highest things. Revelation places peasant and professor on the same level as both being indebted to God for their knowledge of God. This greater knowledge leads to greater human perfection and joy, for man desires to know, and to know the highest thing is to have one's intellect perfected. As Thomas says elsewhere: "[E]ven the most imperfect knowledge about the most noble realities brings the greatest perfection to the soul." *Summa contra Gentiles,* book one, chapter five, section 5.

[8] If the goal of human life is like a target, and this target is union with God, we must have some knowledge of the target in order to reach it. Hence, our salvation cannot take place without faith in God; without some knowledge of our target we cannot order ourselves to the goal.

[9] In order to find perfect happiness, each person must have God's help in terms of both reason and will. Reason needs the help provided by faith in order to know more perfectly who God is, which escapes the power of even the most powerful human intellect unaided. A philosopher like Aristotle could know that there is a God but from the created order could never know that God is a communion of persons, Father, Son, and Holy Spirit, who love each human being.

Objection 1. It would seem unnecessary for salvation to believe any-thing above the natural reason. For the salvation and perfection of a thing seem to be sufficiently insured by its natural endowments. Now matters of faith surpass man's natural reason, since they are things unseen, as stated above (q. 1, a. 4). Therefore to believe seems unnec-essary for salvation.

Reply to Objection 1. Since man's nature is dependent on a higher nature, natural knowledge does not suffice for its perfection, and some supernatural knowledge is necessary, as stated above.

Objection 2. Further, it is dangerous for man to assent to matters wherein he cannot judge whether that which is proposed to him be true or false, according to Job 12:11: "Doth not the ear discern words?" Now a man cannot form a judgment of this kind in matters of faith, since he cannot trace them back to first principles, by which all our judgments are guided. Therefore it is dangerous to believe in such matters. Therefore to believe is not necessary for salvation.

Reply to Objection 2. Just as man assents to first principles, by the natural light of his intellect, so does a virtuous man, by the habit of virtue, judge aright of things concerning that virtue; and in this way, by the light of faith which God bestows on him, a man assents to matters of faith and not to those which are against faith. Conse-quently "there is no" danger or "condemnation to them that are in Christ Jesus," (Rom 8:1) and whom He has enlightened by faith.

Objection 3. Further, man's salvation rests on God, according to Psalm 36:39: "But the salvation of the just is from the Lord." Now "the invisible things" of God "are clearly seen, being understood by the things that are made; His eternal power also and Divinity," according to Romans 1:20: and those things which are clearly seen by the understanding are not an object of belief. Therefore it is not nec-essary for man's salvation that he should believe certain things.

Reply to Objection 3. In many respects faith perceives the invisible things of God in a higher way than natural reason does in proceeding to God from His creatures. Hence it is written (Sir 3:25): "Many things are shown to you above the understandings of man."[10]

ARTICLE 4 ~~ Is it necessary to believe those things which can be proved by natural reason?

Yes, despite objections to the contrary, It is necessary to believe that God is one and incorporeal: which things philosophers prove by natural reason.

I answer that, It is necessary for man to accept by faith not only things which are above reason, but also those which can be known by reason: and this for three motives. First, in order that man may arrive more quickly at the knowledge of Divine truth, because the science to whose province it belongs to prove the existence of God is the last of all to offer itself to human research, since it presupposes many other sciences: so that it would not by until late in life that man would arrive at the knowledge of God. The second reason is, in order that the knowledge of God may be more general. For many are unable to make progress in the study of science, either through dullness of mind, or through having a number of occupations and temporal needs, or even through laziness in learning, all of whom would be altogether deprived of the knowledge of God, unless Divine things were brought to their knowledge under the guise of faith. The third reason is for the sake of certitude.[11] For human reason is very deficient in things concerning

---

[10] Natural reason can only come to understand God as a cause of creation; natural reason cannot come to understand God as Father, Son, and Holy Spirit. Since God is not only Creator, but also Redeemer and Sanctifier, faith teaches us more fully about God than does natural reason.

[11] The gift of faith, unlike opinion or conjecture, includes certitude about what is believed. As Joseph Pieper notes: "Belief in the proper sense really means unqualified assent and unconditional acceptance of the truth of something. . . . To say, 'I believe you but I am not quite certain', is either to use the word believe' in an improper sense or to be talking nonsense." *Faith, Hope, and Love* (San Francisco: Ignatius Press, 1986), 28. At the same time, the certainty of faith does not exclude difficulties. As John Henry Cardinal Newman once said, "Ten thousand difficulties do not make one doubt." John Henry Newman, *Apologia pro vita sua* (London: Longman, 1878), 239. Indeed, believing does not end the quest for knowledge and the asking of questions, but rather prompts further desire for knowledge and deeper questioning.

God. A sign of this is that philosophers in their researches, by natural investigation, into human affairs, have fallen into many errors, and have disagreed among themselves. And consequently, in order that men might have knowledge of God, free of doubt and uncertainty, it was necessary for Divine matters to be delivered to them by way of faith, being told to them, as it were, by God Himself Who cannot lie.[12]

Objection 1. It would seem unnecessary to believe those things which can be proved by natural reason. For nothing is superfluous in God's works, much less even than in the works of nature. Now it is superfluous to employ other means, where one already suffices. Therefore it would be superfluous to receive by faith things that can be known by natural reason.

Reply to Objection 1. The researches of natural reason do not suffice mankind for the knowledge of Divine matters, even of those that can be proved by reason: and so it is not superfluous if these others be believed.

Objection 2. Further, those things must be believed, which are the object of faith. Now science and faith are not about the same object, as stated above (q. 1, aa 4, 5). Since therefore all things that can be known by natural reason are an object of science, it seems that there is no need to believe what can be proved by natural reason.

Reply to Objection 2. Science and faith cannot be in the same subject and about the same object: but what is an object of science for one can be an object of faith for another, as stated above (q. 1, a. 5).[13]

---

[12] Why would God reveal truths that could in principle be known by a philosopher? Aquinas rightly notes that proofs for God's existence are difficult to provide because they presuppose knowledge of many other things that take a great deal of time and ability to know, including Aristotelian physics, metaphysics, and logic. God's revelation of truths that can in principle be known with unaided reason (truths called "preambles of faith" as opposed to "mysteries of faith" like the Trinity, which reason cannot offer arguments to prove) shows God's great mercy. Belief in God is not simply for the super intelligent and the super rich who have the ability and the time for study. Instead, God gives the gift of belief to rich and poor, educated and uneducated alike.

[13] To have science is to have knowledge through demonstration, and therefore by means of one's own power. To have faith is to have knowledge through belief in revelation, and therefore by means of the gift of grace.

Objection 3. Further, all things knowable scientifically[14] would seem to come under one head: so that if some of them are proposed to man as objects of faith, in like manner the others should also be believed. But this is not true. Therefore it is not necessary to believe those things which can be proved by natural reason.

Reply to Objection 3. Although all things that can be known by science are of one common scientific aspect, they do not all alike lead man to beatitude: hence they are not all equally proposed to our belief.

ARTICLE 7 — **Is it necessary for the salvation of all that they should believe explicitly in the mystery of Christ?**[15]

Yes, despite objections to the contrary, Augustine says (*De Corr. et Gratia* vii; *Ep.* cxc): "Our faith is sound if we believe that no man, old or young, is delivered from the contagion of death and the bonds of sin, except by the one Mediator of God and men, Jesus Christ."[16]

---

[14] "Science," as the Dominican Fathers' translation reminds us of the medieval meaning of the word, "is certain knowledge of a demonstrated conclusion through its demonstration." To have science is not only to know *that* something is the case, but to know *why* it is the case.

[15] This query is just as important today as 700 years ago when Thomas examined it. Many in the world remain pre-Christian (say, uneducated peasants in Afghanistan who have never heard the name Jesus), and many have become post-Christian in secular Western society. Are those who do not explicitly believe in Christ, especially those who have never even heard of Christ through no fault of their own, deprived of salvation? If believing in Christ is not needed for salvation, then what is the point of evangelization? Thomas begins to give us resources for tackling these questions in this article.

[16] The Second Vatican Council expressed Augustine's insight as follows: "[A]ll men and women who are saved share, though differently, in the same mystery of salvation in Jesus Christ through his Spirit." *Nostra Aetate,* 2. See also, the Congregation for the Doctrine of the Faith's *Dominus Iesus,* 2000. However, it does not follow from this that those who do not call themselves "Christian" will not be saved. The *Catechism of the Catholic Church* notes: " 'Since Christ died for all, and since all men are in fact called to one and the same destiny, which is divine, we must hold that the Holy Spirit offers to all the possibility of being made partakers, in a way known to God, of the Paschal mystery.' (Vatican Council II, *GS* 22 # 5; cf. *LG* 16; AG 7) Every man who is ignorant of the Gospel of Christ and of his Church, but seeks the truth and does the will of God in accordance with his understanding of

I answer that, As stated above (q. 2, a. 5; q. 1, a. 8), the object of faith includes, properly and directly, that thing through which man obtains beatitude. Now the mystery of Christ's Incarnation and Passion is the way by which men obtain beatitude; for it is written (Acts 4:12): "There is no other name under heaven given to men, whereby we must be saved." Therefore belief of some kind in the mystery of Christ's Incarnation was necessary at all times and for all persons, but this belief differed according to differences of times and persons. The reason of this is that before the state of sin,[17] man believed explicitly in Christ's Incarnation, insofar as it was intended for the consummation of glory, but not as it was intended to deliver man from sin by the Passion and Resurrection, since man had no foreknowledge of his future sin. He does, however, seem to have had foreknowledge of the Incarnation of Christ, from the fact that he said (Gen 2:24): "Wherefore a man shall leave father and mother, and shall cleave to his wife," of which the Apostle says (Eph 5:32) that "this is a great sacrament . . . in Christ and the Church," and it is implausible that the first man was ignorant about this sacrament.

But after sin, man believed explicitly in Christ, not only as to the Incarnation, but also as to the Passion and Resurrection, whereby the human race is delivered from sin and death: otherwise they would not, have foreshadowed Christ's Passion by certain sacrifices both before and after the Law, the meaning of which sacrifices was known by the learned explicitly, while the simple folk, under the veil of those sacrifices, believed them to be ordained by God in reference to Christ's coming, and thus their knowledge was covered with a veil, so to speak. And, as stated above (q. 1, a. 7), the nearer they were to Christ, the more distinct was their knowledge of Christ's mysteries.

After grace had been revealed, both learned and simple folk are bound to explicit faith in the mysteries of Christ, chiefly as regards

_____

it, can be saved. It may be supposed that such persons would have *desired Baptism explicitly* if they had known its necessity." *CCC* 1260. Although Thomas seems to teach in opposition to this, elsewhere Aquinas also notes that only belief in God and God's providence is necessary for salvation (II–II, q. 1, a. 7; see also, reply to objection 3 of this article).

[17] Before the fall, Adam had explicit knowledge of Christ, according to Thomas.

those which are observed throughout the Church, and publicly proclaimed, such as the articles which refer to the Incarnation, of which we have spoken above (q. 1, a. 8). As to other minute points in reference to the articles of the Incarnation, men have been bound to believe them more or less explicitly according to each one's state and office.[18]

Objection 1. It would seem that it is not necessary for the salvation of all that they should believe explicitly in the mystery of Christ. For man is not bound to believe explicitly what the angels are ignorant about: since the unfolding of faith is the result of Divine revelation, which reaches man by means of the angels, as stated above (q. 6; I, q. 111, a. 1). Now even the angels were in ignorance of the mystery of the Incarnation: hence, according to the commentary of Dionysius (*Coel. Hier.* vii), it is they who ask (Ps 23:8): "Who is this king of glory?" and (Is 63:1): "Who is this that comes from Edom?"[19] Therefore men were not bound to believe explicitly in the mystery of Christ's Incarnation.

Reply to Objection 1. The mystery of the Kingdom of God was not entirely hidden from the angels, as Augustine observes (*Gen. ad lit.* v, 19), yet certain aspects thereof were better known to them when Christ revealed them to them.

Objection 2. Further, it is evident that John the Baptist was one of the teachers, and most nigh to Christ, Who said of him (Mt 11:11) that "there has not risen among them that are born of women, a greater than" he. Now John the Baptist does not appear to have known the mystery of Christ explicitly, since he asked Christ (Mt 11:3): "Are You He who is to come, or should we look for another?" Therefore even the teachers were not bound to explicit faith in Christ.

---

[18] Salvation, in other words, does not depend on a test in theology. Not all professors of theology are saints; and not all saints have a great knowledge of academic theology. However, since saints (and saints-in-training) love God, they naturally desire to know as much as they can about their Beloved and so learn about matters of faith to the degree their duties and ability allow.

[19] Esau, the twin brother of Jacob, was another name for Edom. The land given to Esau became known as the "country of Edom."

Reply to Objection 2. It was not through ignorance that John the Baptist inquired of Christ's advent in the flesh, since he had clearly professed his belief therein, saying: "I saw, and I gave testimony, that this is the Son of God" (Jn 1:34). Hence he did not say: "Are You He who has come?" but "Are You He who is to come?" thus saying about the future, not about the past. Likewise it is not to be believed that he was ignorant of Christ's future Passion, for he had already said (Jn 1:39): "Behold the Lamb of God, behold Him who takes away the sins (Vulg.: 'sin') of the world," thus foretelling His future immolation, and since other prophets had foretold it, as may be seen especially in Isaiah 53.[20] We may therefore say with Gregory (*Hom. xxvi in Evang.*) that he asked this question, being in ignorance as to whether Christ would descend into hell in His own Person. But he did not ignore the fact that the power of Christ's Passion would be extended to those who were detained in Limbo,[21] according to Zechariah 9:11: "You also, by

---

[20] Isaiah 53: 3–5: "He was despised and rejected by men, a man of sorrows, and familiar with suffering. Like one from whom men hide their faces, he was despised, and we esteemed him not. Surely he took up our infirmities and carried our sorrows, yet we considered him stricken by God, smitten by him, and afflicted. But he was pierced for our transgressions, he was crushed for our iniquities; the punishment that brought us peace was upon him, and by his wounds we are healed."

[21] Although never a required Catholic belief, "limbo" refers in this case to the hypothesis of some theologians of a temporary state of souls purified from sin but waiting for the passion, death, and resurrection of Christ to enter into the bliss of heaven. Thus, Moses, Abraham, and other holy people of the Old Testament were not enjoying perfect heavenly bliss before the coming of Christ, but neither were they suffering in hell or purgatory. The *limbus patrum*, that bordering place of the holy people waiting for Christ just "outside" heaven, refers to this hypothesis. A related hypothesis, the so-called *limbus puerorum*, refers to the state of unbaptized infants and others who die without serious personal sin but with original sin who remain permanently in the condition temporarily experienced by the holy people of the Old Testament. Although limbo is no longer a popular hypothesis among theologians, the state of unbaptized infants remains a discussed question and a matter of deep concern for many parents. Since God wills that all people be saved (1 Tim 4:10), and since Jesus showed a special love and concern for children (Mt 19:14), these parents can be comforted that, although there is no explicit teaching in Scripture or by the Church that such children enjoy heavenly bliss, God's mercy can be trusted to care for the eternal well-being of such children.

the blood of Your testament have sent forth Your prisoners out of the pit, wherein there is no water"; nor was he bound to believe explicitly, before its fulfillment, that Christ was to descend to that place Himself.

It may also be replied that, as Ambrose observes in his commentary on Luke 7:19, he made this inquiry, not from doubt or ignorance but from devotion: or again, with Chrysostom (*Hom. xxxvi in Matth.*), that he inquired, not as though ignorant himself, but because he wished his disciples to be satisfied on that point, through Christ: hence the latter framed His answer so as to instruct the disciples, by pointing to the signs of His works.

Objection 3. Further, many gentiles obtained salvation through the ministry of the angels, as Dionysius states (*Coel. Hier.* ix). Now it would seem that the gentiles had neither explicit nor implicit faith in Christ, since they received no revelation. Therefore it seems that it was not necessary for the salvation of all to believe explicitly in the mystery of Christ.

Reply to Objection 3. Many of the gentiles received revelations of Christ, as is clear from their predictions. Thus we read (Job 19:25): "I know that my Redeemer lives." The Sibyl too foretold certain things about Christ, as Augustine states (*Contra Faust.* xiii, 15). Moreover, we read in the history of the Romans, that at the time of Constantine Augustus and his mother Irene a tomb was discovered, wherein lay a man on whose breast was a golden plate with the inscription: "Christ shall be born of a virgin, and in Him, I believe. O sun, during the lifetime of Irene and Constantine, you shall see me again."[22] If, however, some were saved without receiving any revelation, they were not saved without faith in a Mediator, for, though they did not believe in Him explicitly, they did, nevertheless, have implicit faith through believing

---

[22] In addition to pre-announcements of Christ's coming in the Old Testament, in his book *Life of Christ*, Bishop Fulton Sheen notes, "Not only were the Jews expecting the birth of a great King, a Wise Man and a Savior, but Plato and Socrates spoke of the *Logos* and the Universal Wise Man 'yet to come.' Confucius spoke of 'the Saint'; the Sibyls, of a 'Universal King'; the Greek Dramatist, of a savior and redeemer to unloose man from the 'primal eldest curse.'" (New York, Toronto, London: McGraw Hill Book Company, Inc., 1958): 13–14. Sheen notes that Tacitus, Suetonius, Aeschylus, Virgil, and Cicero shared in the expectation of a savior.

in Divine providence, since they believed that God would deliver mankind in whatever way was pleasing to Him, and according to the revelation of the Spirit to those who knew the truth, as stated in Job 35:11: "Who teaches us more than the beasts of the earth."[23]

Article 9 ⚬⚬ Is it meritorious to believe?

Yes, despite objections to the contrary, It is written (Heb 11:33) that the saints "by faith . . . obtained promises," which would not be the case if they did not merit by believing. Therefore to believe is meritorious.

I answer that, As stated above (I–II, q. 114, a. 3, a. 4), our actions are meritorious insofar as they proceed from the free-will moved with grace by God. Therefore every human act proceeding from the free-will, if it be referred to God, can be meritorious. Now the act of believing is an act of the intellect assenting to the Divine truth at the command of the will moved by the grace of God, so that it is subject to the free-will in relation to God;[24] and consequently the act of faith can be meritorious.

---

23 Here Thomas points out, as Vatican II would later, that more or less clear revelations of God are given to people even outside the Judeo-Christian tradition. People are saved, if they are saved, through Christ, and we can greatly aid in the possibility of their salvation through spreading the Gospel message. "Nor is God far distant from those who in shadows and images seek the unknown God, for it is He who gives to all men life and breath and all things, and as Savior wills that all men be saved. Those also can attain to salvation who through no fault of their own do not know the Gospel of Christ or His Church, yet sincerely seek God and moved by grace strive by their deeds to do His will as it is known to them through the dictates of conscience. Nor does Divine Providence deny the helps necessary for salvation to those who, without blame on their part, have not yet arrived at an explicit knowledge of God and with His grace strive to live a good life. Whatever good or truth is found amongst them is looked upon by the Church as a preparation for the Gospel." Vatican II, *Lumen Gentium* 13.

24 No argument can ever make someone believe, to *trust* in another. Even if (*per impossibile*) arguments could show the indubitable truth of the material objects of faith (the truths expressed by the propositions of the creed), the formality of faith (*trusting* in God revealing) would be missing if these material truths were believed on account of the force of the arguments. Similarly, faith ceases in heaven for the blessed, since they no longer need to trust in what God has revealed because they see for themselves, "face-to-face." In this life, the importance of desire and free choice is decisive for religious believers

Objection 2. Further, belief is a mean between opinion and scientific knowledge or the consideration of things scientifically known.[25] Now the considerations of science are not meritorious, nor on the other hand is opinion. Therefore belief is not meritorious.

Reply to Objection 2. Two things may be considered in science: namely the assent of the one knowing to the thing known and his consideration of the thing known. Now the assent of the one knowing is not subject to free-will, because the knower is obliged to assent by force of the demonstration, wherefore the assent of the one knowing is not meritorious. But the actual consideration of what a man knows is subject to his free-will, for it is in his power to consider or not to consider. Hence the consideration may be meritorious if it be referred to the end of charity, i.e. to the honor of God or the good of our neighbor. On the other hand, in the case of faith, both these things are subject to the free-will so that in both respects the act of faith can be meritorious,[26] whereas in the case of opinion, there is no firm assent, since it is weak and infirm, as the Philosopher observes (*Poster.* i, 33), so that it does not seem to proceed from a perfect act of the will: and for this reason, as regards the assent, it does not appear to be very meritorious, though it can be as regards the actual consideration.

---

and atheists alike. Just as belief can be meritorious, so disbelief can be unmeritorious. It takes an act of will to believe, and there is often an act of will in not believing. This act of will not to believe seems to be present in the American philosopher Thomas Nagel, who writes: "It isn't just that I don't believe in God. It is that I hope there is no God! I don't want there to be a God, I don't want the universe to be like that."

[25] Again, "science" is meant in its Aristotelian sense as "a certain knowledge of a demonstrated conclusion through its demonstration."

[26] Here Thomas distinguishes two different elements of the will's interaction with the intellect. On the one hand, the will can move the intellect to consider a given topic, and this can be meritorious if done for the love of God and neighbor. Thus, you could move your intellect to consider some topic, say the circulatory system of whales, and this might be meritorious if you undertook investigation of this subject for a worthy reason. On the other hand, the will can move the intellect also with respect to something that is "under-determined." In other words, if given the evidence, one can believe or not believe the statement of a given person: the will can move the intellect to assent or lack of assent.

Objection 3. Further, he who assents to a point of faith, either has a sufficient motive for believing, or he has not. If he has a sufficient motive for his belief, this does not seem to imply any merit on his part, since he is no longer free to believe or not to believe, whereas if he has not a sufficient motive for believing, this is a mark of levity, according to Sirach 19:4: "He that is hasty to give credit, is light of heart," so that, seemingly, he gains no merit thereby. Therefore to believe is by no means meritorious.

Reply to Objection 3. The believer has sufficient motive for believing, for he is moved by the authority of Divine teaching confirmed by miracles, and, what is more, by the inward instinct of the Divine invitation: hence he does not believe lightly. He has not, however, sufficient reason for scientific knowledge, hence he does not lose the merit.[27]

ARTICLE 10 ∼ **Do reasons in support of what we believe lessen the merit of faith?**

No, despite objections to the contrary, It is written (1 Pt 3:15): "Being ready always to satisfy every one that asks you a reason of that faith and hope which is in you."[28] Now the Apostle would not give this advice, if it would imply a diminution in the merit of faith. Therefore reason does not diminish the merit of faith.

---

[27] Although faith does not contradict reason, Thomas indicates here how faith moves beyond reason. Believing, unlike knowing, is not a matter of strict demonstration as in geometry. Rather, a believer trusts and loves God and so accepts what God has revealed. Indeed, because God is so trustworthy, faith is belief without doubt. (As Cardinal Newman said, "ten thousand difficulties do not make a single doubt." Cardinal John Henry Newman, *Apologia Pro Vita Sua* [New York: Cosimo Classics, 2007]: 155.) In the words of Joseph Pieper, "When the word 'belief' is used in its proper sense, when no substitute for it is possible, then it signifies an unrestricted, unreserved, unconditional assent. In respect to knowledge of the subject, the eyewitness and the knower are superior to the believer, but not in respect to the undeterred firmness of assent. It is part of the concept of belief itself that man is certain of that in which he believes." Joseph Pieper, *Faith, Hope, and Love* (San Francisco: Ignatius Press, 1997): 28.

[28] The Dominican editors add: "Vulg.: 'Of that hope which is in you.' St. Thomas' reading is apparently taken from Bede."

I answer that, As stated above (previous article; II–II, q. 3, a. 9), the act of faith can be meritorious, insofar as it is subject to the will, not only as to the use, but also as to the assent. Now human reason in support of what we believe may stand in a twofold relation to the will of the believer: first, as preceding the act of the will, as, for instance, when a man either has not the will, or not a prompt will, to believe, unless he be moved by human reasons: and in this way human reason diminishes the merit of faith. In this sense it has been said above (I–II, q. 24, a. 3, ad 1; I–II, q. 77, a. 6, ad 2) that, in moral virtues, a passion which precedes choice makes the virtuous act less praiseworthy. For just as a man ought to perform acts of moral virtue on account of the judgment of his reason, and not on account of a passion, so ought he to believe matters of faith, not on account of human reason, but on account of the Divine authority.[29] Secondly, human reasons may be consequent to the will of the believer. For when a man's will is ready to believe, he loves the truth he believes, he thinks out and takes to heart whatever reasons he can find in support thereof; and in this way human reason does not exclude the merit of faith but is a sign of greater merit. Thus again, in moral virtues a consequent passion is the sign of a more prompt will, as stated above (I–II, q. 24, a. 3, ad 1). We have an indication of this in the words of the Samaritans to the woman, who is a type of human reason: "We now believe, not for your saying" (Jn 4:42).

Objection 1. It would seem that reasons in support of what we believe lessen the merit of faith. For Gregory says (*Hom. xxvi in Evang.*) that "there is no merit in believing what is shown by reason." If, therefore, human reason provides sufficient proof, the merit of faith is altogether

---

[29] In other words, a person who believed in the Trinity solely because struck by the beauty, cogency, and coherence of Thomas's discussion (addressed in *Summa theologiae* I, qq. 27–43) would not believe in the Trinity with the formality of faith. True faith is an acceptance of a divine gift and not the result of human arguments. Nevertheless, if a person does have faith, it is important to share that gift, perhaps at certain times making use of reasons accessible to those without faith, as Thomas himself ably did in the *Summa contra Gentiles* and the *Summa theologiae* itself. With respect to the articles of faith, natural reason can remove objections to believing, showing that believing is not contrary to reason, but, with the exceptions of the preambles of faith, it can never demonstrate the truth of belief.

taken away. Therefore it seems that any kind of human reasoning in support of matters of faith, diminishes the merit of believing.

Reply to Objection 1. Gregory is referring to the case of a man who has no will to believe what is of faith, unless he be induced by reasons. But when a man has the will to believe what is of faith on the authority of God alone, although he may have reasons in demonstration of some of them, e.g. of the existence of God, the merit of his faith is not, for that reason, lost or diminished.

Objection 2. Further, whatever lessens the measure of virtue, lessens the amount of merit, since "happiness is the reward of virtue," as the Philosopher states (Ethic. i, 9). Now human reasoning seems to diminish the measure of the virtue of faith, since it is essential to faith to be about the unseen, as stated above (q. 1, a. 4, a. 5).[30] Now the more a thing is supported by reasons the less is it unseen. Therefore human reasons in support of matters of faith diminish the merit of faith.

---

[30] In this article, Thomas writes: "[I]t is impossible that one and the same thing should be believed and seen by the same person. Hence it is equally impossible for one and the same thing to be an object of science and of belief for the same person. It may happen, however, that a thing which is an object of vision or science for one, is believed by another: since we hope to see some day what we now believe about the Trinity, according to 1 Cor 13:12: 'We see now through a glass in a dark manner; but then face to face': which vision the angels possess already, so that what we believe, they see. In like manner it may happen that what is an object of vision or scientific knowledge for one man, even in the state of a wayfarer, is, for another man, an object of faith, because he does not know it by demonstration. Nevertheless that which is proposed to be believed equally by all, is equally unknown by all as an object of science: such are the things that are of faith simply. Consequently faith and science are not about the same things." We cannot *believe* and *know* the very same thing, for *to believe* is to accept that something is the case on account of the testimony of another whereas *to know* is to accept that something is the case on account of one's own understanding. An analogy may illuminate the matter. I *believe* you that you feel sick; but I know that I feel sick. I do not believe you that I feel sick, for I know from my own bodily sensations that I either feel sick or I don't. On the other hand, I do not know that you feel sick but can only *believe* that you feel sick based on what you communicate to me about yourself through bodily or verbal signs. We cannot have knowledge and belief about the very same thing, for if we believe something we do not know it, and if we know it we do not merely believe it.

Reply to Objection 2. The reasons which are brought forward in support of the authority of faith are not demonstrations which can bring intellectual vision to the human intellect; wherefore they do not cease to be unseen.

But they remove obstacles to faith, by showing that what faith proposes is not impossible; wherefore such reasons do not diminish the merit or the measure of faith. On the other hand, though demonstrative reasons in support of the preambles of faith, but not of the articles of faith,[31] diminish the measure of faith, since they make the thing believed to be seen, yet they do not diminish the measure of charity, which makes the will ready to believe them, even if they were unseen; and so the measure of merit is not diminished.

Objection 3. Further, contrary things have contrary causes. Now an inducement in opposition to faith increases the merit of faith, whether it consist in persecution inflicted by one who endeavors to force a man to renounce his faith, or in an argument persuading him to do so. Therefore reasons in support of faith diminish the merit of faith.

Reply to Objection 3. Whatever is in opposition to faith, whether it consist in a man's thoughts, or in outward persecution, increases the merit of faith, insofar as the will is shown to be more prompt and firm in believing. Hence the martyrs had more merit of faith, through not renouncing faith on account of persecution; and even the wise have greater merit of faith, through not renouncing their faith on account of the reasons brought forward by philosophers or heretics in opposition to faith. On the other hand, things that are favorable to faith do not always diminish the promptness of the will to believe, and therefore they do not always diminish the merit of faith.

---

[31] The contrast here seems to be between, on the one hand, the "preambles of faith," which natural reason can in principle know, though often fails to know—such as the existence of God and basic moral truths—and, on the other hand, the "mysteries of faith," which could not be known unless God revealed them. Put another way, although ancient philosophers came to knowledge that God existed, they could never have come to know God as a Communion of Persons, Father, Son, and Holy Spirit, nor could they have known the identity and reality of Jesus. These "mysteries of faith," like so many disclosures of a lover to a beloved, would and could never be known unless they were revealed.

QUESTION **4**

~~~~~~~~~~~~~~~~~~~~~~~

THE VIRTUE ITSELF
OF FAITH

ARTICLE 3 ⤙ **Is charity the form of faith?**

Yes, despite objections to the contrary, Each thing works through its form. Now faith works through charity. Therefore the love of charity is the form of faith.

    I answer that, As appears from what has been said above (I–II, q. 1, a. 3; I–II, q. 18, a. 6), voluntary acts take their species from their end which is the will's object. Now that which gives a thing its species is after the manner of a form in natural things. Wherefore the form of any voluntary act is, in a manner, the end to which that act is directed, both because it takes its species therefrom, and because the mode of an action should correspond proportionately to the end.[1] Now it is evident from what has been said (a. 1) that the act of faith is directed to the object of the will, i.e. the good, as to its end: and this good which is the end of faith, viz. the Divine Good, is the proper object of charity. Therefore charity is called the form of faith insofar as the act of faith is perfected and formed by charity.

---

[1] Thomas writes elsewhere that someone who commits adultery in order to steal is more a thief than an adulterer (*ST* I–II, q. 18, a. 6), though, one should note, he is both. In other words, an agent's remote goals "form" the agent's proximate means to those goals. Love of God is the goal of faith and so "forms" faith. In Aquinas's terminology, just as the form of the human body is the soul that makes it living, so charity is the form of faith that makes faith living. Put differently, without charity faith is dead.

Objection 1. It would seem that charity is not the form of faith. For each thing derives its species from its form. When, therefore, two things are opposite members of a division, one cannot be the form of the other. Now faith and charity are stated to be opposite members of a division, as different species of virtue (1 Cor 13:13). Therefore charity is not the form of faith.

Reply to Objection 1. Charity is called the form of faith because it quickens the act of faith. Now nothing hinders one act from being quickened by different habits, so as to be reduced to various species in a certain order, as stated above (I–II, q. 18, a. 6, a. 7; I–II, q. 61, a. 2) when we were treating of human acts in general.

ARTICLE 5 ✢ Is faith a virtue?

Yes, despite objections to the contrary, Man is justified by the virtues, since "justice is all virtue," as the Philosopher states (*Ethic.* v, 1). Now man is justified by faith according to Romans 5:1: "Being justified therefore by faith let us have peace," etc. Therefore faith is a virtue.

 I answer that, As shown above, it is by human virtue that human acts are rendered good; hence, any habit that is always the principle of a good act may be called a human virtue. Such a habit is living faith. For since to believe is an act of the intellect assenting to the truth at the command of the will, two things are required that this act may be perfect: one of which is that the intellect should infallibly tend to its object, which is the true; while the other is that the will should be infallibly directed to the last end, on account of which it assents to the true: and both of these are to be found in the act of living faith. For it belongs to the very essence of faith that the intellect should ever tend to the true,[2] since nothing false can be the object of faith, as proved

---

 [2] Stephen Brown notes the centrality of truth for faith: "In short, the First Truth is not only the ground of faith. The First Truth is also the end or goal of faith. In his *Exposition on the 'De Trinitate' of Boethius,* Thomas argues: 'Consequently, since the goal of human life is perfect happiness, which consists in the full knowledge of divine realities, the direction of human life toward perfect happiness from the very beginning requires faith in the divine, the complete knowledge of which we look forward to in our final state of perfection.'" Stephen Brown, "The Theological Virtue of Faith" in *The Ethics of*

above (q. 1, a. 3): while the effect of charity, which is the form of faith, is that the soul ever has its will directed to a good end. Therefore living faith is a virtue.

On the other hand, lifeless faith is not a virtue, because, though the act of lifeless faith is duly perfect on the part of the intellect, it has not its due perfection as regards the will: just as if temperance be in the concupiscible, without prudence being in the rational part, temperance is not a virtue, as stated above (I–II, q. 65, a. 1), because the act of temperance requires both an act of reason, and an act of the concupiscible faculty, even as the act of faith requires an act of the will, and an act of the intellect.[3]

Objection 1. It would seem that faith is not a virtue. For virtue is directed to the good, since "it is virtue that makes its subject good," as the Philosopher states (*Ethic.* ii, 6). But faith is directed to the true. Therefore faith is not a virtue.

Reply to Objection 1. The truth is itself the good of the intellect, since it is its perfection: and consequently faith has a relation to some good insofar as it directs the intellect to the true. Furthermore, it has a relation to the good considered as the object of the will, inasmuch as it is formed by charity.

Objection 2. Further, infused virtue is more perfect than acquired virtue. Now faith, on account of its imperfection, is not placed among the acquired intellectual virtues, as the Philosopher states (*Ethic.* vi, 3). Much less, therefore, can it be considered an infused virtue.

Aquinas, ed. Stephen Pope (Washington DC: Georgetown University Press, 2002), 223–24.

[3] This distinction is an important one for healing the divisions between Protestants and Catholics. When Protestants say that believers are saved by "faith alone," this could be understood as true if by faith is meant "living faith," which includes charity, and therefore the works of charity. A "dead faith" separated from charity does not save. For more, see Avery Cardinal Dulles, "Two Languages of Salvation: The Lutheran–Catholic Joint Declaration," *First Things* 98 (December 1999): 25–30; see, too, "The Gift of Salvation," a joint Catholic-Evangelical declaration in *First Things* 79 (January 1998): 20–23.

Reply to Objection 2. The faith of which the Philosopher speaks is based on human reasoning in a conclusion which does not follow, of necessity, from its premisses, and which is subject to be false: hence such like faith is not a virtue. On the other hand, the faith of which we are speaking is based on the Divine Truth, which is infallible, and consequently its object cannot be anything false, so that faith of this kind can be a virtue.

Objection 3. Further, living and lifeless faith are the same species, as stated above (a. 4). Now lifeless faith is not a virtue, since it is not connected with the other virtues. Therefore neither is living faith a virtue.

Reply to Objection 3. Living and lifeless faith do not differ specifically, as though they belonged to different species. But they differ as perfect and imperfect within the same species. Hence lifeless faith, being imperfect, does not satisfy the conditions of a perfect virtue, for "virtue is a kind of perfection" (Aristotle, *Phys.* vii, text. 18).

THOSE WHO HAVE FAITH

ARTICLE 3 ⟶ **Can a man who disbelieves one article of faith have living faith in the other articles?**

No, despite objections to the contrary, Just as mortal sin is contrary to charity, so is disbelief in one article of faith contrary to faith. Now charity does not remain in a man after one mortal sin.[1] Therefore neither does faith, after a man disbelieves one article.

I answer that, Neither living nor lifeless faith remains in a heretic who disbelieves one article of faith. The reason of this is that the species of every habit depends on the formal aspect of the object, without which the species of the habit cannot remain. Now the formal object of faith is the First Truth, as manifested in Holy Writ and the teaching of the Church, which proceeds from the First Truth. Consequently whoever does not adhere, as to an infallible and Divine rule, to the teaching of the Church, which proceeds from the First

---

[1] A mortal sin is one that extinguishes divine life within a person. A person dying in the condition of mortal sin remains permanently outside communion with God. For a sin to be mortal, it must be something seriously wrong and it must be done knowingly and willingly. Sometimes what is done is seriously wrong, such as killing an innocent person, but there is no mortal sin committed if the agent through no fault of his own did not realize what he was doing (e.g., he didn't know the gun was loaded) or he did not willingly commit the act (e.g., the gun went off because somebody bumped into him). Of course, sometimes it may be a "grey area" whether someone has understood and consented to a sin due to factors of fear, violent emotion, or some other disabling characteristic.

Truth manifested in Holy Writ, has not the habit of faith, but holds that which is of faith otherwise than by faith. Even so, it is evident that a man whose mind holds a conclusion without knowing how it is proved has not scientific knowledge, but merely an opinion about it. Now it is manifest that he who adheres to the teaching of the Church, as to an infallible rule, assents to whatever the Church teaches; otherwise, if, of the things taught by the Church, he holds what he chooses to hold, and rejects what he chooses to reject, he no longer adheres to the teaching of the Church as to an infallible rule, but to his own will. Hence it is evident that a heretic, who obstinately disbelieves one article of faith, is not prepared to follow the teaching of the Church in all things; but if he is not obstinate, he is no longer in heresy but only in error.[2] Therefore it is clear that such a heretic with regard to one article has no faith in the other articles, but only a kind of opinion in accordance with his own will.

Objection 1. It would seem that a heretic who disbelieves one article of faith can have lifeless faith in the other articles. For the natural intellect of a heretic is not more able than that of a Catholic. Now a Catholic's intellect needs the aid of the gift of faith in order to believe any article whatever of faith. Therefore it seems that heretics cannot believe any articles of faith without the gift of lifeless faith.

Reply to Objection 1. A heretic does not hold the other articles of faith about which he does not err, in the same way as one of the faithful does, namely by adhering simply to the Divine Truth, because in order to do so, a man needs the help of the habit of faith; but he holds the things that are of faith by his own will and judgment.[3]

---

[2] Heresy, in other words, is not confusion or misunderstanding or even difficulty in accepting some teaching of the Church. Heresy involves obstinately adhering to one's own view in preference to the Church's and so manifests a form of pride and a lack of humility in one's own limitations.

[3] The earlier distinction between formal and material faith is again here present. A heretic and a Catholic may believe the same thing materially, say that Jesus was raised on the third day, but they differ formally because the Catholic believes this because of God's revelation, and the heretic perhaps solely because, having read the arguments pro and con, he believes the case for resurrection is stronger.

Objection 2. Further, just as faith contains many articles, so does one science, viz. geometry, contain many conclusions. Now a man may possess the science of geometry as to some geometrical conclusions, and yet be ignorant of other conclusions. Therefore a man can believe some articles of faith without believing the others.

Reply to Objection 2. The various conclusions of a science have their respective means of demonstration, one of which may be known without another, so that we may know some conclusions of a science without knowing the others. On the other hand, faith adheres to all the articles of faith by reason of one mean, viz. on account of the First Truth proposed to us in Scriptures, according to the teaching of the Church who has the right understanding of them.[4] Hence whoever abandons this mean is altogether lacking in faith.

Objection 3. Further, just as man obeys God in believing the articles of faith, so does he also in keeping the commandments of the Law. Now a man can obey some commandments, and disobey others. Therefore he can believe some articles, and disbelieve others.

Reply to Objection 3. The various precepts of the Law may be referred either to their respective proximate motives, and thus one can be kept without another, or to their primary motive, which is perfect obedience to God, in which a man fails whenever he breaks one commandment, according to James 2:10: "Whosoever shall . . . offend in one point is become guilty of all."

---

[4] Implicitly, Thomas critiques the idea that scripture alone, *sola scriptura,* is sufficient for knowledge of God's revelation. No text, including Scripture, can interpret itself. If the Bible and the Bible alone is the rule of faith, then it is really no rule at all, for various interpretations of Scripture contradict and undermine one another. This approach leads not to a united confession of one Lord, one faith, and one baptism but to thousands of denominations at odds with each other. For Scripture to remain truly authoritative, an authoritative interpreter is needed. In addition, *sola scriptura* runs into the difficulty that there is no passage in the entire Bible that states that the Bible and the Bible alone is the rule of faith. In other words, *sola scriptura* is itself not scriptural.

ARTICLE 4 ⟿ **Can faith be greater in one person than in another?**

Yes, despite objections to the contrary, Wherever we find great and little, there we find more or less. Now in the matter of faith we find great and little, for Our Lord said to Peter (Mt 14:31): "O you of little faith, why did you doubt?" And to the woman he said (Mt 15:28): "O woman, great is your faith!" Therefore faith can be greater in one than in another.[5]

I answer that, As stated above (I–II, q. 52, a. 1, a. 2; I–II, q. 112, a. 4), the quantity of a habit may be considered from two points of view: first, on the part of the object; secondly, on the part of its participation by the subject.

Now the object of faith may be considered in two ways: first, in respect of its formal aspect; secondly, in respect of the material object which is proposed to be believed. Now the formal object of faith is one and simple, namely the First Truth, as stated above (q. 1, a. 1). Hence in this respect there is no diversity of faith among believers, but it is specifically one in all, as stated above (q. 4, a. 6). But the things which are proposed as the matter of our belief are many and can be received more or less explicitly; and in this respect one man can believe explicitly more things than another, so that faith can be greater in one man on account of its being more explicit.

If, on the other hand, we consider faith from the point of view of its participation by the subject, this happens in two ways, since the act of faith proceeds both from the intellect and from the will, as stated above (q. 2, a. 1, a. 2; q. 4, a. 2). Consequently a man's faith may be described as being greater, in one way, on the part of his intellect, on account of its greater certitude and firmness, and, in another way, on the part of his will, on account of his greater promptitude, devotion, or confidence [See **Table 1**, page 59].

Objection 1. It would seem that faith cannot be greater in one man than in another. For the quantity of a habit is taken from its object.

---

[5] This article, along with so many others, highlights the signal importance of Sacred Scripture for Thomas. Philosophy, especially Aristotle, and the writings of Church Fathers are key authorities for Aquinas, but Sacred Scripture is the most important source guiding his reflection.

Now whoever has faith believes everything that is of faith, since by failing in one point, a man loses his faith altogether, as stated above (a. 3). Therefore it seems that faith cannot be greater in one than in another.

Reply to Objection 1. A man who obstinately disbelieves a thing that is of faith has not the habit of faith, and yet he who does not explicitly believe all, while he is prepared to believe all, has that habit. In this respect, one man has greater faith than another, on the part of the object, insofar as he believes more things, as stated above.

Objection 2. Further, those things which consist in something supreme cannot be "more" or "less." Now faith consists in something supreme, because it requires that man should adhere to the First Truth above all things. Therefore faith cannot be "more" or "less."

Reply to Objection 2. It is essential to faith that one should give the first place to the First Truth. But among those who do this, some submit to it with greater certitude and devotion than others; and in this way faith is greater in one than in another.

Objection 3. Further, faith is to knowledge by grace, as the understanding of principles is to natural knowledge, since the articles of faith are the

TABLE 1

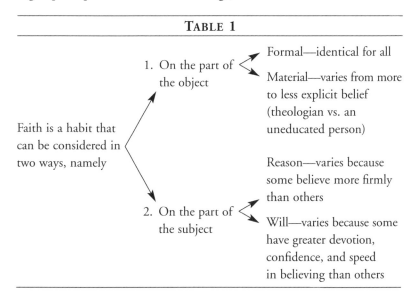

first principles of knowledge by grace, as was shown above (q. 1, a. 7). Now the understanding of principles is possessed in equal degree by all men. Therefore faith is possessed in equal degree by all the faithful.

Reply to Objection 3. The understanding of principles results from man's very nature, which is equally shared by all: whereas faith results from the gift of grace, which is not equally in all, as explained above (I–II, q. 112, a. 4). Hence the comparison fails.

Nevertheless the truth of principles is more known to one than to another, according to the greater capacity of intellect.[6]

---

[6] Faith is not a virtue found equally in all the faithful. Like hope and love, our faith can grow. With God's help, we can and should increase our faith through prayer and continued education. In *Living a Christian Life: The Way of the Lord Jesus*, vol. 2, (Quincy, IL: Franciscan Press, 1983), 38–76. Germain Grisez suggests a number of ways to do so. First, "people should continue to learn about their faith" since even the professional theologian can continue to explore the riches of theological tradition. Second, "it is necessary to respond to challenges to faith" arising from colleagues, news events, or personal experiences. Such challenges can be the occasion of growing more mature in the faith. Third, "finding the response to challenges should be a communal effort" (p. 56). A solution to any given difficulty may elude one person but be found by believers thinking, talking, and praying together. Sometimes, a fitting response to a problem of faith will be found only after a long time and a great deal of effort. This time and effort can also contribute to the development of faith. One should also note that "spontaneous doubts," mere possibilities popping into mind, do not involve sin, but simply the play of the mind considering various possibilities (section J, d). On the other hand, other things being equal, persons or occasions that may weaken a person's faith should be avoided.

QUESTION **6**

THE CAUSE OF FAITH

ARTICLE 1 **Is faith infused into a human being by God?**

Yes, despite objections to the contrary, It is written (Eph 2:8, 9): "By grace you are saved through faith, and that not of yourselves . . . that no man may glory . . . for it is the gift of God."

I answer that, Two things are requisite for faith. First, that the things which are of faith should be proposed to man: this is necessary in order that man believe anything explicitly. The second thing requisite for faith is the assent of the believer to the things which are proposed to him. Accordingly, as regards the first of these, faith must be from God, because those things which are of faith surpass human reason, hence they do not come to man's knowledge, unless God reveal them. To some, indeed, they are revealed by God immediately, as those things which were revealed to the apostles and prophets, while to some they are proposed by God in sending preachers of the faith, according to Romans 10:15: "How shall they preach, unless they be sent?"[1]

As regards the second, viz. man's assent to the things which are of faith, we may observe a twofold cause, one of external inducement, such as seeing a miracle, or being persuaded by someone to embrace the faith: neither of which is a sufficient cause, since of those who see the

---

[1] Truths of faith sometimes are revealed immediately by God, as God communicated with Moses or in Jesus with the apostles. Often, however, that which is revealed is mediated by apostles, successors to the apostles, or other messengers, such as parents or teachers who propose for our belief something revealed by God.

same miracle, or who hear the same sermon, some believe, and some do not. Hence we must assert another internal cause, which moves man inwardly to assent to matters of faith.[2]

The Pelagians held that this cause was nothing else than man's free-will:[3] and consequently they said that the beginning of faith is from ourselves, inasmuch as, to wit, it is in our power to be ready to assent to things which are of faith, but that the consummation of faith is from God, Who proposes to us the things we have to believe. But this is false, for, since man, by assenting to matters of faith, is raised above his nature, this must accrue to him from some supernatural principle moving him inwardly; and this is God. Therefore faith, as regards the assent which is the chief act of faith, is from God moving man inwardly by grace.

Objection 1. It would seem that faith is not infused into man by God. For Augustine says (*De Trin.* xiv) that "science begets faith in us, and nourishes, defends and strengthens it." Now those things which science begets in us seem to be acquired rather than infused. Therefore faith does not seem to be in us by Divine infusion.

Reply to Objection 1. Science begets and nourishes faith, by way of external persuasion afforded by science; but the chief and proper cause of faith is that which moves man inwardly to assent.[4]

---

2 External inducements are not sufficient for faith. Sophisticated arguments, even astonishing miracles, cannot move someone who is not open to belief. Some would not believe even if a person rose from the dead (cf. Lk 16:31).

3 Pelagianism, a heresy originating in the fifth century, denied original sin and the need for grace in salvation. The importance of Christ for Pelagius, from whom the heresy takes its name, was merely as a teacher and as an example. The suffering, death, and resurrection of Christ did not save us, but rather our own virtue and will power led to salvation. Against this view, St. Augustine of Hippo wrote in a number of works including *On the Spirit and the Letter, On Nature and Grace, On Man's Perfection in Righteousness, On the Proceedings of Pelagius, On the Grace of Christ and Original Sin, On the Merits and Remission of Sins and the Baptism of Infants, On Grace and Free Will,* and *On the Gift of Perseverance.* These works of Augustine, and more writings against Pelagianism, are found in the *Nicene and Post-Nicene Fathers,* vol. 5 (Grand Rapids, MI: Eerdmans, 1956).

4 The word "science" in this article and throughout the *Summa theologiae* does not mean the same thing as empirical twenty-first-century science. Thomas

Objection 2. Further, that to which man attains by hearing and see-ing seems to be acquired by him. Now man attains to belief, both by seeing miracles, and by hearing the teachings of faith: for it is written (Jn 4:53): "The father . . . knew that it was at the same hour, that Jesus said to him, Your son lives; and himself believed, and his whole house"; and (Rom 10:17) it is said that "faith is through hearing." Therefore man attains to faith by acquiring it.

Reply to Objection 2. This argument again refers to the cause that proposes outwardly the things that are of faith, or persuades man to believe by words or deeds.

Objection 3. Further, that which depends on a man's will can be acquired by him. But "faith depends on the believer's will," according to Augustine (*De Praedest. Sanct.* v). Therefore faith can be acquired by man.

Reply to Objection 3. To believe does indeed depend on the will of the believer: but man's will needs to be prepared by God with grace, in order that he may be raised to things which are above his nature, as stated above (q. 2, a. 3).[5]

---

is talking about a systematic and certain understanding, described in Aristo-tle's *Posterior Analytics*, that surpasses what empirical science can provide. For a scholarly treatment, see John I. Jenkins, *Knowledge and Faith in Aquinas* (Cambridge: Cambridge University Press, 1997). Commenting on this reply, Stephen Brown notes: "God uses human instruments, such as preachers and teachers, to beget, nourish, defend, and strengthen faith, but such instru-ments are not sufficient on their own to produce faith. If they were, then every competent preacher would be effective in leading his or her listeners to affirm the faith preached, and every teacher would be successful in his or her faith endeavors." Stephen Brown, "The Theological Virtue of Faith" in *The Ethics of Aquinas*, ed. Stephen Pope (Washington DC: Georgetown Univer-sity Press, 2002), 226.

[5] Faith depends on both grace and the human will, but of the two causes grace is the initial and more important one. It is possible, however, for the human will to reject the gift of grace.

QUESTION *7*

THE EFFECTS OF FAITH

ARTICLE 1 ⟿ **Is fear an effect of faith?**

Yes, despite objections to the contrary, It is written (Jas 2:19): "The devils . . . believe and tremble."

I answer that, Fear is a movement of the appetitive power, as stated above (I–II, q. 41, a. 1). Now the principle of all appetitive movements is the good or evil apprehended: and consequently the principle of fear and of every appetitive movement must be an apprehension. Again, through faith there arises in us an apprehension of certain penal evils, which are inflicted in accordance with the Divine judgment. In this way, then, faith is a cause of the fear whereby one dreads to be punished by God; and this is servile fear.

It is also the cause of filial fear, whereby one dreads to be separated from God,[1] or whereby one shrinks from equaling oneself to Him[2] and holds Him in reverence, inasmuch as faith makes us appreciate God as an unfathomable and supreme good, separation from which is the greatest evil, and to which it is wicked to wish to be equaled. Of the first fear, viz. servile fear, lifeless faith is the cause, while living faith is the cause of the second, viz. filial fear, because it makes man adhere to God and to be subject to Him by charity.[3]

---

[1] Filial fear is not fear of God in Himself, Thomas notes, but fear of being separated from God through sin.

[2] Filial fear moves the believer away from pride.

[3] In addition to this healthy "fear of the Lord," faith also purifies the heart: "A thing is impure through being mixed with baser things: for silver is not called

Objection 1. It would seem that fear is not an effect of faith. For an effect does not precede its cause. Now fear precedes faith: for it is written (Sir 2:8): "You that fear the Lord, believe in Him." Therefore fear is not an effect of faith.

Reply to Objection 1. Fear of God cannot altogether precede faith, because if we knew nothing at all about Him, with regard to rewards and punishments, concerning which faith teaches us, we should nowise fear Him. If, however, faith be presupposed in reference to certain articles of faith, for example the Divine excellence, then reverential fear follows, the result of which is that man submits his intellect to God, so as to believe in all the Divine promises. Hence the text quoted continues: "And your reward shall not be made void."

Objection 2. Further, the same thing is not the cause of contraries. Now fear and hope are contraries, as stated above (I–II, q. 23, a. 2): and faith begets hope, as a gloss observes on Matthew 1:2. Therefore fear is not an effect of faith.

Reply to Objection 2. The same thing in respect of contraries can be the cause of contraries, but not under the same aspect. Now faith begets hope, insofar as it enables us to appreciate the prize which God awards to the just, while it is the cause of fear, insofar as it makes us appreciate the punishments which He intends to inflict on sinners.

Objection 3. Further, one contrary does not cause another. Now the object of faith is a good, which is the First Truth, while the object of fear is an evil, as stated above (I–II, q. 42, a. 1). Again, acts take their species

---

impure, when mixed with gold, which betters it, but when mixed with lead or tin. Now it is evident that the rational creature is more excellent than all transient and corporeal creatures; so that it becomes impure through subjecting itself to transient things by loving them. From this impurity the rational creature is purified by means of a contrary movement, namely, by tending to that which is above it, viz. God. The first beginning of this movement is faith: since 'he that cometh to God must believe that He is,' according to Hebrews 11:6. Hence the first beginning of the heart's purifying is faith; and if this be perfected through being quickened by charity, the heart will be perfectly purified thereby" (II–II, q. 7, a. 2).

from the object, according to what was stated above (I–II, q. 18, q. 2). Therefore faith is not a cause of fear.

Reply to Objection 3. The primary and formal object of faith is the good which is the First Truth; but the material object of faith includes also certain evils:[4] for instance, that it is an evil either not to submit to God, or to be separated from Him, and that sinners will suffer penal evils from God: in this way faith can be the cause of fear.

---

[4] Building on what he wrote previously, Thomas holds that fear is always of something perceived as evil. God, as First Truth of faith and highest Good, is in no way evil. However, unlike the formal object of faith, the material object of faith includes things that should be feared, in particular the eternal separation from God, called hell.

QUESTION **10**

UNBELIEF

ARTICLE 1 ⇒ **Is unbelief a sin?**

Yes, despite objections to the contrary, Vice is opposed to virtue. Now faith is a virtue, and unbelief is opposed to it. Therefore unbelief is a sin.

I answer that, Unbelief may be taken in two ways: first, by way of pure negation, so that a man be called an unbeliever, merely because he has not the faith. Secondly, unbelief may be taken by way of opposition to the faith, in which sense a man refuses to hear the faith, or despises it, according to Isaiah 53:1: "Who has believed our report?" It is this that completes the notion of unbelief, and it is in this sense that unbelief is a sin.[1]

---

[1] Since faith is an adherence to God, to refuse faith or despise faith is to refuse or despise God. Disbelief in this sense is always a sin, a separation from God. However, it is possible that a person could so misunderstand the faith that the person does not truly reject the faith, but rather rejects (perhaps quite properly) a mistaken understanding of faith. For example, someone might believe that to be a Catholic requires giving divine honor and worship to Mary. Such a person does not reject the Catholic faith, but rather a mistaken understanding of Catholic faith. Whether or not rejecting faith is a sin in any particular case would depend upon the knowledge and will of the particular person involved and would not generally be an easy matter to judge. As Pieper notes, "Unbelief in the precise sense of the term is only that mental act in which someone deliberately refuses assent to a truth that he has recognized with sufficient plainness to be God's speech." *Faith, Hope, and Love* (San Francisco: Ignatius Press, 1986), 72. Put a different way, unbelief of both a sinful and innocent kind poses a challenge for Christians. In the words of Richard John Neuhaus:

If, however, we take it by way of pure negation, as we find it in those who have heard nothing about the faith, it bears the character, not of sin, but of punishment, because such like ignorance of Divine things is a result of the sin of our first parent.[2] If such like unbelievers are damned, it is on account of other sins,[3] which cannot be taken away without faith, but not on account of their sin of unbelief. Hence Our Lord said (Jn 15:22): "If I had not come, and spoken to them, they would not have sin," which Augustine expounds (Tract. lxxxix in Joan.) as "referring to the sin whereby they believed not in Christ."

Objection 1. It would seem that unbelief is not a sin. For every sin is contrary to nature, as Damascene proves (*De Fide Orth.* ii, 4).[4] Now unbelief seems not to be contrary to nature; for Augustine says (*De Praedest. Sanct.* v) that "to be capable of having faith, just as to be capable of having charity, is natural to all men, whereas to have faith, even as to have charity belongs to the grace of the faithful." Therefore not to have faith, which is to be an unbeliever, is not a sin.

"If Christians exhibited more intellectual patience, modesty, curiosity, and sense of adventure, there would be fewer atheists in the world, both of the modern rationalist and postmodern irrationalist varieties. I have never met an atheist who rejects the God in whom I believe. I have met many who decline to commit intellectual suicide, and maybe spiritual suicide as well, by accepting a God proposed by Christians who claim to know more than they can possibly know." Richard John Neuhaus, "Naked Public Square," *First Things* 86 (October 1998), 83.

[2] The sin of Adam, original sin, darkens the intellect so that human beings have greater difficulty knowing God.

[3] Here Thomas makes implicit reference to natural law, the providential guidance God gives to all humans whether they be persons of faith or not. Natural law guides believer and non-believer alike to avoid evil and to do good, as well as provides basic knowledge about what is good and evil to do. Hence, persons who do not believe could nevertheless sin against the natural light given them by God and knowingly do wrong. Human wrongdoing cannot always be excused as inculpable ignorance, even among those not benefiting from revelation.

[4] St. John Damascene was a Greek Father of the Church who wrote in the first half of the eighth century. His works were not translated into Latin until the eleventh century but soon after became very influential and important in the West among theologians writing in Latin.

Reply to Objection 1. To have the faith is not part of human nature, but it is part of human nature that man's mind should not thwart his inner instinct and the outward preaching of the truth. Hence, in this way, unbelief is contrary to nature.

Objection 2. Further, no one sins in that which he cannot avoid, since every sin is voluntary. Now it is not in a man's power to avoid unbelief, for he cannot avoid it unless he have faith, because the Apostle says (Rom 10:14): "How shall they believe in Him, of Whom they have not heard? And how shall they hear without a preacher?" Therefore unbelief does not seem to be a sin.

Reply to Objection 2. This argument takes unbelief as denoting a pure negation.[5]

Objection 3. Further, as stated above (I–II, q. 84, a. 4), there are seven capital sins, to which all sins are reduced. But unbelief does not seem to be comprised under any of them. Therefore unbelief is not a sin.

Reply to Objection 3. Unbelief, insofar as it is a sin, arises from pride, through which man is unwilling to subject his intellect to the rules of faith, and to the sound interpretation of the Fathers. Hence

---

[5] In the words of Vatican II: "Those also can attain to salvation who through no fault of their own do not know the Gospel of Christ or His Church, yet sincerely seek God and moved by grace strive by their deeds to do His will as it is known to them through the dictates of conscience. Nor does Divine Providence deny the helps necessary for salvation to those who, without blame on their part, have not yet arrived at an explicit knowledge of God and with His grace strive to live a good life." *Lumen Gentium* 16. On the other hand, some people report that they willfully disbelieve. Aldous Huxley in *Ends and Means* says: "I had motives for not wanting the world to have meaning; consequently assumed that it had none, and was able without any difficulty to find satisfying reasons for this assumption. . . . We don't know because we don't want to know. It is our will that decides how and upon what subjects we shall use our intelligence. Those who detect no meaning in the world generally do so because, for one reason or another, it suits their books that the world should be meaningless. . . . For myself . . . the philosophy of meaninglessness was essentially an instrument of liberation." (New York: Harper, 1937): 273. This "liberation" from a relationship with a loving Father, "freedom" from God's plan of personal fulfillment, is actually a mere license that leads to unhappiness for oneself and almost invariably for others.

Gregory says (*Moral.* xxxi, 45) that "presumptuous innovations arise from vainglory."

It might also be replied that just as the theological virtues are not reduced to the cardinal virtues, but precede them, so too, the vices opposed to the theological virtues are not reduced to the capital vices.

ARTICLE 12 ∾ Should the children of Jews and other unbelievers be baptized against their parents' will?

No, despite objections to the contrary, Injustice should be done to no man. Now it would be an injustice to Jews if their children were to be baptized against their will, since they would lose the rights of parental authority over their children as soon as these were Christians. Therefore these should not be baptized against their parents' will.

I answer that, The custom of the Church has very great authority and ought to be jealously observed in all things, since the very doctrine of catholic doctors derives its authority from the Church. Hence we ought to abide by the authority of the Church rather than by that of an Augustine or a Jerome or of any doctor whatever.[6] Now it was never the custom of the Church to baptize the children of the Jews against the will of their parents, although at times past there have been many very powerful catholic princes like Constantine and Theodosius, with whom most holy bishops have been on most friendly terms, as Sylvester with Constantine, and Ambrose with Theodosius, who would certainly not have failed to obtain this favor from them if it had been at all reasonable. It seems therefore hazardous to repeat this assertion, that the children of Jews should be baptized against their parents' wishes, in contradiction to the Church's custom observed hitherto.

There are two reasons for this custom. One is on account of the danger to the faith. For children baptized before coming to the use of reason, afterwards when they come to perfect age, might easily be per-

---

6 Thomas has tremendous respect for the Fathers of the Church, in particular for St. Augustine. His point is that the teaching of the Church is an even greater authority. In other words, one should not follow the teaching of any given theologian, even a theologian as renowned as Augustine, if following such teaching would be in opposition to what the Church teaches.

suaded by their parents to renounce what they had unknowingly embraced; and this would be detrimental to the faith.

The other reason is that it is against natural justice. For a child is by nature part of its father: thus, at first, it is not distinct from its parents as to its body, so long as it is enfolded within its mother's womb; and later on after birth, and before it has the use of its free-will, it is enfolded in the care of its parents, which is like a spiritual womb, for so long as man has not the use of reason, he differs not from an irrational animal; so that even as an ox or a horse belongs to someone who, according to the civil law, can use them when he likes, as his own instrument, so, according to the natural law, a son, before coming to the use of reason, is under his father's care. Hence it would be contrary to natural justice, if a child, before coming to the use of reason, were to be taken away from its parents' custody, or if anything were done to it against its parents' wish.[7] As soon, however, as it begins to have the use of its free-will, it begins to belong to itself, and is able to look after itself, in matters concerning the Divine or the natural law, and then it should be induced, not by compulsion but by persuasion, to embrace the faith: it can then consent to the faith and be baptized, even against its parents' wish, but not before it comes to the use of reason. Hence it is said of the children of the fathers of old that they were saved in the faith of their parents; whereby we are given to understand that it is the parents' duty to look after the salvation of their children, especially before they come to the use of reason.

Objection 2. Further, one is more bound to succor a man who is in danger of everlasting death, than one who is in danger of temporal death. Now it would be a sin, if one saw a man in danger of temporal

---

[7] Aquinas's teaching presupposes the truth of the Pauline maxim that one may not do evil that good may come, even when the good is the greatest good of all, salvation. Such teaching is especially opposed to a moral method known as "proportionalism," which determines the rightness or wrongness of any given act by taking into consideration all the circumstances involved, including likely outcomes. For more on proportionalism, see Pope John Paul II, *Veritatis Splendor,* as well as Christopher Kaczor, *Proportionalism and the Natural Law Tradition* (Washington, DC: The Catholic University of America Press, 2002).

death and failed to go to his aid. Since, then, the children of Jews and other unbelievers are in danger of everlasting death, should they be left to their parents who would imbue them with their unbelief, it seems that they ought to be taken away from them and baptized, and instructed in the faith.

Reply to Objection 2. No one should be snatched from natural death against the order of civil law: for instance, if a man were condemned by the judge to temporal death, nobody ought to rescue him by violence: hence no one ought to break the order of the natural law, whereby a child is in the custody of its father, in order to rescue it from the danger of everlasting death.

QUESTION **11**

HERESY

ARTICLE 2 ⟶ **Is heresy properly about matters of faith?**

Yes, despite objections to the contrary, Augustine says against the Manichees (Cf. *De Civ. Dei* xviii, 51): "In Christ's Church, those are heretics who hold mischievous and erroneous opinions, and, when rebuked that they may think soundly and rightly, offer a stubborn resistance, and, refusing to mend their pernicious and deadly doctrines, persist in defending them." Now pernicious and deadly doctrines are none but those which are contrary to the dogmas of faith, whereby "the just man lives" (Rom 1:17). Therefore heresy is about matters of faith, as about its proper matter.

    I answer that, We are speaking of heresy now as denoting a corruption of the Christian faith. Now it does not imply a corruption of the Christian faith, if a man has a false opinion in matters that are not of faith, for instance, in questions of geometry and so forth, which cannot belong to the faith by any means, but only when a person has a false opinion about things belonging to the faith.

    Now a thing may be of the faith in two ways, as stated above (I, q. 32, a. 4; I–II, q. 1, a. 6, ad 1; I–II, q. 2, a. 5): in one way, directly and principally, e.g. the articles of faith;[1] in another way, indirectly and

---

[1] An example of a denial of an article of faith would be not believing in the resurrection of Christ.

secondarily, e.g. those matters, the denial of which leads to the corruption of some article of faith;[2] and there may be heresy in either way, even as there can be faith.

Objection 1. It would seem that heresy is not properly about matters of faith. For just as there are heresies and sects among Christians, so were there among the Jews and Pharisees, as Isidore[3] observes (*Etym.* viii, 3, 4, 5). Now their dissensions were not about matters of faith. Therefore heresy is not about matters of faith, as though they were its proper matter.

Reply to Objection 1. Just as the heresies of the Jews and Pharisees were about opinions relating to Judaism or Pharisaism, so also heresies among Christians are about matter touching the Christian faith.

Objection 3. Further, we find the holy doctors differing even about matters pertaining to the faith, for example Augustine and Jerome, on the question about the cessation of the legal observances: and yet this was without any heresy on their part. Therefore heresy is not properly about the matter of faith.

Reply to Objection 3. As Augustine says (*Ep.* xliii) and we find it stated in the Decretals (xxiv, qu. 3, can. *Dixit Apostolus*): "By no means should we accuse of heresy those who, however false and perverse their opinion may be, defend it without obstinate fervor, and

---

2 For example, though there is no article of the creed "there is truth," nevertheless a general denial of truth corrupts articles of faith since if there is no truth, then none of the articles of faith can be true. If someone were to deny the reality of death, again although the reality of death is not explicitly stated in the creed, such a denial would nevertheless undermine the creed since Christ could not have died. In these ways, and a variety of others, corrupt philosophy can undermine religious belief.

3 Saint Isidore served as Archbishop of Seville for more than 30 years until his death in 636. A great scholar, Isidore helped transmit classical learning to medieval thinkers especially through his most famous work, the *Etymologies* in which he taught that the earth was round as well as addressed many other matters encompassing all areas of learning.

seek the truth with careful anxiety, ready to mend their opinion, when they have found the truth," because, to wit, they do not make a choice in contradiction to the doctrine of the Church. Accordingly, certain doctors seem to have differed either in matters the holding of which in this or that way is of no consequence, so far as faith is concerned, or even in matters of faith, which were not as yet defined by the Church,[4] although if anyone were obstinately to deny them after they had been defined by the authority of the universal Church, he would be deemed a heretic. This authority resides chiefly in the Sovereign Pontiff. For we read (Decret. xxiv, qu. 1, can. *Quoties*): "Whenever a question of faith is in dispute, I think that all our brethren and fellow bishops ought to refer the matter to none other than Peter, as being the source of their name and honor, against whose authority neither Jerome nor Augustine nor any of the holy doctors defended their opinion." Hence Jerome says:[5] "This, most blessed Pope, is the faith that we have been taught in the Catholic Church. If anything therein has been incorrectly or carelessly expressed, we beg that it may

---

[4] Aquinas implicitly refers here to development of doctrine. He talks about erring Fathers of the Church in the preface to one of his other works *Contra errores Graecorum*, and says that they should be interpreted reverently because some truths and some ways of expressing truths were not as clear in their time as in later times.

[5] Although this quotation does not actually come from St. Jerome, but was erroneously attributed to him, the thoughts expressed have been taught by many saints. In his *Spiritual Exercises*, the founder of the Society of Jesus (the Jesuits), St. Ignatius Loyola, wrote: "To be right in everything, we ought always to hold that the white which I see, is black, if the Hierarchical Church so decides it, believing that between Christ our Lord, the Bridegroom, and the Church, His Bride, there is the same Spirit which governs and directs us for the salvation of our souls. Because by the same Spirit and our Lord Who gave the ten Commandments, our holy Mother the Church is directed and governed" (Rule 13). St. Thomas Aquinas himself on his deathbed after receiving his final Holy Communion said: "I have written and taught much about this very holy Body, and about the other sacraments in the faith of Christ, and about the Holy Roman Church, to whose correction I expose and submit everything I have written" (As cited in Vernon Bourke, *Aquinas's Search for Wisdom* [Milwaukee: Bruce Publishing Co., 1965], 193).

be set aright by you who hold the faith and see of Peter. If however this, our profession, be approved by the judgment of your apostleship, whoever may blame me, will prove that he himself is ignorant, or malicious, or even not a Catholic but a heretic."[6]

---

[6] In addition to the works cited in the notes, readers may also want to consult the following works about the virtue of faith: Romanus Cessario, *Christian Faith and the Theological Life* (Washington, DC: The Catholic University of America Press, 1994), and Robert Sokolowski, *The God of Faith and Reason: Foundations of Christian Theology* (Notre Dame, IN: University of Notre Dame Press, 1982).

ON HOPE

INTRODUCTION
TO HOPE

〜〜〜〜〜〜〜〜〜〜〜〜〜

SUFFERING, pain, and loss are a part of every human life. We experience minor setbacks and major ones. Some of us experience catastrophic events in which all hope appears extinguished. Consider, for example, those who suffered in concentration camps, physically abused, daily threatened by murderous death, enduring the loss of all property and privacy, and mourning the extinction of so many friends and relatives. In his book *Man's Search for Meaning*, Victor Frankel pointed out that people in these horrible circumstances nevertheless reacted in radically different ways. Some killed themselves; others praised God even as they walked into certain death.

As if enduring present hardships were not burden enough, we also fear the suffering that has not yet come. In dark times, it is easy to imagine a future filled with even greater affliction, debilitating loss, and destroyed dreams. Indeed, the foreboding future can darken the present. Man needs hope to live.

In his second encyclical letter, *Spe salvi* (*Saved by Hope*), Pope Benedict XVI emphasizes the indispensability of hope for all human lives in the encounter with suffering of whatever depth: "the present, even if it is arduous, can be lived and accepted if it leads towards a goal, if we can be sure of this goal, and if this goal is great enough to justify the effort of the journey."[1]

---

[1] Pope Benedict XVI, *Spe Salvi* (November 30, 2007), 1.

Despite all difficulties, Christians need never fear the future. Pope Benedict writes: "We see as a distinguishing mark of Christians the fact that they have a future: it is not that they know the details of what awaits them, but they know in general terms that their life will not end in emptiness. Only when the future is certain as a positive reality does it become possible to live the present as well."[2] Man needs hope, not only for the future, but also for the present.

But what exactly is hope? Hope is a word often on our lips: I hope to achieve this goal; I hope this or that situation turns out well; I hope my friend feels better soon. We have many hopes of greater or lesser importance. However, all of our small hopes are geared to a bigger hope, the hope of happiness, the hope of perfect happiness. The greatest hope that we can have is the hope of eternal happiness forever. If we do not achieve this happiness, everything else will be meaningless. If we can have this happiness, all the losses and setbacks in life will seem minor by comparison.

Thomas Aquinas holds that faith, hope, and love are theological virtues, gifts given by God to help us in our journey to heaven where alone we can find perfect happiness. The theological virtues are so called both because they are received as gifts through God's power (as opposed to acquired virtues attained through human effort) and because they focus in distinct ways on God himself. Faith believes in God and in what God has revealed. Love or charity is a friendly union with God himself, which begins now but reaches its culmination in the life to come. Hope grows out of faith and is a manifestation of love, since by hope we move towards perfect union with God in heaven. The *Catechism of the Catholic Church* defines hope as "the theological virtue by which we desire the kingdom of heaven and eternal life as our happiness, placing our trust in Christ's promises and relying not on our own strength, but on the help of the grace of the Holy Spirit" (*CCC* 1817).

Aquinas teaches that hope is a virtue that lies in a mean between the extremes of two vices, presumption and despair. With *presumption*, a person assumes that he will be saved, presuming on his own

---

2 Pope Benedict XVI, *Spe Salvi*, 2.

capacities or seeking forgiveness of sins without repentance. The dictum "once saved, always saved" expresses a kind of presumption, for it holds that even if a person commits and persists in mortal sin (which is a deadly destruction of our friendship with God) he or she can maintain a good relationship with God both now and into eternity. In despair, a person ceases to hope for salvation from God, considering sinfulness too great or God's mercy too little. We may despair at the loss of many sought goods, but there is no despair like believing that one will forever lose the greatest of all goods, perfect happiness. In presumption, salvation is considered automatic; in despair, salvation is thought to be impossible. Both presumption and despair contradict authentic hope. Salvation is always possible with God's help, for God's love and mercy extends even to the most hardened, vicious sinner. Salvation is not automatic, however, for God cannot contradict himself by giving people the liberty to freely believe in him and love him both now and forever and also not giving people that freedom.

For Thomas Aquinas, hope is indeed always linked to faith, since one cannot have a living faith without also having both love and hope. Even though hope primarily focuses on the perfect happiness of heaven attained through the help of God, we also have earthly hopes that are related to our great hope of salvation. Infused with hope, human beings can endure even the worst of circumstances. Lacking hope, even an earthly palace can feel like a prison.

QUESTION **17**

THE NATURE, OBJECT, AND CAUSE OF HOPE

ARTICLE 1 ∾ **Is hope a virtue?**

Yes, despite objections to the contrary, Gregory says (*Moral.* i, 33) that the three daughters of Job signify these three virtues: faith, hope and charity.[1] Therefore hope is a virtue.

I answer that, According to the Philosopher (*Ethic.* ii, 6) "the virtue of a thing is that which makes its subject good, and its work good likewise." Consequently wherever we find a good human act, it must correspond to some human virtue. Now in all things measured and ruled, the good is that which attains its proper rule: thus we say that a coat is good if it neither exceeds nor falls short of its proper measurement. But, as we stated above (q. 8, a. 3, ad 3) human acts have a twofold measure: one is proximate and homogeneous, viz. the reason, while the other is remote and excelling, viz. God: wherefore every human act is good, which attains reason or God Himself. Now the act of hope, whereof we speak now, attains God. For, as we have already stated (I–II, q. 40, a. 1), when we were treating of the passion of hope, the object of hope is a future good,[2] difficult but possible to

---

[1] In a book that was to be tremendously influential in the Middle Ages, Pope St. Gregory the Great commented on the book of Job and saw symbolic meanings in various events in Job's life, here suggesting that the three daughters of Job symbolize the three theological virtues.

[2] As with the virtue of faith, understanding the "object" of hope is vital to appreciating this theological virtue. Acts are known by their objects in that we would not know about the act of sight were it not for visible things that

85

obtain.[3] Now a thing is possible to us in two ways: first, by ourselves; secondly, by means of others, as stated in *Ethic.* iii. Wherefore, insofar as we hope for anything as being possible to us by means of the Divine assistance, our hope attains God Himself on Whose help it leans. It is therefore evident that hope is a virtue, since it causes a human act to be good and to attain its due rule.[4]

---

can be seen activating our potentiality to see. We would not know about the act of hearing without "objects," such as music, that are audible. Likewise, habits are known by their acts. The habit of justice is made known and formed by acts of justice. So, for example, in order to know what the virtue of faith is, we must know what the act of faith is, and to know what the act of faith is, we must know the object of faith. The same holds true for the other theological virtues, such as hope, and for Thomas's analysis of things in general, including the human soul. Habits are known by acts; acts are known by objects.

[3] Romanus Cessario, O.P., highlights the unique characteristics of hope so briefly mentioned by Thomas: "In Aquinas' writings, one finds four characteristics common to every kind of hoping. First, hope concerns only the movement towards what perfects the human person, toward good objects or ends that enhance the personal dignity of the one endowed with spiritual powers. On the other hand, when a person encounters something destructive, the reaction takes a different shape, such as the repugnance or fear we experience in the face of evil. Second, hope looks toward the future, for a person never hopes for what he or she already possesses. Hope seeks a good object that still lies in the future; the person who presently and actually realizes the attainment of something desired reacts with joy. Third, one speaks of hoping only when the attainment of the good, future object involves some difficulty or an element of arduousness. Otherwise, when it is a case of someone seeking a good that is easily achieved, the person experiences the simple emotion of desire, which properly pertains to the concupiscible appetite. . . . Finally, only something that is attainable elicits hope; a person must judge that the hoped for reality lies within the realm of possible options. When this is not the case, the individual definitively impeded from obtaining some good that is required for human perfection experiences instead the emotion of despair." Romanus Cessario, O.P., "The Theological Virtue of Hope," in *The Ethics of Aquinas*, ed. Stephen Pope (Washington, DC: Georgetown University Press, 2002), 232–33.

[4] Today, hope may be the most neglected of all the virtues. As Thomas notes, the object of hope is a future good, difficult but possible to attain. Hope as a theological virtue has God as its object, and hope is most neglected today since many people act as if the attainment of heaven were inevitable and therefore not difficult to obtain (presumption) and other people act as if God were impossible to obtain (despair). The former idea, that all people or almost all (save Hitler perhaps) go to heaven, is widely believed, but has sparse basis in Scripture or the Catholic tradition. For more on how many

Objection 1. It would seem that hope is not a virtue. For "no man makes ill use of a virtue," as Augustine states (*De Lib. Arb.* ii, 18). But one may make ill use of hope, since the passion of hope, like the other passions, is subject to a mean and extremes. Therefore hope is not a virtue.

Reply to Objection 1. In the passions, the mean of virtue depends on right reason being attained, wherein also consists the essence of virtue [See **Table 2**, below]. Wherefore in hope too, the good of virtue depends on a man's attaining, by hoping, the due rule, viz. God. Consequently man cannot make ill use of hope that attains God, as neither can he make ill use of moral virtue that attains reason, because to attain thus is to make good use of virtue. Nevertheless, the hope of which we speak now is not a passion but a habit of the mind, as we shall show further on (q. 18, a. 1).

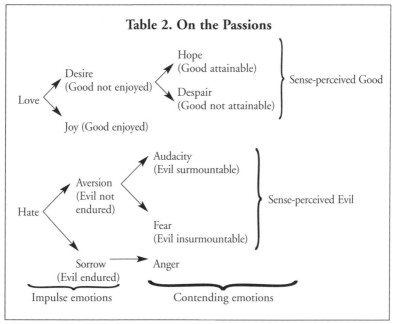

Table 2. On the Passions

SOURCE: St. Thomas Aquinas, *Summa theologiae,* Blackfriars ed. (Springfield, MO: W. J. Hill, 1966).

people are (or are not) saved, see Avery Cardinal Dulles, "The Population of Hell," *First Things* 133 (May 2003): 36–41.

Objection 3. Further, "virtue is the disposition of a perfect thing" (Aristotle, *Phys.* vii, text. 17, 18). But hope is the disposition of an imperfect thing; of one, namely, that lacks what it hopes to have. Therefore hope is not a virtue.

Reply to Objection 3. He who hopes is indeed imperfect in relation to that which he hopes to obtain, but has not as yet; yet he is perfect, insofar as he already attains his proper rule, viz. God, on Whose help he leans.

ARTICLE 2~~Is eternal happiness the proper object of hope?

Yes, despite objections to the contrary, The Apostle says (Heb 6:19) that we have hope "which enters in," i.e. makes us to enter . . . "within the veil," i.e. into the happiness of heaven, according to the interpretation of a gloss[5] on these words. Therefore the object of hope is eternal happiness.

　　I answer that, As stated above (1), the hope of which we speak now, attains God by leaning on His help in order to obtain the hoped for good. Now an effect must be proportionate to its cause.[6] Wherefore the good that we ought to hope for from God properly and chiefly is the infinite good, which is proportionate to the power of our divine helper, since it belongs to an infinite power to lead anyone to an infinite good. Such a good is eternal life, which consists in the enjoyment of God Himself. For we should hope from Him for noth-

---

　　[5] A "gloss" is a commentary, explanation, or clarification written in the margins of the primary text as an interpretive aid. These footnotes themselves, for example, are a kind of "gloss" on the text of the *Summa*. Some scholars would take issue with the interpretation given in the gloss above by arguing that the veil spoken of in this passage is actually referring to the veil that separated the Holy and Most Holy Place in the Hebrew sanctuary. The Most Holy Place was the innermost part of the sanctuary where the Ark of the Covenant and the presence of God were. Only the high priest was allowed in this chamber once a year. The theological point seems to be that through Christ we have direct access to God.

　　[6] This fundamental metaphysical principle states that no effect is greater than its cause. A human being can do many things, but it is beyond causal human power to achieve and enjoy the infinite good of God. To achieve this infinite effect, an infinite and divine cause is needed.

ing less than Himself, since His goodness, whereby He imparts good things to His creature, is no less than His Essence. Therefore the proper and principal object of hope is eternal happiness.[7]

Objection 1. It would seem that eternal happiness is not the proper object of hope. For a man does not hope for that which surpasses every movement of the soul, since hope itself is a movement of the soul. Now eternal happiness surpasses every movement of the human soul, for the Apostle says (1 Cor 2:9) that it has not "entered into the heart of man." Therefore happiness is not the proper object of hope.

Reply to Objection 1. Eternal happiness does not enter into the heart of man perfectly, i.e. so that it be possible for a wayfarer[8] to know its nature and quality; yet, under the general notion of the perfect good,[9] it is possible for it to be apprehended by a man, and it is in this way that the movement of hope towards it arises. Hence the Apostle says

---

[7] Joseph Pieper notes: "In the virtue of hope more than in any other, man understands and affirms that he is a creature, that he has been created by God." Joseph Pieper, *Faith, Hope, and Love* (San Francisco: Ignatius Press, 1997), 98. While on earth, a human being, notes Pieper, is in the *status viatoris*, in the condition of a traveler heading toward the goal but not yet there. As a creature, each human person is created out of nothing and is headed toward the fulfillment of human existence. Hope highlights this "in between" state of human beings on earth as created for heavenly bliss but not yet having attained eternal happiness.

[8] A "wayfarer" is one still "on the way" *in via* to eternal rest in heaven or hell. Thus, all those in the earthly life are called "wayfarers." The issue at hand in this article is in what sense the hope of salvation of someone on earth is certain.

[9] The distinction between "notion of the perfect good" and "that which realizes the notion of the perfect good" is similar to the distinction between the "ideal spouse" and "various candidates for ideal spouse." We can all imagine the characteristics of the ideal spouse (loving, smart, fun, reliable, good looking, etc.) and then we can consider various people and the degree to which they live up or fail to live up to this ideal. Similarly, the "notion of the perfect good" is a happiness that satisfies us in every way. It is an end rather than a means, and excludes all evil, including being lost. All people want a good like this, but people seek various candidates as "that which realizes the perfect good," some trying bodily pleasure, others power, fame, or money. As indicated in the introduction, only God realizes the notion of perfect happiness. For Thomas's own analysis, see *ST* I–II, q. 1, a. 7, as well as I–II, questions 2–5.

pointedly (Heb 6:19) that hope "enters in, even within the veil," because that which we hope for is as yet veiled, so to speak.

Objection 2. Further, prayer is an expression of hope, for it is written (Ps 36:5): "Commit your way to the Lord, and trust in Him, and He will do it." Now it is lawful for man to pray to God not only for eternal happiness, but also for the goods, both temporal and spiritual, of the present life, and, as evidenced by the Lord's Prayer, to be delivered from evils that will no longer be in eternal happiness. Therefore eternal happiness is not the proper object of hope.

Reply to Objection 2. We ought not to pray to God for any other goods, except in reference to eternal happiness. Hence hope regards eternal happiness chiefly, and other things, for which we pray to God, it regards secondarily and as referred to eternal happiness:[10] just as faith regards God principally, and, secondarily, those things which are referred to God, as stated above (II–II, q. 1, a. 1).

ARTICLE 5 ⁕ Is hope a theological virtue?

Yes, despite objections to the contrary, Hope is enumerated (1 Cor 13) together with faith and charity, which are theological virtues.[11]

---

[10] We may hope for non-eternal goods, for example, to pass an exam, to meet the right person to marry, or to be healed of an illness. However, we should want these things only insofar as obtaining them is compatible with and conducive to the primary object of hope, the enjoyment of God. Prayer arises out of hope for eternal happiness and other goods helpful to attaining heavenly bliss: "Despair and presumption block the approach to true prayer. For prayer, even if in its original form is expressed as a prayer of petition, is nothing other than the voicing of hope. One who despairs does not petition, because he assumes that his prayer will not be granted. One who is presumptuous petitions, indeed, but his petition is not genuine because he fully anticipates its fulfillment." Joseph Pieper, *Faith, Hope, and Love* (San Francisco: Ignatius Press, 1997), 127.

[11] Like faith and love, the virtue of hope can increase in an individual through prayer and reception of the sacraments, especially Confession and Holy Communion. In times of trial, or in moments when we feel "hopeless," we can also recall God's fidelity in Scripture to his people. Again and again, God kept his promises: rewarding Abraham's hope of having children lasting through the ages, the hope of the Hebrews to escape Egyptian bondage, and the hope of the chosen people that a Messiah would come. Scripture abounds with testimonies

I answer that, Since specific differences, by their very nature, divide a genus,[12] in order to decide under what division we must place hope, we must observe whence it derives its character of virtue.

Now it has been stated above (a. 1) that hope has the character of virtue from the fact that it attains the supreme rule of human actions: and this it attains both as its first efficient cause, in as much as it leans on its assistance, and as its last final cause, in as much as it expects happiness in the enjoyment thereof.[13] Hence it is evident that God is the principal object of hope, considered as a virtue. Since, then, the very idea of a theological virtue is one that has God for its object, as stated above (I–II, q. 62, a. 1), it is evident that hope is a theological virtue.[14]

Objection 1. It would seem that hope is not a theological virtue. For a theological virtue is one that has God for its object. Now hope has for its object not only God but also other goods which we hope to obtain from God. Therefore hope is not a theological virtue.

---

of God's fidelity and gives ample grounds for our hope. For a useful retelling of the grand Scriptural narrative, see Scott Hahn's *A Father Who Keeps His Promises: God's Covenant Love in Scripture* (Ann Arbor, MI: Servant Publications, 1998). In moments when hope seems dim, we can also recall the many Christian saints who struggled against various sins and powerful temptations (such as Augustine with holy purity and Jerome with foul temper), but who nevertheless achieved the goal of all human life—becoming saints. With God's help, they did it and so can we.

12 For example, the genus of animal is divided by specific differences, such as "rational" and "non-rational," that mark out different kinds of things that nevertheless share the same genus.

13 God is both what we hope to gain (final cause or goal) and the power by which we can achieve what we hope for (efficient cause or moving force).

14 We might also say, with Pieper, that hope is a specifically Christian virtue: "Christ is the actual foundation of hope. . . . Christ is, at the same time, the actual fulfillment of our hope. . . . This inherent linking of our hope to Christ is so crucial that one who is not in Christ has no hope (1 Thess 4:13)." Joseph Pieper, *Faith, Hope, and Love* (San Francisco: Ignatius Press, 1997), 106. Christ is the foundation of hope because without the saving action of Christ's incarnation, passion, death, and resurrection, no one could be saved. Christ is the actual fulfillment of our hope because through our being united to Christ in the sacraments, through our incorporation into the Body of Christ, the Church, we fulfill our longing for salvation, imperfectly during our journey on earth and perfectly in heaven. One who is not in Christ, whether consciously or not, has no hope because one who is not in Christ cannot be saved.

Reply to Objection 1. Whatever else hope expects to obtain, it hopes for it in reference to God as the last end, or as the first efficient cause.[15]

Objection 2. Further, a theological virtue is not a mean between two vices, as stated above (I–II, q. 64, a. 4). But hope is a mean between presumption and despair. Therefore hope is not a theological virtue.

Reply to Objection 2. In things measured and ruled the mean consists in the measure or rule being attained; if we go beyond the rule, there is excess, if we fall short of the rule, there is deficiency. But in the rule or measure itself there is no such thing as a mean or extremes. Now a moral virtue is concerned with things ruled by reason, and these things are its proper object; wherefore it is proper to it to follow the mean as regards its proper object. On the other hand, a theological virtue is concerned with the First Rule not ruled by another rule, and that Rule is its proper object. Wherefore it is not proper for a theological virtue, with regard to its proper object, to follow the mean, although this may happen to it accidentally with regard to something that is referred to its principal object. Thus faith can have no mean or extremes in the point of trusting to the First Truth, in which it is impossible to trust too much; whereas on the part of the things believed, it may have a mean and extremes; for instance, one truth is a mean between two false-hoods.[16] So too, hope has no mean or extremes, as regards its principal object, since it is impossible to trust too much in the Divine assistance; yet it may have a mean and extremes, as regards those things a man

---

[15] Pieper explains: "In a certain sense, the virtue of hope brings order and direction in its wake even for man's natural hope, which is bound thereby to its proper and final 'not yet': [Thomas writes] 'In our orientation toward eternal life, we hope to receive help from God not only for spiritual but also for corporal deeds.' On the clear basis of this sentence from Saint Thomas Aquinas . . . he plainly says that it is permitted us to surround even the natural goods of life with supernatural hope, that is, with a hope directly infused by God." Joseph Pieper, *Faith, Hope, and Love* (San Francisco: Ignatius Press, 1997), 109.

[16] We can never have too much faith in God. However, it is possible to be too credulous (believing in things in which one ought not believe) or to be too skeptical (not believing what should be believed).

trusts to obtain, insofar as he either presumes above his capability,[17] or despairs of things of which he is capable.[18]

Objection 4. Further, the object of hope is something arduous. But it belongs to magnanimity, which is a moral virtue, to tend to the arduous. Therefore hope is a moral, and not a theological virtue.

Reply to Objection 4. Magnanimity tends to something arduous in the hope of obtaining something that is within one's power, wherefore its proper object is the doing of great things. On the other hand hope, as a theological virtue, regards something arduous, to be obtained by another's help, as stated above (a.1).[19]

ARTICLE 6 ∼ **Is hope distinct from faith and love?**

Yes, despite objections to the contrary, There cannot be numbers without distinction.[20] Now hope is numbered with the other theological

---

[17] This would be the sin of presumption in which one assumes salvation without the possibility of loss. Presumption is defined in the 1908 Catholic encyclopedia (online at www.newadvent.org) as "the condition of a soul which, because of a badly regulated reliance on God's mercy and power, hopes for salvation without doing anything to deserve it, or for pardon of his sins without repenting of them."

[18] This would be the sin of despair, in which one assumes that salvation is in no way possible.

[19] Hope is a theological virtue, but the theological virtue of "infused hope" can also be distinguished from the emotion of hope and the acquired virtue of hope. "The emotion of hope shares in the general dynamics of human longing and expectation. As part of the psychological makeup of the human person, hope expresses itself in two ways. First of all, hope exists at the level of basic sense appetites, specifically as one of the five irascible or contending emotions that serve to strengthen one against difficult situations that life presents. . . . This expectation compromises the simple, primordial movement of the person toward an expected good. . . . But in the form of a moral virtue, hope specifically affects the human appetite, strengthening the irascible or contending appetites to withstand whatever threatens its well being in the world. In other words, moral hope begets courage." Romanus Cessario, O.P., "The Theological Virtue of Hope," in *The Ethics of Aquinas*, ed. Stephen Pope (Washington DC: Georgetown University Press, 2002), 233.

[20] For example, if you are going to count various people, there has to be some distinction among them such as that they are in different places and have different bodies. You and I are in different places and have different bodies, so on the

virtues: for Gregory says (*Moral.* i, 16) that the three virtues are faith, hope, and charity. Therefore hope is distinct from the theological virtues.

I answer that, A virtue is said to be theological from having God for the object to which it adheres. Now one may adhere to a thing in two ways: first, for its own sake; secondly, because something else is attained thereby. Accordingly charity makes us adhere to God for His own sake, uniting our minds to God by the emotion of love.

On the other hand, hope and faith make man adhere to God as to a principle wherefrom certain things accrue to us. Now we derive from God both knowledge of truth and the attainment of perfect goodness. Accordingly faith makes us adhere to God, as the source whence we derive the knowledge of truth, since we believe that what God tells us is true: while hope makes us adhere to God, as the source whence we derive perfect goodness, i.e. insofar as, by hope, we trust to the Divine assistance for obtaining happiness.[21]

Objection 1. It would seem that hope is not distinct from the other theological virtues. For habits are distinguished by their objects, as stated above (I–II, q. 54, a. 2). Now the object of hope is the same as of the other theological virtues. Therefore hope is not distinct from the other theological virtues.

---

    basis of these differences (as well as many others) you would count me as one person and yourself as another. If there were no differences between you and me, you could not begin to number us. Cicero, Tully, the author of the *Tusculan Disputations*, and the man murdered by Herennius on December 7, 43 B.C. are not counted as four people because there is no distinction among these four. Cicero, Tully, the author, and the victim in question are all various names or descriptions of the very same person, namely Marcus Tullius Cicero. Thus, as Thomas notes, there cannot be numbering without distinction among the things numbered.

[21] Though distinct, the theological virtues are interrelated. In the order of generation, faith comes first since one cannot hope in a God that one does not believe exists. Hope comes next for one does not love that which one only fears, and charity is the crowning virtue based upon both faith and hope. However, in the order of excellence and perfection, charity is first, for it is the greatest virtue as well as the only one of the theological virtues that will remain in heaven. In the final state, we will "see" God. Faith will become intimate experience, and hope will be fulfilled beyond expectation. Love will still remain, indeed will be maximally intense.

Reply to Objection 1. God is the object of these virtues under different aspects, as stated above: and a different aspect of the object suffices for the distinction of habits, as stated above (I–II, q. 54, a. 2).

Objection 2. Further, in the symbol of faith,[22] whereby we make profession of faith, we say: "I expect the resurrection of the dead and the life of the world to come." Now expectation of future happiness belongs to hope, as stated above (a.5). Therefore hope is not distinct from faith.

Reply to Objection 2. Expectation is mentioned in the symbol of faith, not as though it were the proper act of faith, but because the act of hope presupposes the act of faith, as we shall state further on (q. 17, a. 7).[23] Hence an act of faith is expressed in the act of hope.

---

[22] As noted in the previous chapter on faith, the symbol of faith is the creed.

[23] In the article cited here, Thomas says, "Absolutely speaking, faith precedes hope. For the object of hope is a future good, arduous but possible to obtain. In order, therefore, that we may hope, it is necessary for the object of hope to be proposed to us as possible. Now the object of hope is, in one way, eternal happiness, and in another way, the Divine assistance, as explained above ['Hope makes us tend to God, as to a good to be obtained finally, and as to a helper strong to assist' (q. 17, a. 6, ad 3 and q. 17, a. 2):] and both of these are proposed to us by faith, whereby we come to know that we are able to obtain eternal life, and that for this purpose the Divine assistance is ready for us, according to Hebrews 11:6: 'He that cometh to God, must believe that He is, and is a rewarder to them that seek Him.' Therefore it is evident that faith precedes hope." We cannot hope to win the race unless we believe that the race is possible; similarly we cannot hope to obtain God unless we believe in a God that could be reached.

The question of whether faith precedes hope, like the question of whether hope precedes or is prior to charity (q. 17, a. 8) is one way of approaching the relationship among the theological virtues. How are these virtues related to one another? Must one have faith to have hope? Does one need hope to have charity? Does one need charity to have hope? Does the possessor of one virtue always have the others? The question of the "priority" of one virtue to another is a complex one about their relationship. As Aristotle points out in his *Categories* (12), one thing can be prior to another in a variety of ways. Chronological sequence is one sense of priority (e.g., a father is prior to his son), but also there is priority in a certain order (e.g., "apple" is prior to "man" in alphabetical order), priority in being (e.g., surface is prior to color, since every color is supervenient upon a surface), or priority in importance (e.g., securing safety comes prior to playing horseshoes).

Objection 3. Further, by hope man tends to God. But this belongs properly to charity. Therefore hope is not distinct from charity.

Reply to Objection 3. Hope makes us tend to God, as to a good to be obtained finally, and as to a helper strong to assist: whereas charity, properly speaking, makes us tend to God, by uniting our affections to Him, so that we live, not for ourselves, but for God.

QUESTION **18**

THE SUBJECT
OF HOPE

ARTICLE 2 ⚓ **Is there hope in those who are in heaven?**

No, despite objections to the contrary, The Apostle says (Rom 8:24): "What a man sees, why does he hope for?" Now the blessed enjoy the sight of God.[1] Therefore hope has no place in them.

    I answer that, If what gives a thing its species be removed, the species is destroyed, and that thing cannot remain the same; just as when a natural body loses its form, it does not remain the same specifically.[2] Now hope takes its species from its principal object, even as the other virtues do, as was shown above (II–II, q. 17, a. 5, a. 6; I–II, q. 54, a. 2): and its principal object is eternal happiness as being possible to obtain by the assistance of God, as stated above (II–II, q. 17, a. 2).

    Since, then, the arduous possible good cannot be an object of hope except insofar as it is something future, it follows that when happiness is no longer future, but present, it is incompatible with the virtue of hope. Consequently hope, like faith, is voided in heaven, and neither of them can be in the blessed.

Objection 1. It would seem that in the blessed there is hope. For Christ was a perfect comprehensor from the first moment of His conception.[3]

---

  [1] By the "blessed," Thomas means those in heaven.

  [2] When the human body loses its form, the soul, it ceases to be a human body and becomes a mere corpse.

  [3] Thomas later in the *Summa* explores Christ's knowledge (see *ST* III, questions 9–12), concluding that he enjoyed full fellowship and communion and

Now He had hope, since, according to a gloss, the words of Psalm 30:2, "In You, O Lord, have I hoped," are said in His person. Therefore in the blessed there can be hope.

Reply to Objection 1. Although Christ was a comprehensor[4] and therefore blessed as to the enjoyment of God, nevertheless He was, at the same time, a wayfarer, as regards the possibility of nature,[5] to which He was still subject. Hence it was possible for Him to hope for the glory of impassibility and immortality, yet not so as to the virtue of hope, the principal object of which is not the glory of the body but the enjoyment of God.

Objection 2. Further, even as the obtaining of happiness is an arduous good, so is its continuation. Now, before they obtain happiness, men hope to obtain it. Therefore, after they have obtained it, they can hope to continue in its possession.

Reply to Objection 2. The happiness of the saints is called eternal life, because through enjoying God they become partakers, as it were, of God's eternity which surpasses all time: so that the continuation of happiness does not differ in respect of present, past and future. Hence the blessed do not hope for the continuation of their happiness (for as regards this there is no future), but are in actual possession thereof.[6]

---

understanding of God and remained God throughout the incarnation (that is, even while within the womb). He remained therefore a "comprehensor," one who has the vision of God, even in the incarnation (*ST* III, 9, 2).

[4] Christ comprehended God himself and enjoyed heavenly bliss on earth, but he was also like us in journeying to the Father, a journey which was completed at the Ascension. (Jn 14:28)

[5] By "passibility," Thomas means that Christ in his humanity could suffer, undergo change, and develop. Jesus is fully God and fully man, and so in his humanity endured human weakness, emotion, pain, and growth. Though he had the weakness belonging to human nature, he did not have the weakness of original or actual sin.

[6] Persons in heaven enjoy one eternal "now," of which our greatest experiences on earth, such as a thrilling victory, an intense experience of love, a triumph against the odds, are a mere foreshadowing. For more on what heaven may be like, see Peter Kreeft's *Heaven: The Heart's Deepest Longing* (San Francisco: Ignatius Press, 1989) and his *Everything You Ever Wanted to Know about Heaven* (San Francisco: Ignatius Press, 1990).

Objection 3. Further, by the virtue of hope, a man can hope for happiness, not only for himself, but also for others, as stated above (q. 17, a. 3). But the blessed who are in heaven hope for the happiness of others, else they would not pray for them. Therefore there can be hope in them.

Reply to Objection 3. So long as the virtue of hope lasts, it is by the same hope that one hopes for one's own happiness and for that of others. But when hope is voided in the blessed, whereby they hoped for their own happiness, they hope for the happiness of others indeed, yet not by the virtue of hope, but rather by the love of charity. Even so, he that has Divine charity, by that same charity loves his neighbor, and yet a man may love his neighbor without having the virtue of charity, but by some other love.

Objection 4. Further, the happiness of the saints implies not only glory of the soul but also glory of the body. Now the souls of the saints in heaven look yet for the glory of their bodies (Apoc. 6:10; Augustine, *Gen. ad lit.* xii, 35). Therefore in the blessed there can be hope.

Reply to Objection 4. Since hope is a theological virtue having God for its object, its principal object is the glory of the soul, which consists in the enjoyment of God, and not the glory of the body. Moreover, although the glory of the body is something arduous in comparison with human nature, yet it is not so for one who has the glory of the soul, both because the glory of the body is a very small thing as compared with the glory of the soul, and because one who has the glory of the soul has already the sufficient cause of the glory of the body.

ARTICLE 3 ⊷ **Is hope in those who are in hell?**

No, despite objections to the contrary, Hope causes joy, according to Romans 12:12, "Rejoicing in hope." Now the damned have no joy,[7] but sorrow and grief, according to Isaiah 65:14, "My servants shall praise for joyfulness of heart, and you shall cry for sorrow of heart, and shall howl for grief of spirit." Therefore no hope is in the damned.

I answer that, Just as it is a condition of happiness that the will should find rest therein, so is it a condition of punishment that what is

---

[7] By the "damned," Thomas means those who are in hell.

inflicted in punishment should go against the will. Now that which is not known can neither be restful nor repugnant to the will: wherefore Augustine says (*Gen. ad lit.* xi, 17) that the angels could not be perfectly happy in their first state before their confirmation, or unhappy before their fall, since they had no foreknowledge of what would happen to them. For perfect and true happiness requires that one should be certain of being happy for ever, else the will would not rest.[8]

In like manner, since the everlastingness of damnation is a necessary condition of the punishment of the damned, it would not be truly penal unless it went against the will; and this would be impossible if they were ignorant of the everlastingness of their damnation.[9] Hence it

---

[8] It is important that perfect happiness lasts forever and cannot be lost. In I–II, q. 5, a. 4, Thomas writes: "For since happiness is the 'perfect and sufficient good,' it must set man's desire at rest and exclude every evil. Now man naturally desires to hold to the good that he has, and to have the surety of his holding: else he must of necessity be troubled with the fear of losing it, or with the sorrow of knowing that he will lose it. Therefore it is necessary for true Happiness that man have the assured opinion of never losing the good that he possesses. If this opinion be true, it follows that he never will lose happiness: but if it be false, it is in itself an evil that he should have a false opinion: because the false is the evil of the intellect, just as the true is its good, as stated in *Ethic.* vi, 2. Consequently he will no longer be truly happy, if evil be in him. . . . Moreover, neither can he lose Happiness, through God taking it away from him. Because, since the withdrawal of Happiness is a punishment, it cannot be enforced by God, the just Judge, except for some fault; and he that sees God cannot fall into a fault, since rectitude of the will, of necessity, results from that vision. Thus, heaven once had cannot be lost. Since servile fear is the fear of punishment, and heaven excludes all evils, including the evil of punishment, servile fear is not experienced by the blessed in heaven." Perfect happiness must be everlasting, for if it were not, and one knew it, then one would dread the possibility of its loss. On the other hand, if the happiness were not everlasting and one did not know it, then one's happiness would be based on ignorance of this fact and insofar as the intellect would not be perfected, the human person would not be perfected, and therefore not perfectly happy.

[9] In his *Summa contra Gentiles*, Thomas argues that hell must be everlasting because once bodily life is over, the soul's journey is "fixed." (*Summa contra Gentiles* III, 145). See also, Avery Cardinal Dulles, "The Population of Hell," *First Things* 133 (May 2003): 36–41.

belongs to the unhappy state of the damned that they should know that they cannot by any means escape from damnation and obtain happiness. Wherefore it is written (Job 15:22): "He believes not that he may return from darkness to light." It is, therefore, evident that they cannot apprehend happiness as a possible good, as neither can the blessed apprehend it as a future good. Consequently there is no hope either in the blessed or in the damned. On the other hand, hope can be in wayfarers, whether of this life or in purgatory, because in either case they apprehend happiness as a future possible thing.

Objection 1. It would seem that there is hope in the damned. For the devil is damned and prince of the damned, according to Matthew 25:41: "Depart . . . you cursed, into everlasting fire, which was prepared for the devil and his angels." But the devil has hope, according to Job 40:28, "Behold his hope shall fail him." Therefore it seems that the damned have hope.

Reply to Objection 1. As Gregory says (*Moral.* xxxiii, 20) this is said of the devil as regards his members, whose hope will fail utterly: or, if it be understood of the devil himself, it may refer to the hope whereby he expects to vanquish the saints, in which sense we read just before (Job 40:18): "He trusts that the Jordan may run into his mouth": this is not, however, the hope of which we are speaking.

Objection 2. Further, just as faith is either living or dead, so is hope. But lifeless faith can be in the devils and the damned, according to James 2:19: "The devils . . . believe and tremble." Therefore it seems that lifeless hope also can be in the damned.

Reply to Objection 2. As Augustine says (*Enchiridion* viii), "faith is about things, bad or good, past, present, or future, one's own or another's, whereas hope is only about good things, future and concerning oneself." Hence it is possible for lifeless faith to be in the damned, but not hope, since the Divine goods are not for them future possible things, but far removed from them.

ARTICLE 4 ⁓ **Is there certainty in the hope of those on earth?**

Yes, despite objections to the contrary, "Hope is the certain expectation of future happiness," as the Master[10] states (*Sent.* iii, D, 26): and this may be gathered from 2 Timothy 1:12, "I know Whom I have believed, and I am certain that He is able to keep that which I have committed to Him."

I answer that, Certainty is found in a thing in two ways, essentially and by participation. It is found essentially in the cognitive power; by participation in whatever is moved infallibly to its end by the cognitive power. In this way we say that nature works with certainty, since it is moved by the Divine intellect which moves everything with certainty to its end. In this way too, the moral virtues are said to work with greater certainty than art, in as much as, like a second nature, they are moved to their acts by the reason: and thus too, hope tends to its end with certainty, as though sharing in the certainty of faith which is in the cognitive faculty.[11]

---

[10] The "Master," as noted earlier, is Peter Lombard, author of the influential *Sentences*, a collection of patristic teachings on various points of disagreement that Lombard sought to reconcile.

[11] W. J. Hill distinguishes the *certitude of tendency*, the certainty involved in the virtue of hope, from *the certitude of faith* and *the certitude of event*. The certitude of faith is primarily cognitive about what the intellect knows, while the certainty of tendency involved in the virtue of hope is primarily affective about what the will desires, since as Thomas noted, hope is primarily in the will, not the intellect (q. 18, a. 1). The certainty of faith concerns things that cannot be other than they are. (God cannot be anything other than God.) The certainty of hope concerns things of the practical order that can be other than they currently are. (I am not yet enjoying the beatific vision in heaven, but I might be able to in the future.) True faith cannot be erroneous, whereas we may fail to achieve that for which we hope. Nor is hope a certainty of event, an assurance that in fact we will be saved. In other words, the certainty of hope for Aquinas is not a "once saved, always saved" teaching as proposed by some Protestant denominations. The doctrine of "perseverance of the saints" as articulated by some Reformed/Calvinistic churches can be compared to the variety of views offered during the Middle Ages by different Catholic theologians, such as Gabriel Biel or Johann von Staupitz. Franciscans and Dominican thinkers argued about such matters. The root of the issue is in the free will/determinism debate. Can one that is elected by God to salvation fall away from God's divine election? Thomas attempts to articulate a mediating position that preserves both God's sovereignty as well as

Objection 2. Further, hope is based on grace and merits, as stated above (q. 17, a. 1). Now it is impossible in this life to know for certain that we are in a state of grace, as stated above (I–II, q. 112, a. 5). Therefore there is no certainty in the hope of a wayfarer.

Reply to Objection 2. Hope does not trust chiefly in grace already received, but on God's omnipotence and mercy, whereby even he that has not grace, can obtain it, so as to come to eternal life. Now whoever has faith is certain of God's omnipotence and mercy.[12]

Objection 3. Further, there can be no certainty about that which may fail. Now many a hopeful wayfarer fails to obtain happiness. Therefore the wayfarer's hope has no certainty.

Reply to Objection 3. That some who have hope fail to obtain happiness is due to a fault of the free will in placing the obstacle of sin, but not to any deficiency in God's power or mercy, in which hope places its trust. Hence this does not prejudice the certainty of hope.

---

human free-will. As Hill notes: "Were such assurance verified then one would not hope for salvation; one would merely wait for it. . . . In the natural order, the plant may fail to bear fruit because of such counter-agents as frost, but it cannot fail to tend in accord with the vital conditions of its own life towards fructification. Analogously, the certainty that the Christian experiences in his hope is precisely his untroubled assurance that the power and mercy of God orders him (though fallibly) to salvation." W. J. Hill in St. Thomas Aquinas, *Summa theologiae,* vol. 33 (New York: Blackfriars, 1966), 163–64. Nevertheless, there are strong grounds for a firm hope that we will indeed be saved, as Scott Hahn illuminates in his remarks on hope quoted in the footnotes for *ST* II–II, q. 21, a. 2, note 52 of this chapter.

12 There are at least two ways to deny God's mercy—either by denying that sins committed could be forgiven or by denying that sins are committed.

QUESTION **19**

THE GIFT OF FEAR

ARTICLE 1 ~ **Can God be feared?**

Yes, despite objections to the contrary, It is written (Jer 10:7): "Who shall not fear You, O King of nations?" and (Mal 1:6): "If I be a master, where is My fear?"

I answer that, Just as hope has two objects, one of which is the future good itself that one expects to obtain, while the other is someone's help, through whom one expects to obtain what one hopes for, so too, fear may have two objects, one of which is the very evil which a man shrinks from, while the other is that from which the evil may come. Accordingly, in the first way God, Who is goodness itself, cannot be an object of fear; but He can be an object of fear in the second way, insofar as there may come to us some evil either from Him or in relation to Him.

From Him there comes the evil of punishment, but this is evil not absolutely but relatively, and, absolutely speaking, is a good, because, since a thing is said to be good through being ordered to an end, while evil implies lack of this order, that which excludes the order to the last end is altogether evil, and such is the evil of fault. On the other hand, the evil of punishment is indeed an evil, insofar as it is the privation of some particular good, yet absolutely speaking, it is a good, insofar as it is ordained to the last end.

In relation to God the evil of fault can come to us,[1] if we be separated from Him: and in this way God can and ought to be feared.[2]

Objection 1. It would seem that God cannot be feared. For the object of fear is a future evil, as stated above (I–II, q. 41, a. 2, a. 3). But God is free of all evil, since He is goodness itself. Therefore God cannot be feared.

Reply to Objection 1. This objection considers the object of fear as being the evil that a man shuns.

---

[1] Thomas here distinguishes two different kinds of evils, the evil of fault (*malum culpae*) and the evil of punishment, penalty, or pain (*malum poenae*). As Thomas explains elsewhere (I, q. 48, a. 5; *Disputed Questions on Evil,* question 1, article 4), evil of fault is a deficiency of the moral goodness of a person (a moral defect) and evil of punishment is deprivation of some non-moral good, such as health (no moral defect). In other words, the evil of fault is an evil that cannot be endured against a person's will. The evil of fault is an evil that agents bring upon themselves and only upon themselves, for to sin is by definition a voluntary act. On the other hand, an evil of punishment, such as suffering death or loss of bodily goods, can be inflicted on other people against their wills. Since evil of punishment and evil of fault are different kinds of evils, non-moral evil and moral evil, and since fear is in response to evil, from these two kinds of evil different kinds of fear arise. Filial fear is in response to moral evil; it is the fear of doing evil by choice, the fear of losing or damaging friendship with God. Servile fear is in response to non-moral evil; it is the fear of suffering evil against one's choice.

[2] Pieper explains that there is a link between authentic hope and fear of the Lord: "Fear of the Lord assures the genuineness of hope. It eliminates the danger that hope may be turned into its *falsa similitudo*, its false image: into the presumptuous anticipation of fulfillment. Fear of the Lord keeps ever before the mind of the one who hopes the fact that fulfillment has 'not yet' been accomplished. Fear of the Lord is a constant reminder that human existence, although destined for and oriented toward fulfillment by the Highest Being, is, nevertheless, perpetually threatened in the *status viatoris* by the closeness of nothingness." Joseph Pieper, *Faith, Hope, and Love* (San Francisco: Ignatius Press, 1997), 138. The blessed in heaven are freed from every fault and flaw, but even in heaven a creature does not become the Creator; the finite does not become the Infinite; the dependent being does not become the Necessary Being. In heaven, we remain who we are, created, finite, dependent beings. As such, even in heaven, there will always exist a fear of the Lord, not a "negative" fear incompatible with perfect happiness, but a reverential awe of Perfect Goodness, Power, and Love.

Objection 2. Further, fear is opposed to hope. Now we hope in God. Therefore we cannot fear Him at the same time.

Reply to Objection 2. In God, we may consider both His justice, in respect of which He punishes those who sin, and His mercy, in respect of which He sets us free: in us the consideration of His justice gives rise to fear, but the consideration of His mercy gives rise to hope, so that, accordingly, God is the object of both hope and fear, but under different aspects.[3]

Objection 3. Further, as the Philosopher states (*Rhet.* ii, 5), "we fear those things whence evil comes to us." But evil comes to us, not from God, but from ourselves, according to Hosea 13:9: "Destruction is your own, O Israel: your help is . . . in Me." Therefore God is not to be feared.

Reply to Objection 3. The evil of fault is not from God as its author but from us, insofar as we forsake God: while the evil of punishment is from God as its author, insofar as it has the character of a good, since it is something just, through being inflicted on us justly, although originally this is due to the demerit of sin: thus it is written (Wis 1:13, 16): "God made not death . . . but the wicked with works and words have called it to them."

ARTICLE 2 ➺ **Is fear fittingly divided into filial, initial, servile and worldly fear?**

Yes, despite objections to the contrary, Stands the authority of the Master (*Sent.* iii, D, 34).

I answer that, We are speaking of fear now, insofar as it makes us turn, so to speak, to God or away from Him. For, since the object of fear is an evil, sometimes, on account of the evils he fears, man withdraws from God,[4] and this is called human fear, while sometimes, on account

---

[3] God is one, and so God's mercy and justice are not competing "parts," so to speak, of God. To use an analogy borrowed from Bishop Sheen, just as the same sun melts wax but hardens clay, so too, one and the same God is viewed and experienced as either merciful or justly punishing depending on the condition of the human person in relationship to God.

[4] Worldly fear in which a person fears losing worldly goods such as life, pleasure, riches, or health, is always sinful because it is based, by definition, on treating

of the evils he fears, he turns to God and adheres to Him. This latter evil is twofold, viz. evil of punishment, and evil of fault.

Accordingly if a man turn to God and adhere to Him, through fear of punishment, it will be servile fear; but if it be on account of fear of committing a fault, it will be filial fear, for it becomes a child to fear offending his father. If, however, it be on account of both, it will be initial fear, which is between both these fears.[5] As to whether it is possible to fear the evil of fault, the question was treated above (I–II, q. 42, a. 3)[6] when we were considering the passion of fear.

ARTICLE 7 ⁓ Is fear the beginning of wisdom?

Yes, despite objections to the contrary, It is written in the Psalm 110:10: "The fear of the Lord is the beginning of wisdom."[7]

---

    worldly goods as if they were the most important goods of all. However, fear considered in itself is not a moral defect.

[5] Servile fear of God is fear of God's punishment; filial fear of God is fear of sin whereby one is separated from God; initial fear is of both kinds. Servile fear leads to imperfect contrition, sorrow for sin because of fear of the punishment due to sin. Filial fear leads to perfect contrition, sorrow for sin because one does not want to offend God but rather desires to be united with God.

[6] Here, Thomas writes: "As the object of hope is a future good difficult but possible to obtain, so the object of fear is a future evil, arduous and not to be easily avoided. From this we may gather that whatever is entirely subject to our power and will, is not an object of fear, and that nothing gives rise to fear save what is due to an external cause. Now human will is the proper cause of the evil of sin: and consequently evil of sin, properly speaking, is not an object of fear. But since the human will may be inclined to sin by an extrinsic cause, if this cause have a strong power of inclination, in that respect, a man may fear the evil of sin insofar as it arises from that extrinsic cause: as when he fears to dwell in the company of wicked men, lest he be led by them to sin. But, properly speaking, a man thus disposed fears being led astray rather than the sin considered in its proper nature, that is, as a voluntary act; for considered in this light it is not an object of fear to him."

[7] Thomas was passionately concerned about gaining wisdom. In chapter two of the opening book of *Summa contra Gentiles*, he notes that wisdom is intimately linked to our happiness. The pursuit of wisdom is the most perfect because it fulfills or perfects our noblest faculty with the most noble object; it is the most noble because through gaining wisdom we become like God, who has perfect wisdom; and it is the most useful because through it we attain that which will make us happiest—immortality. In his praise of wisdom, Thomas echoes Aristotle's maxim: "All men by nature desire to

I answer that, A thing may be called the beginning of wisdom in two ways: in one way because it is the beginning of wisdom itself as to its essence; in another way, as to its effect. Thus the beginning of an art as to its essence consists in the principles from which that art proceeds, while the beginning of an art as to its effect is that wherefrom it begins to operate: for instance, we might say that the beginning of the art of building is the foundation because that is where the builder begins his work.

Now, since wisdom is the knowledge of Divine things, as we shall state further on (II–II, q. 45, a. 1), it is considered by us in one way, and in another way by philosophers. For, seeing that our life is ordained to the enjoyment of God, and is directed thereto according to a participation of the Divine Nature, conferred on us through grace, wisdom, as we look at it, is considered not only as being cognizant of God, as it is with the philosophers, but also as directing human conduct, since this is directed not only by the human law, but also by the Divine law, as Augustine shows (*De Trin.* xii, 14). Accordingly the beginning of wisdom as to its essence consists in the first principles of wisdom, i.e. the articles of faith, and in this sense faith is said to be the beginning of wisdom. But as regards the effect, the beginning of wisdom is the point where wisdom begins to work, and in this way fear is the beginning of wisdom, yet servile fear in one way, and filial fear in another. For servile fear is like a principle disposing a man to wisdom from without, insofar as he refrains from sin through fear of punishment, and is thus fashioned for the effect of wisdom, according to Sirach 1:27, "The fear of the Lord drives out sin." On the other hand, chaste or filial fear is the beginning of

---

know" and also the teaching of scripture: "Do not forsake wisdom, and she will protect you; love her, and she will watch over you. Wisdom is supreme; therefore get wisdom. Though it cost all you have, get understanding. Esteem her, and she will exalt you; embrace her, and she will honor you" (Prov 4:6–8). "Happy the man who meditates on wisdom and reasons intelligently, who reflects in his heart on her ways and ponders her secrets. He pursues her like a hunter and lies in wait on her paths. He peers through her windows and listens at her doors. He camps near her house and fastens his tent-peg to her walls; he pitches his tent near her and so finds an excellent resting-place; he places his children under her protection and lodges under her boughs; by her he is sheltered from the heat and he dwells in the shade of her glory" (Sir 14:20–27).

wisdom, as being the first effect of wisdom. For since the regulation of human conduct by the Divine law belongs to wisdom, in order to make a beginning, man must first of all fear God and submit himself to Him: for the result will be that in all things he will be ruled by God.[8]

Objection 1. It would seem that fear is not the beginning of wisdom. For the beginning of a thing is a part thereof. But fear is not a part of wisdom, since fear is seated in the appetitive faculty, while wisdom is in the intellect. Therefore it seems that fear is not the beginning of wisdom.

Reply to Objection 1. This argument proves that fear is not the beginning of wisdom as to the essence of wisdom.

Objection 2. Further, nothing is the beginning of itself. "Now fear of the Lord, that is wisdom," according to Job 28:28. Therefore it seems that fear of God is not the beginning of wisdom.

Reply to Objection 2. The fear of God is compared to a man's whole life that is ruled by God's wisdom, as the root to the tree: hence it is written (Sir 1:25): "The root of wisdom is to fear the Lord, for (Vulg.: 'and') the branches thereof are long lived." Consequently, as the root is said to be virtually the tree, so the fear of God is said to be wisdom.

Objection 3. Further, nothing is prior to the beginning. But something is prior to fear, since faith precedes fear. Therefore it seems that fear is not the beginning of wisdom.

Reply to Objection 3. As stated above, faith is the beginning of wisdom in one way, and fear, in another. Hence it is written (Sir 25:16): "The fear of God is the beginning of love: and the beginning of faith is to be fast joined to it."

---

8 Fear of the Lord can seem like a "negative" thing, but, according to Thomas, even Christ had fear of the Lord, indeed to a greater degree than anyone else. "For Christ as man had this act of reverence towards God in a fuller sense and beyond all others. And hence Scripture attributes to Him the fullness of the fear of the Lord" (*ST* III, 7, 6). Fear is the beginning of wisdom by restraining the wrongdoing of human beings through fear of divine punishment (servile fear) and through fear of injuring one's relationship with God and the loss of sanctifying grace by which a person becomes an adopted child of God (filial fear).

ARTICLE 9 ⤳ Is fear a gift of the Holy Spirit?

Yes, despite objections to the contrary, The fear of the Lord is numbered among the seven gifts of the Holy Spirit (Is 11:3).[9]

I answer that, Fear is of several kinds, as stated above (a. 2). Now it is not "human fear," according to Augustine (*De Gratia et Lib. Arb.* xviii), "that is a gift of God"—for it was by this fear that Peter denied Christ—but that fear of which it was said (Mt 10:28): "Fear Him that can destroy both soul and body into hell."

Again servile fear is not to be reckoned among the seven gifts of the Holy Spirit, though it is from Him, because according to Augustine (*De Nat. et Grat.* lvii), it is compatible with the will to sin: whereas the gifts of the Holy Spirit are incompatible with the will to sin, as they are inseparable from charity, as stated above (I–II, q. 68, a. 5).

It follows, therefore, that the fear of God, which is numbered among the seven gifts of the Holy Spirit, is filial or chaste fear. For it was stated above (I–II, q. 68, a. 1, a. 3) that the gifts of the Holy Spirit are certain habitual perfections of the soul's powers,[10] whereby these are rendered amenable to the motion of the Holy Spirit, just as, by the moral virtues, the appetitive powers are rendered amenable to the motion of reason.[11] Now for a thing to be amenable to the motion of

---

[9] Since fear of the Lord is the beginning of wisdom, and since gaining wisdom is part of our becoming happy, it is truly a gift to have fear of the Lord. As Thomas notes later in this article, this fear is not just any kind of fear but rather a "filial" fear, the fear of a good son who wants to please his loving father and fears any injury coming to their relationship.

[10] The powers of the soul are the vegetative, sensitive, appetitive, locomotive, and intellectual powers. Each person has only one soul, but the individual soul has five different kinds of operations that it performs: growth (vegetative power), receiving "data" of various kinds (sensitive power), seeking (appetitive power), moving (locomotive power), and rationality (intellectual power). For more, see *ST* I, questions 75–78.

[11] As Augustine Waldron puts it: "[T]he proper function of the moral virtues is to rectify the appetitive powers, i.e., to dispose them to act in accordance with right reason; there are principally three moral virtues: justice, which perfects the rational appetite or will; fortitude and temperance, which moderate the lower or sensuous appetite. Prudence, as we have observed, is called a moral virtue, not indeed essentially, but by reason of its subject matter, inasmuch as it is directive of the acts of the moral virtues."

a certain mover, the first condition required is that it be a non-resistant subject of that mover, because resistance of the movable subject to the mover hinders the movement. This is what filial or chaste fear does, since thereby we revere God and avoid separating ourselves from Him. Hence, according to Augustine (*De Serm. Dom. in Monte* i, 4), filial fear holds the first place, as it were, among the gifts of the Holy Spirit, in the ascending order, and the last place, in the descending order.[12]

Objection 1. It would seem that fear is not a gift of the Holy Spirit. For no gift of the Holy Spirit is opposed to a virtue, which is also from the Holy Spirit, else the Holy Spirit would be in opposition to Himself. Now fear is opposed to hope, which is a virtue. Therefore fear is not a gift of the Holy Spirit.

Reply to Objection 1. Filial fear is not opposed to the virtue of hope: since thereby we fear, not that we may fail of what we hope to obtain

---

[12] About the gifts of the Holy Spirit, Thomas writes: "The gifts are perfections of man, whereby he becomes amenable to the promptings of the Holy Spirit. Now it is evident from what has been already said (q. 56, a. 4; q. 58, a. 2) that the moral virtues perfect the appetitive power according as it partakes somewhat of the reason, insofar, to wit, as it has a natural aptitude to be moved by the command of reason. Accordingly the gifts of the Holy Spirit, as compared with the Holy Spirit Himself, are related to man even as the moral virtues, in comparison with the reason, are related to the appetitive power. Now the moral virtues are habits whereby the powers of appetite are disposed to obey reason promptly. Therefore the gifts of the Holy Spirit are habits whereby man is perfected to obey readily the Holy Spirit" (*ST* I–II, q. 68, a. 3). These gifts (understanding, counsel, wisdom, knowledge, piety, fortitude, and fear) are necessary for salvation (*ST* I–II, q.68, a. 2). Each of these gifts brings to completion an aspect of the human person. "Accordingly, for the apprehension of truth, the speculative reason is perfected by 'understanding,' the practical reason, by 'counsel.' In order to judge aright, the speculative reason is perfected by 'wisdom,' the practical reason by 'knowledge.' The appetitive power, in matters concerning a man's relations to another, is perfected by 'piety'; in matters concerning himself, it is perfected by 'fortitude' against the fear of dangers; and against inordinate lust for pleasures, by 'fear.' . . . Hence it is clear that these gifts extend to all those things to which the virtues, both intellectual and moral, extend" (*ST* I–II, q. 68, a. 4). The gifts of the Holy Spirit are infused by God and help man to reach an end that surpasses the ends achievable by human power alone, namely divine adoption.

by God's help, but lest we withdraw ourselves from this help. Wherefore filial fear and hope cling together, and perfect one another.

Objection 2. Further, it is proper to a theological virtue to have God for its object. But fear has God for its object, insofar as God is feared. Therefore fear is not a gift, but a theological virtue.

Reply to Objection 2. The proper and principal object of fear is the evil shunned, and in this way, as stated above (a. 1), God cannot be an object of fear. Yet He is, in this way, the object of hope and the other theological virtues, since, by the virtue of hope, we trust in God's help, not only to obtain any other goods, but, chiefly, to obtain God Himself, as the principal good. The same evidently applies to the other theological virtues.

Objection 3. Further, fear arises from love. But love is reckoned a theological virtue. Therefore fear also is a theological virtue, being connected with the same matter, as it were.

Reply to Objection 3. From the fact that love is the origin of fear, it does not follow that the fear of God is not a distinct habit from charity, which is the love of God, since love is the origin of all the emotions, and yet we are perfected by different habits in respect of different emotions. Yet love is more of a virtue than fear is, because love regards good, to which virtue is principally directed by reason of its own nature, as was shown above (I–II, q. 55, a. 3, a. 4), for which reason hope is also reckoned as a virtue, whereas fear principally regards evil, the avoidance of which it denotes, wherefore it is something less than a theological virtue.

Objection 4. Further, Gregory says (*Moral.* ii, 49) that "fear is bestowed as a remedy against pride." But the virtue of humility is opposed to pride. Therefore again, fear is a kind of virtue.

Reply to Objection 4. According to Sirach 10:14, "the beginning of the pride of man is to fall off from God," that is to refuse submission to God, and this is opposed to filial fear, which reveres God. Thus fear cuts off the source of pride, for which reason it is bestowed as a remedy against pride. Yet it does not follow that it is the same as the virtue of humility, but that it is its origin. For the gifts of the Holy Spirit are the origin of the intellectual and moral virtues, as stated above (I–II, q. 68, a. 4), while the theological virtues are the origin of the gifts, as stated above (I–II, q. 69, a. 4, ad 3).

QUESTION **20**

DESPAIR

ARTICLE 1 ⟿ Is despair a sin?

Yes, despite objections to the contrary, That which leads men to sin, seems not only to be a sin itself, but a source of sins. Now such is despair, for the Apostle says of certain men (Eph 4:19): "Who, despairing, have given themselves up to lasciviousness, unto the working of all uncleanness and (Vulg.: 'unto') covetousness." Therefore despair is not only a sin but also the origin of other sins.

I answer that, According to the Philosopher (*Ethic.* vi, 2) affirmation and negation in the intellect correspond to search and avoidance in the appetite; while truth and falsehood in the intellect correspond to good and evil in the appetite. Consequently every appetitive movement which is conformed to a true intellect is good in itself, while every appetitive movement which is conformed to a false intellect is evil in itself and sinful. Now the true opinion of the intellect about God is that from Him comes salvation to mankind, and pardon to sinners, according to Ezekiel 18:23, "I desire not the death of the sinner, but that he should be converted, and live" (Vulg.: 'Is it My will that a sinner should die . . . and not that he should be converted and live?' Cf. Ez 33:11), while it is a false opinion that He refuses pardon to the repentant sinner, or that He does not turn sinners to Himself by sanctifying grace. Therefore, just as the movement of hope, which is in conformity with the true opinion, is praiseworthy

and virtuous, so the contrary movement of despair,[1] which is in conformity with the false opinion about God, is vicious and sinful.[2]

Objection 1. It would seem that despair is not a sin. For every sin
includes conversion to a mutable good, together with aversion from the
immutable good, as Augustine states (*De Lib. Arb.* ii, 19). But despair
includes no conversion to a mutable good. Therefore it is not a sin.

Reply to Objection 1. In every mortal sin there is, in some way, aversion from the Immutable Good, and conversion to a mutable good, but
not always in the same way, since the theological virtues have God for
their object, the sins which are contrary to them, such as hatred of God,
despair and unbelief, consist principally in aversion from the Immutable
Good; but, consequently, they imply conversion to a mutable good,
insofar as the soul that is a deserter from God must necessarily turn to
other things.[3] Other sins, however, consist principally in conversion to a

---

[1] Despair as well as its opposite, presumption, seems rather common today.
Many people believe in a deistic God, who perhaps initiated the Big Bang but
is removed from everyday life. They have no hope in a God who is a living
Trinity of Persons, loving and saving people. They despair of a loving, living,
saving God.

[2] Pieper notes: "Today when we speak of despair we are usually referring to a
psychological state into which an individual 'falls' almost against his will. As
it is used here, however, the term describes a decision of the will. Not a
mood, but an act of intellect. Hence not something into which one falls, but
something one posits." Joseph Pieper, *Faith, Hope, and Love* (San Francisco:
Ignatius Press, 1997), 114. To despair is an act, a sinful act, and all sin must
involve the will. Moods however do not (at least usually) involve the will,
but rather arise from a variety of factors (including weather and hormonal
shifts) that cannot be controlled by the will. To be in a hopeful or unhope-
ful, cheerful or uncheerful mood is not sinful in itself, but what one does
with one's mood is subject to moral evaluation.

[3] As Thomas says elsewhere, "the generation of one thing is the corruption of
another" (I, q. 72, a. 1, ad 5). The soul more deeply and firmly adhering to
God is to that degree less fixated on other things; the more a soul is fixated
on lesser things, the less deeply and firmly it can adhere to God. In a way
though, true love of God does not corrupt love of other people or things,
insofar as they are loved as God's creation. Indeed, we will love other people
and all of God's creation more when we love God more. However, in the
sense that Thomas means here, as true love of God increases, a false love that
idolizes people or things decreases.

mutable good, and, consequently, in aversion from the Immutable Good: because the fornicator intends, not to depart from God, but to enjoy carnal pleasure, the result of which is that he departs from God.[4]

Objection 2. Further, that which grows from a good root seems to be no sin, because "a good tree cannot bring forth evil fruit" (Mt 7:18). Now despair seems to grow from a good root, viz. fear of God, or from horror at the greatness of one's own sins. Therefore despair is not a sin.

Reply to Objection 2. A thing may grow from a virtuous root in two ways: first, directly and on the part of the virtue itself, even as an act proceeds from a habit: and in this way no sin can grow from a virtuous root, for in this sense Augustine declared (*De Lib. Arb.* ii, 18, 19) that "no man makes evil use of virtue." Secondly, a thing proceeds from a virtue indirectly, or is occasioned by a virtue, and in this way nothing hinders a sin proceeding from a virtue: thus sometimes men pride themselves of their virtues, according to Augustine (*Ep.* ccxi): "Pride lies in wait for good works that they may die." In this way fear of God or horror of one's own sins may lead to despair,[5] insofar as

---

[4] In other words, not all sins involve a conscious, deliberate, and willful rejection of God in Himself. Often, sin is to prefer some lesser good, even if this involves separation from God, which of itself is not desired.

[5] We all sin, but despite this we all have reason to hope that we will be saved, forever children of God in heaven. In the words of Scott Hahn: "I don't know about you, but I struggle with sin, I struggle with my temper, and I say to God, 'How can I be your son if I'm still struggling with these sins I was struggling with 10, 15 or 20 years ago? How can I know that I'm one of your children?' The response that I got in my own heart, my own mind, was this: Do your kids ever wonder whose kids they are? If God asked me how my kids know they're mine, I could make a list: first of all, they live in my house. But sometimes we have students living with us, so it's not enough just to live in the house. My kids are also called by my name, and the students aren't. They also sit at our table, every night. . . . If the kids still had doubts, they could do some DNA testing. Genetic testing would show them that they share my flesh and blood. Besides that, my bride is their mother and no one else's. . . . Plus, my kids know they're my kids because I discipline them and not the neighbors' kids. Another proof: we're always celebrating together as a family, birthdays, saints' days, vacations.

"And then it was like my guardian angel tapped me on the shoulder and said, 'Do you think God has given you anything less?' It dawned on me how

man makes evil use of those good things by allowing them to be an occasion of despair.

Objection 3. Further, if despair were a sin, it would be a sin also for the damned to despair. But this is not imputed to them as their fault but as part of their damnation. Therefore neither is it imputed to wayfarers as their fault, so that it is not a sin.

Reply to Objection 3. The damned are outside the pale of hope on account of the impossibility of returning to happiness: hence it is not imputed to them that they hope not, but it is a part of their damnation. Even so, it would be no sin for a wayfarer to despair of obtaining that which he had no natural capacity for obtaining, or which was not due to be obtained by him; for instance, if a physician were to despair of healing some sick man, or if anyone were to despair of ever becoming rich.[6]

---

we can know we are God's sons: We live in his house, the Church. We're called by his name, and we have been ever since we were reborn as his children, because we were baptized in the name of the Father, the Son and the Holy Spirit. We sit at his table every time we gather for the Mass. What do we receive from this table? We share his flesh and his blood. Jesus said, 'He who eats my flesh and drinks my blood abides in me and I in him.' . . . Besides that, his bride is our mother. Who is the Bride of Christ? The Church. Plus, he disciplines us. And we are always celebrating together as a family (Christmas, Easter, etc)." Scott Hahn, "The Family of God," *The Catholic Home Educator* 6 (Pentecost 1999): 3.

[6] Thus, not every kind of despair is sinful, for example, despair of being elected president. However, for people to despair of the possibility of their salvation is always sinful.

QUESTION 21

PRESUMPTION

ARTICLE 1 ⟶ Does presumption trust in God or in our own power? [1]

Yes, despite objections to the contrary, Just as, through despair, a man despises the Divine mercy, on which hope relies, so, through presumption, he despises the Divine justice, which punishes the sinner. Now justice is in God even as mercy is.[2] Therefore, just as despair consists in aversion from God, so presumption consists in inordinate conversion to Him.

I answer that, Presumption seems to imply immoderate hope. Now the object of hope is an arduous possible good: and a thing is possible to

---

[1] As W. J. Hill notes, presumption, in the sense used by Thomas here, does not have to do with a legal determination as to who has the burden of proof in a case ("the presumption of innocence"). Rather, presumption is a disordered hope for salvation, for example, that one will be saved and also be able to continue in serious sin.

[2] Both despair and presumption share a lack of love of God as God really is. They "trim" the living God down to size by neglecting his mercy or his justice. Pieper explains: "By describing both despair and presumption as 'anticipation', we disclose the fact that both of them destroy the pilgrim character of human existence in the *status viatoris* (the state of one 'on the way'). For they are both opposed to man's true becoming. Against all reality, they transform the 'not yet' of hope into either the 'not' or the 'already' of fulfillment. In despair, as in presumption, that which is genuinely human—which alone is able to preserve the easy flow of hope—is paralyzed and frozen. Both forms of hopelessness are, in the last analysis, unnatural and deadly." Joseph Pieper, *Faith, Hope, and Love* (San Francisco: Ignatius Press, 1997), 113.

a man in two ways: first by his own power; secondly, by the power of God alone. With regard to either hope, there may be presumption owing to lack of moderation. As to the hope whereby a man relies on his own power, there is presumption if he tends to a good as though it were possible to him, whereas it surpasses his powers, according to Judith 6:15: "You humble them that presume of themselves." This presumption is contrary to the virtue of magnanimity which holds to the mean in this kind of hope.[3]

But as to the hope whereby a man relies on the power of God, there may be presumption through immoderation in the fact that a man tends to some good as though it were possible by the power and mercy of God, whereas it is not possible, for instance, if a man hope to obtain pardon without repenting, or glory without merits.[4] This presumption is, properly, the sin against the Holy Spirit, because, to wit, by presuming thus a man removes or despises the assistance of the Holy Spirit, whereby he is withdrawn from sin.

Objection 3. Further, sin arises from the inordinate conversion to a mutable good. Now presumption is a sin. Therefore it arises from turning to human power, which is a mutable good, rather than from turning to the power of God, which is an immutable good.

Reply to Objection 3. Presumption on God's mercy implies both conversion to a mutable good, insofar as it arises from an inordinate desire of one's own good, and aversion from the immutable good, in

---

[3] Pieper writes: "[This Pelagian error] is characterized by the more or less explicit thesis that man is able by his own human nature to win eternal life and the forgiveness of sins." Pieper also notes the relationship between magnanimity and humility: "Magnanimity directs this hope on its true possibilities; humility, with its gaze fixed on the infinite distance between man and God, reveals the limitations of these possibilities and preserves them from sham realization and for true realization." Joseph Pieper, *Faith, Hope, and Love* (San Francisco: Ignatius Press, 1997), 126, 102.

[4] Presumption is not wrong because it hopes too much in God, for one cannot trust too much in God. Presumption is to trust wrongly that God would act against his own will by, for instance, forcing someone to be friends with him in charity.

as much as it ascribes to the Divine power that which is unbecoming to it, for thus man turns away from God's power.

ARTICLE 2 ⬗ Is presumption a sin?

Yes, despite objections to the contrary, It is reckoned a species of sin against the Holy Spirit.[5]

I answer that, As stated above (q. 20, a. 1) with regard to despair, every appetitive movement that is conformed to a false intellect is evil in itself and sinful. Now presumption is an appetitive movement, since it denotes an inordinate hope. Moreover it is conformed to a false intellect, just as despair is: for just as it is false that God does not pardon the repentant, or that He does not turn sinners to repentance, so is it false that He grants forgiveness to those who persevere in their sins,[6] and that He gives glory to those who cease from good works: and it is to this estimate that the movement of presumption is conformed.

Consequently presumption is a sin, but less grave than despair, since, on account of His infinite goodness, it is more proper to God to have mercy and to spare, than to punish: for the former becomes God in Himself, the latter becomes Him by reason of our sins.

Objection 1. It would seem that presumption is not a sin. For no sin is a reason why man should be heard by God. Yet, through presumption

---

[5] Thomas noted earlier (II–II, q. 14, a. 1) that various interpretations of the sin against the Holy Spirit (Mt 12:32, Mk 3:29, Lk 12:10) have been proposed.

[6] This is not a failure of God's infinite mercy. God cannot do anything that is self-contradictory, such as make a square circle, or grant human beings free-will and simultaneously not grant humans free-will, for such things are not logically possible, and God is a reasonable God. The laws of logic are not "above" God, as if God had to consult a logic text to find out what He could and could not do. Rather, such laws are implicit within the fabric of reality, the reality of God and what God creates, and God does not contradict himself. If God were to make a thing exist and not exist at the same time and in the same respect, God would be willing and not willing the very same thing, and there would be a contradiction within the Being Who is Complete Unity. Since sin is a separation from God, sin (a separation from God) and mercy (a reuniting with God) cannot as it were exist together at the same time and in the same respect.

some are heard by God, for it is written (Jud 9:17): "Hear me, a poor wretch making supplication to You, and presuming of Your mercy." Therefore presumption on God's mercy is not a sin.

Reply to Objection 1. Presumption sometimes stands for hope, because even the right hope which we have in God seems to be presumption, if it be measured according to man's estate: yet it is not, if we look at the immensity of the goodness of God.

Objection 2. Further, presumption denotes excessive hope. But there cannot be excess of that hope which is in God, since His power and mercy are infinite. Therefore it seems that presumption is not a sin.

Reply to Objection 2. Presumption does not denote excessive hope, as though man hoped too much in God, but through man hoping to obtain from God something unbecoming to Him, which is the same as to hope too little in Him, since it implies a depreciation of His power, as stated above (a. 1, ad 1).[7]

Objection 3. Further, that which is a sin does not excuse from sin: for the Master says (*Sent.* ii, D, 22) that "Adam sinned less, because he sinned in the hope of pardon," which seems to indicate presumption. Therefore presumption is not a sin.

Reply to Objection 3. To sin with the intention of persevering in sin and through the hope of being pardoned, is presumptuous, and this

---

[7] Some Protestant groups, but not all, claim that believers in Christ have salvation secured regardless of what they do. This idea is sometimes expressed by the phrase: "once saved, always saved." Thomas and the Catholic tradition reject this understanding of salvation as currently understood by some Protestants. In Philippians 2:12, Paul exhorts Christians to "work out your own salvation with fear and trembling," but if salvation cannot be lost, why should we fear and tremble? If Christians could not lose salvation, why would Paul warn Christians that a certain kind of sin, namely "mortal," excludes one from the Kingdom of God (1 Cor 6:9)? In speaking of the final judgment, Jesus says that it is necessary to do the will of his Father to enter heaven (Mt 7:21), but unfortunately some people do not have mercy on the "least of these" and so despite saying "Lord, Lord" will not enter the Kingdom.

does not diminish, but increases sin. To sin, however, with the hope of obtaining pardon some time, and with the intention of refraining from sin and of repenting of it, is not presumptuous, but diminishes sin, because this seems to indicate a will less hardened in sin.[8]

---

[8] For more on the subject of hope, see Pope Benedict XVI, *Spe Salvi*; Joseph Ratzinger, *To Look on Christ: Exercises in Faith, Hope, and Love*, trans. Robert Nowell (New York: Crossroad Publishing Co., 1991); Bernard N. Schumacher, *A Philosophy of Hope: Josef Pieper and the Contemporary Debate on Hope*, trans. D. C. Schindler (New York: Fordham University Press, 2003).

On Love
(Charity)

INTRODUCTION
TO LOVE

~~~~~~~~~~~~~~~~~~~~~~~~~~

FOR THOMAS AQUINAS, love or charity (*caritas* in Latin, *agape* in Greek) is the most important of all virtues. Any discussion of love faces the difficulty that the one English word "love" has many different meanings, reflected by different words used in Greek. People may say they love their best friend (*philia*), love their fiancé (*eros*), and love God (*agape*), and they clearly do not mean exactly the same thing by 'love' in these various contexts. Over the last few hundred years, there has been a lively debate about how these different kinds of love relate to one another, in particular how *eros* relates to *agape*. Roughly speaking, *eros* (desiring love) is exemplified by Romeo and Juliet or Rose and Jack Dawson from the movie *Titanic. Agape* (self-giving love) is exemplified by Mother Teresa of Calcutta's dedication to alleviating the suffering of the poor for love of God. How are these kinds of love related to one another? Are they opposites, one being a purely selfish love and the other a purely giving love? How does friendship fit into the discussion? How do the longings of the human heart for love (*eros, agape,* and *philia*) relate to the divine?

In Catholic thought, these loves come together in God. God's *eros* differs from human eros in that for us erotic desire arises from our incompleteness and imperfection. We are akin to an empty jar that wishes to be filled with the other. God's *eros* arises from his perfection and completeness. He is akin to an overflowing fountain, enjoying such super-abundance that it spills over to benefit others. We tend to use the word "lover" to pertain only to human beings, and yet God is a "lover" of each one of us. In his encyclical, *Deus Caritas Est* (*God is Love*), Pope Benedict XVI puts the point as follows: "God is the absolute and ultimate source of all being; but this universal principle of creation—the *Logos*, primordial reason—is at the same time a lover with all the passion of a true love. *Eros* is thus supremely ennobled, yet at the same time it is so purified as to become one with *agape*"[1] The idea startles: God as our erotic lover. Yet, the Song of Solomon, chapter four in particular, has been read for centuries as not merely a man's praise of a woman's beautiful body, but as a metaphor of God's taking delight in us. In the New Testament as well, Jesus the bridegroom takes the Church as his immaculate bride (Mk 2:19-20, Eph 5:25–27). Ancient Christian authors, such as Pseudo-Dionysius, understood "God is love" not just as "God is *agape*" but also as "God is *eros*." Mystics, like St. Teresa of Avila, experience a mystical union with God described in language reminiscent of the union of man and wife in the act of marriage. The poet John Donne put it this way:

> Batter my heart, three-personed God . . .
> Take me to you, imprison me, for I,
> Except you enthrall me, never shall be free,
> Nor ever chaste, except you ravish me.[2]

God loves us—not with the cold, calculating, mechanistic love of a distant Creator, but with the urgent, personal, and overwhelming love of a passionate groom for his beautiful bride.

God also loves us as a friend. For Thomas Aquinas, love, or charity, is properly defined as the friendship of man for God. At the last supper, Jesus said to his disciples, "I will not now call you servants . . . but my friends" (Jn 15:15). Love in this sense, or charity, is the friendship between God and human beings that arises from a gift of God. By nature, a human being cannot be friends with God but for a divine gift. It would be unusual for a five-star general to become

---

[1] Pope Benedict XVI, *Deus Caritas Est* (December 25, 2005), 10.

[2] X. J. Kennedy and Dana Gioia, *Literature: An Introduction to Fiction, Poetry and Drama* 9th Ed. (New York: Pearson Longman, 2005), 753.

friends, real friends, with a private. Should this unlikely relationship arise, surely it would be on the initiative of the general. Imagine, then, how much more unlikely it is that the infinite distance between God and man, a distance unfathomably greater than the distance between a general and a private, could be traversed by human effort and desire. God thus takes the initiative to establish friendship with man. For this friendship to be real, however, the human person must not reject God's offering of friendship. Friendship by its nature cannot be simply one way. We can have good will for another, but if that good will is not reciprocated then we cannot be said to be friends. God's love never fails, but the human response to this love can fail. This failure is called "mortal sin," and unless the situation is remedied before death, the separation of God and an individual human remains eternally. Like heaven, hell begins on earth and after death continues—intensified and uninterrupted—forever.

As faith is primarily a matter of the intellect, love is primarily a matter of the will for Aquinas. Emotions are involved with love, but one can freely choose (in some cases against one's emotions and inclinations) to love someone for the love of God, as Mother Teresa did for so many people. It was not that Mother Teresa had "an emotional connection," so to speak, with all the poor people that she served. It is likely that she often did, but sometimes did not. We cannot choose to always have pleasant emotions about our enemies or to delight in their company, but we can choose to do what is best for them and so to love them. Love, in this sense, is a decision rather than a feeling, though persons advanced in virtue normally also enjoy the acts themselves. Our acts of love should be most particularly aimed at those with whom we find ourselves daily. It is right and good to love people in far off lands and to do what we can to help them. However, we should especially extend our charitable efforts each day to those with whom we live, work, and associate in our daily lives. For Aquinas, our love should not be limited to special "volunteer hours," but should center on where our activity usually takes place in our circle of family, friends, acquaintances, and neighbors. Love in dreams is much less costly and effective than love in our daily living.

For Thomas, love for God above all and love for neighbor because of God is the most important virtue of the Christian life. The vices opposed to this virtue include hatred, which is properly opposed to love itself. Likewise, sadness and apathy towards the spiritual good (sloth) or the good of others (envy) are opposed to joy, an act of love. Vices opposed to the peace arising from love include discord, contention, schism, war, strife, and scandal. Just as the pursuit of health is aided by a knowledge of disease (and how to avoid it), Thomas explores each of these vices so as to better illuminate the value and goodness of love.

Ultimately, love itself motivated Thomas to write the *Summa theologiae*. Thomas's deep love for God led to a care and concern also for all human beings. Since human beings are guided at least in part by their understanding, Thomas sought to pass on what he had learned in his contemplation and study about God, man, and human happiness to enable and increase the love other people have for God and for each other, so that we may experience a taste of heaven while still on earth and then the fullness of heaven after our sojourn here is complete.

QUESTION 23

CHARITY CONSIDERED IN ITSELF

ARTICLE 1 ⤳ **Is charity friendship?**

Yes, despite objections to the contrary, It is written (Jn 15:15): [Jesus said to his Apostles] "I will not now call you servants . . . but My friends." This was said to them by reason of nothing else than charity. Therefore charity is friendship.[1]

I answer that, According to the Philosopher (*Ethic.* viii, 2, 3) not every love has the character of friendship, but love that is together with benevolence, when, to wit, we love someone so as to wish good to him. If, however, we do not wish good to what we love, but wish its good for ourselves, (thus we are said to love wine, or a horse, or the like), it

---

[1] The relationship among various kinds of love—such as charity, philia (friendship), and eros—is subject to some dispute. Some scholars see charity and eros as radically opposed: charity is a supernatural gift from God, while eros is merely carnal, a result of fallen human nature. Others, such as Joseph Pieper, recognize compatibility among various kinds of love: "Above all, *caritas* (charity) in the Christian sense does not invalidate any of the love and affirmation we are able to feel on our own and frequently do feel as a matter of course. Rather, *caritas* comprehends all forms of human love (*dilectio caritatis sub se comprehendit omnes dilectiones humanas,* Thomas Aquinas's *Disputed Questions on Charity,* 7)." Joseph Pieper, *Faith, Hope, and Love* (San Francisco: Ignatius Press, 1997), 277–78. Even more valuable is the discussion of Pope Benedict XVI in *Deus Caritas Est* (*God is Love*) in which he explores the relationship between eros and agape deftly in the first half of his encyclical.

is love, not of friendship, but of a kind of concupiscence. For it would be absurd to speak of having friendship for wine or for a horse.[2]

Yet neither does well-wishing suffice for friendship, for a certain mutual love is requisite,[3] since friendship is between friend and friend: and this well-wishing is founded on some kind of communication.

Accordingly, since there is a communication between man and God, inasmuch as He communicates His happiness to us, some kind of friendship must be based on this same communication, of which it is written (1 Cor 1:9): "God is faithful: by Whom you are called unto the fellowship of His Son." The love which is based on this communication is charity: wherefore it is evident that charity is the friendship of man for God.[4]

Objection 1. It would seem that charity is not friendship. For nothing is so appropriate to friendship as to dwell with one's friend, according to the Philosopher (*Ethic.* viii, 5). Now charity is of man towards God

---

[2] When someone "loves wine" this differs radically from "loving a friend." A true friend wants what is good for his friend for his friend's own sake, not his own sake. By contrast, no one wishes good to the wine for the wine's own sake, but for the sake of those who will drink the wine. Pieper helpfully remarks, "It remains now, to shed further light on the relationship between hope and love by means of a distinction—a distinction, namely, between the perfect love of friendship (*amor amicitiae*) and the imperfect love of 'concupiscence' (*amor concupiscentiae*), that is, between a love that loves the beloved for his sake and one that loves him for its own sake. The virtue of hope is associated primarily with that *im*perfect love of God that desires God, the Highest Good, only for its own sake. . . . And the perfect love of God, which is the theological virtue of love and, at the same time, the mother and root of all Christian virtues, flows back again on hope to mold and enhance it." Joseph Pieper, *Faith, Hope, and Love* (San Francisco: Ignatius Press, 1997), 103–4.

[3] We may be very friendly to another, but if he is not friendly back to us, we will never be friends. Friendship is always a two-way street, but mere good will for another can be entirely one-sided.

[4] The idea that man and God could be friends is unthinkable, in for instance Islam, where the relationship of God and man is of master to slave, or in pantheistic religions where "God" is an impersonal "force" with whom no personal friendship is possible.

and the angels, "whose dwelling is not with men"[5] (Dan 2:11). Therefore charity is not friendship.

Reply to Objection 1. Man's life is twofold. There is his outward life in respect of his sensitive and corporeal nature: and with regard to this life there is no communication or fellowship between us and God or the angels. The other is man's spiritual life in respect of his mind, and with regard to this life there is fellowship between us and both God and the angels, imperfectly indeed in this present state of life, wherefore it is written (Phil 3:20): "Our conversation is in heaven."[6] But this "conversation" will be perfected in heaven, when "His servants shall serve Him, and they shall see His face" (Apoc 22:3, 4). Therefore charity is imperfect here, but will be perfected in heaven.

Objection 2. Further, there is no friendship without return of love (*Ethic.* viii, 2). But charity extends even to one's enemies, according to Matthew 5:44: "Love your enemies." Therefore charity is not friendship.

Reply to Objection 2. Friendship extends to a person in two ways: first in respect of himself, and in this way friendship never extends but to one's friends; secondly, it extends to someone in respect of another, as, when a man has friendship for a certain person, for his sake he loves all belonging to him, be they children, servants, or connected with him in any way. Indeed so much do we love our friends that for their sake we love all who belong to them, even if they hurt or hate us, so that, in this way, the friendship of charity extends even to our enemies,[7] whom

---

[5] Here Thomas takes into account an objection derived from Aristotle's *Ethics*. Friends live together, or at least in close proximity, whereas God and human beings do not. Hence, a divine-human friendship is impossible.

[6] Prayer is a conversation with God whereby we communicate with Him, and He with us. In prayer, we raise our minds and hearts (our spiritual faculties) to God, so every true prayer is a foretaste of heaven, where our communication with God will be perfect. Friends spend time with one another, so truly close friends of God spend much time in prayer.

[7] After being elected president, Abraham Lincoln was encouraged by some to take revenge and destroy his enemies rather than cooperate with his opponents. Lincoln answered, "The best way to destroy an enemy is to make him a friend."

we love out of charity in relation to God, to Whom the friendship of charity is chiefly directed.[8]

Objection 3. Further, according to the Philosopher (*Ethic.* viii, 3) there are three kinds of friendship, directed respectively towards the delightful, the useful, or the virtuous.[9] Now charity is not the friendship for the useful or delightful; for Jerome says in his letter to Paulinus, which is to be found at the beginning of the Bible:[10] "True friendship, cemented by Christ, is where men are drawn together, not by household interests, not by mere bodily presence, not by crafty and cajoling flattery, but by the fear of God, and the study of the Divine Scriptures." No more is it friendship for the virtuous, since by charity we love even sinners, whereas friendship based on the virtuous is only for virtuous men (*Ethic.* viii). Therefore charity is not friendship.

Reply to Objection 3. The friendship that is based on the virtuous is directed to none but a virtuous man as the principal person, but for his sake we love those who belong to him, even though they be not virtuous: in this way charity, which above all is friendship based on the virtuous, extends to sinners, whom, out of charity, we love for God's sake.

---

[8] True friendship must be mutual. Nevertheless, one can have charity for another, such as an enemy, even if the good will is not returned. The mutuality of friendship is found in loving the person in God and for God's sake, and although the "enemy" may not love us, the love is mutual since God does love us in return. Since every single human person is made in God's image, our friendship with God should always include a charity toward the image of God in each human person. In this way, certain "loves" apparently in tension can find a unity. As R. J. Batten puts it: "Charity is more than the loving of the good-for-you, and more than loving the good for another; it is a loving shared by you and another of such sort that the terms 'egoism' and 'altruism' are irrelevant." "Introduction" in St. Thomas Aquinas, *Summa theologiae* (New York: Blackfriars, 1975), xvii–xviii.

[9] Human beings love that which is useful, that which is pleasurable, and that which is excellent (*areté, virtus*), the core meaning of virtue. Virtues are perfections, "excellences" of various aspects of the human person.

[10] St. Jerome (d. 420) translated the Old Testament from the Hebrew and the New Testament from Greek into Latin, the most widely used language of his time. This translation came to be known as the Vulgate. St. Jerome, a Father and Doctor of the Church, also wrote many commentaries on Scripture as well as polemical works of disputation.

ARTICLE 6 ⇝ **Is charity the most excellent of the virtues?**

Yes, despite objections to the contrary, It is written (1 Cor 13:13): "The greatest of these is charity."

I answer that, Since good, in human acts, depends on their being regulated by the due rule, human virtue, which is a principle of good acts, must consist in attaining the rule of human acts. Now the rule of human acts is twofold, as stated above (II–II, q. 17, a. 1), namely, human reason and God: yet God is the first rule, whereby even human reason must be regulated. Consequently the theological virtues, which consist in attaining this first rule, since their object is God, are more excellent than the moral, or the intellectual virtues, which consist in attaining human reason: and it follows that among the theological virtues themselves, the first place belongs to that which attains God most.[11]

Now that which is of itself always ranks before that which is by another. But faith and hope attain God indeed insofar as we derive from Him the knowledge of truth or the acquisition of good, whereas charity attains God Himself that it may rest in Him, but not that something may accrue to us from Him. Hence charity is more excellent than faith or hope, and, consequently, than all the other virtues, just as prudence, which by itself attains reason, is more excellent than the other moral virtues, which attain reason insofar as it [prudence] appoints the mean in human operations or passions.[12]

Objection 1. It would seem that charity is not the most excellent of the virtues because the higher power has the higher virtue even as it has a higher operation. Now the intellect is higher than the will, since it

---

[11] The human judgment of conscience is the proximate guide for human action, but conscience is itself to be formed and informed by a higher rule—God's own wisdom.

[12] Moral virtues such as temperance, courage, and justice participate in and are ordered by practical reason, prudence. Prudence, human reasoning in the practical realm as well as the judgment of conscience, is in turn a participation in the wisdom of God and is ordered to God. Since the theological virtues have God as their object, they are greater than practical wisdom, and practical wisdom in turn is a greater virtue than temperance, courage, and justice. The theological virtues themselves are not equal, as Thomas here notes, since love excels faith and hope by attaining God more perfectly.

directs the will. Therefore, faith, which is in the intellect, is more excellent than charity which is in the will.

Reply to Objection 1. The operation of the intellect is completed by the thing understood being in the intellectual subject, so that the excellence of the intellectual operation is assessed according to the measure of the intellect.[13] On the other hand, the operation of the will and of every appetitive power is completed in the tendency of the appetite towards a thing as its term, wherefore the excellence of the appetitive operation is gauged according to the thing which is the object of the operation.[14] Now those things which are beneath the soul are more excellent in the soul than they are in themselves, because a thing is contained according to the mode of the container (*De Causis* xii). On the other hand, things that are above the soul are more excellent in themselves than they are in the soul. Consequently it is better to know than to love the things that are beneath us, for which reason the Philosopher gave the preference to the intellectual virtues over the moral virtues (*Ethic.* x, 7, 8): whereas the love of the things that are above us, especially of God, ranks before the knowledge of such things.[15] Therefore charity is more excellent than faith.

Objection 2. Further, the thing by which another works seems the less excellent of the two, even as a servant, by whom his master works,

---

[13] When that which is understood is present in the intellect, when reality is present to the mind, then the operation of the intellect is said to be successful. The goal of the mind is to attain the truth. When the mind and reality correspond, the intellect has achieved its goal.

[14] The goal of the will is to attain that which it seeks, its "term."

[15] In the order of being Thomas has in mind, God is the greatest, followed by angels, human beings, non-rational animals, plants, and finally inanimate objects. For a human to know an object below in the order of being is in a way to raise that object in the order of being to a higher plane. When I know a plant, the plant exists in my mind, and that existence in my mind is a higher order of being than the plant enjoys in itself. But when I know an object above me, my knowledge of that object does not ennoble that object. So our love of those objects "ranks above" our knowledge of those objects. What Thomas may be getting at is that in a certain way we become that which we love, so in loving God, not just knowing him, we achieve our highest aim.

is beneath his master. Now "faith . . . works by charity," according to Galatians 5:6. Therefore faith is more excellent than charity.

Reply to Objection 2. Faith works by love, not instrumentally, as a master by his servant, but as by its proper form: hence the argument does not prove.

ARTICLE 7 ↠ Is any true virtue possible without charity?

No, despite objections to the contrary, The Apostle says (1 Cor 13:3): "If I should distribute all my goods to the poor, and if I should deliver my body to be burned, and have not charity, it profits me nothing." And yet true virtue is very profitable, according to Wisdom 8:7: "She teaches temperance, and prudence, and justice, and fortitude, which are such things as men can have nothing more profitable in life." Therefore no true virtue is possible without charity.[16]

    I answer that, Virtue is ordered to the good, as stated above (I–II, q. 55, a. 4). Now the good is chiefly an end, for things directed to the end are not said to be good except in relation to the end. Accordingly, just as the end is twofold, the last end, and the proximate end, so also is good twofold, one, the ultimate and universal good, the other, proximate and particular. The ultimate and principal good of man is the enjoyment of God, according to Psalm 72:28: "It is good for me to adhere to God," and to this good man is ordered by charity. Man's secondary and, as it were, particular good may be twofold: one is truly good, because, considered in itself, it can be directed to the principal good, which is the last end, while the other is good apparently and not truly, because it leads us away from the final good. Accordingly it is evident that simply true virtue is that which is directed to man's principal good; thus also the Philosopher says (Aristotle, *Phys.* vii, text. 17)

---

16 Thomas cites Scripture here but he could also have appealed to the work of St. Augustine, in particular, *On the Morals of the Catholic Church*. In this work, Augustine argues that there is no true virtue without charity. Without charity, we cannot attain God and without attaining God we cannot be happy. The virtues, to be true virtues, help us to attain not just any goal but our true and highest goal—happiness. So, without charity, we can only imitate or feign true virtue.

that "virtue is the disposition of a perfect thing to that which is best": and in this way no true virtue is possible without charity.

If, however, we take virtue as being ordered to some particular end, then we speak of virtue being where there is no charity, insofar as it is directed to some particular good. But if this particular good is not a true, but an apparent good, it is not a true virtue that is ordered to such a good, but a counterfeit virtue. Even so, as Augustine says (*Contra Julian.* iv, 3), "the prudence of the miser, whereby he devises various roads to gain, is no true virtue; nor the miser's justice, whereby he scorns the property of another through fear of severe punishment; nor the miser's temperance, whereby he curbs his desire for expensive pleasures; nor the miser's fortitude, whereby as Horace says, 'he braves the sea, he crosses mountains, he goes through fire, in order to avoid poverty'" (*Epis. lib,* 1; *Ep.* i, 45). If, on the other hand, this particular good be a true good, for instance the welfare of the state, or the like, it will indeed be a true virtue, imperfect, however, unless it be referred to the final and perfect good. Accordingly no strictly true virtue is possible without charity.[17]

Objection 1. It would seem that there can be true virtue without charity. For it is proper to virtue to produce a good act. Now those who have not charity do some good actions, as when they clothe the naked, or feed the hungry and so forth. Therefore true virtue is possible without charity.

---

17 "Virtue" in English is derived through Latin from the Greek "areté," meaning excellence. The true excellence of anything consists in its reaching its goal, end, or telos. An excellent watch keeps accurate time, an excellent car drives well, and an excellent human being is one who has found what every human being searches for—happiness. Aquinas argues in the First Part of the Second Part of the *Summa*, in questions one through five, that only God can perfectly satisfy our deepest human desire that innately craves perfect Love, perfect Truth, and Perfect Goodness. Since it is charity by which we are united to God, no human person without charity can be said to be truly virtuous because without charity it is impossible to reach the final human end. Before Thomas, Augustine provided a defense that there is no true virtue without charity in his *On the Morals of the Catholic Church.* St. Paul, as the "to the contrary" or *sed contra* shows, also made this clear. Some interpreters, however, also see in Thomas's treatment of charity a subtle correction of Augustinian views; see Eberhard Schockenhoff, "The Theological Virtue of Charity" in *The Ethics of Aquinas*, ed. Stephen Pope (Washington DC: Georgetown University Press), 248–51.

Reply to Objection 1. The act of one lacking charity may be of two kinds; one is in accordance with his lack of charity, as when he does something that is referred to that whereby he lacks charity. Such an act is always evil: thus Augustine says (*Contra Julian.* iv, 3) that the actions which an unbeliever performs as an unbeliever[18] are always sinful, even when he clothes the naked, or does any like thing, and directs it to his unbelief as end.[19]

There is, however, another act of one lacking charity, not in accordance with his lack of charity, but in accordance with his possession of some other gift of God, whether faith, or hope, or even his natural good, which is not completely taken away by sin, as stated above (q. 10, a. 4; I–II, q. 85, a. 2). In this way it is possible for an act, without charity, to be generically good, but not perfectly good, because it lacks its due order to the last end.

Objection 2. Further, charity is not possible without faith, since it comes of "an unfeigned faith," as the Apostle says (1 Tim 1:5). Now, in unbelievers, there can be true chastity, if they curb their concupiscence, and true justice, if they judge rightly. Therefore true virtue is possible without charity.

Reply to Objection 2. Since the end is in practical matters what the principle is in speculative matters, just as there can be no strictly true science if a right estimate of the first indemonstrable principle be lacking,

---

[18] As Batten notes, by "unbeliever" Thomas means not merely someone lacking faith (a pure negation of faith) but someone who knowingly and willingly rejects what he knows to be the true faith.

[19] A bad end always vitiates an action that in other aspects is good. If a politician donates money to the poor, this act considered in itself is good, but if this donation is done in order to take advantage of others, which is clearly a bad end, the action considered as a whole (proximate end, remote intention, and circumstances) is wrong. Earlier in the *Summa*, in question 18 of the *Prima secundae pars*, Thomas explained that for an action to be good, all three aspects of it must be good: proximate end, remote intention, and circumstances. Just as an airline pilot lacking just one of three essential characteristics (experience flying, sobriety, and good eyesight) is a bad pilot, so also an action that is not good in all three essential respects is evil. For more, see John Paul II in *Veritatis Splendor* (74–83), who reaffirmed this teaching found in Thomas as well as elsewhere in the Catholic tradition.

so there can be no strictly true justice, or chastity, without that due ordering to the end, which is effected by charity, however rightly a man may be affected about other matters.

Objection 3. Further, science and art are virtues, according to *Ethic.* vi. But they are to be found in sinners who lack charity. Therefore true virtue can be without charity.

Reply to Objection 3. Science and art of their very nature imply a relation to some particular good, and not to the ultimate good of human life, as do the moral virtues, which make man good simply, as stated above (I–II, q. 56, a. 3). Hence the comparison fails.

QUESTION 24

THE SUBJECT
OF CHARITY

ARTICLE 2 ⤳ Is charity caused in us by divine infusion?

Yes, despite objections to the contrary, The Apostle says (Rom 5:5):
"The charity of God is poured forth in our hearts by the Holy Spirit,
Who is given to us."

I answer that, As stated above (q. 23, a. 1), charity is a friendship
of man for God, founded upon the fellowship of everlasting happiness.
Now this fellowship is in respect, not of natural, but of gratuitous gifts,
for, according to Romans 6:23, "the grace of God is life everlasting":
wherefore charity itself surpasses our natural faculties. Now that which
surpasses the faculty of nature cannot be natural or acquired by the
natural powers,[1] since a natural effect does not transcend its cause.

Therefore charity can be in us neither naturally, nor through
acquisition by the natural powers, but by the infusion of the Holy
Spirit, Who is the love of the Father and the Son, and the participation of Whom in us is created charity, as stated above (q. 23, a. 2).[2]

---

[1] By our natural powers of intellect, Thomas believes we can come to knowledge
of God. But this knowledge is not the same as the vision of God in which
heaven consists. Rather than direct vision of God, our natural or philosophical
knowledge of God in this life is indirect and partial, through *effects* coming
from God, as indicated in the famous "five ways" arguing for God's existence. It
is proper naturally to God alone to know himself, but through the gift of grace
we can share in this supernatural knowledge insofar as we, as humans, are able.

[2] Charity is an infused virtue, not acquired by human effort but rather given
by God. Acquired virtues on the other hand are gained through repeated acts

Objection 1. It would seem that charity is not caused in us by infusion. For that which is common to all creatures, is in man naturally. Now, according to Dionysius (*Div. Nom.* iv),[3] the "Divine good," which is the object of charity, "is for all an object of dilection and love." Therefore charity is in us naturally, and not by infusion.

Reply to Objection 1. Dionysius is speaking of the love of God that is founded on the fellowship of natural goods, wherefore it is in all naturally. On the other hand, charity is founded on a supernatural fellowship, so the comparison fails.[4]

Objection 2. Further, the more lovable a thing is the easier it is to love it. Now God is supremely lovable, since He is supremely good. Therefore it is easier to love Him than other things. But we need no infused habit in order to love other things. Neither, therefore, do we need one in order to love God.

Reply to Objection 2. Just as God is supremely knowable in Himself yet not to us, on account of a defect in our knowledge which depends on sensible things, so too, God is supremely lovable in Himself, in as much as He is the object of happiness. But He is not supremely lovable to us in this way, on account of the inclination of our appetite towards visible goods. Hence it is evident that for us to love God above all things in this way, it is necessary that charity be infused into our hearts.[5]

---

of a given kind. So, for example, the habit of justice is gained through repeatedly performing just acts because they are just. Charitable acts might dispose a person to received infused charity, but they do not create the virtue that is created in us, as Thomas notes, by the infusion of the Holy Spirit.

3 Thomas wrote an unfinished commentary on the *De divinis nominibus.*

4 God loves all people; indeed God loves all creatures, since He made them to exist. But charity, a friendship with God, goes beyond the love God has for all creatures naturally to include the supernatural plane. All human beings naturally are loved by God, but not all human beings, it would seem, accept God's gift of supernatural charity establishing a friendship with Him.

5 Pieper notes that although charity is an infused virtue, it is not set in opposition to natural love, proper to human beings in virtue of their creation. "Even if *agape* (*caritas*) is explicitly defined as 'supernatural', that is, as a 'virtue' nourished not by our own strength alone but by some divine power communicated to us through grace, still must not be thought of as strictly separated

Objection 3. Further, the Apostle says (1 Tim 1:5): "The end of the commandment is charity from a pure heart, and a good conscience, and an unfeigned faith." Now these three have reference to human acts. Therefore charity is caused in us from preceding acts, and not from infusion.

Reply to Objection 3. When it is said that in us charity proceeds from "a pure heart, and a good conscience, and an unfeigned faith," this must be referred to the act of charity which is aroused by these things. Or again, this is said because the aforesaid acts dispose man to receive the infusion of charity. The same remark applies to the saying of Augustine (*Tract. ix in prim. canon. Joan.*): "Fear leads to charity," and of a gloss on Matthew 1:2: "Faith begets hope, and hope charity."

ARTICLE 4 ～ **Can charity increase?**

Yes, despite objections to the contrary, Augustine says (*Tract. lxxiv in Joan.*) (cf. Ep. clxxxv) that "charity merits increase that by increase it may merit perfection."

I answer that, The charity of a wayfarer can increase.[6] For we are called wayfarers by reason of our being on the way to God, Who is the last end of our happiness. In this way we advance as we get near to God, Who is approached, "not by steps of the body but by the affections of the soul" (St. Augustine, *Tract. in Joan. xxxii*): and this approach is the result of charity, since it unites man's mind to God. Consequently it is

---

from nature-given self-love directed towards happiness and the fulfillment of existence. Three impulses, that which springs from nature, that which springs from ethical freedom and that which springs from grace, are in harmony with one another. If you row a boat in the same direction as the wind is driving it—how are you to distinguish between the motion that is caused by your own efforts and what is caused by the wind?" Joseph Pieper, *Faith, Hope, and Love* (San Francisco: Ignatius Press, 1997), 242. Pieper is anxious to make clear the difference between Thomas's conception of love and the conception of the Lutheran theologian Anders Nygren, who in his famous work *Eros and Agape* contrasts these two kinds of love as having an absolutely distinct character.

6 As noted in the previous chapter, by "wayfarer" Thomas means a human being in this life before death, or in purgatory, a person "on the way" to eternal reward.

essential to the charity of a wayfarer that it can increase,[7] for if it could not, all further advance along the way would cease. Hence the Apostle calls charity the way, when he says (1 Cor 12:31): "I show unto you yet a more excellent way."

Objection 2. Further, that which consists in something extreme receives no increase. But charity consists in something extreme, being the greatest of the virtues, and the supreme love of the greatest good. Therefore charity cannot increase.

Reply to Objection 2. Charity consists in an extreme with regard to its object, insofar as its object is the Supreme Good, and from this it follows that charity is the most excellent of the virtues. Yet not every charity consists in an extreme, as regards the intensity of the act.

ARTICLE 12 ❧ Is charity lost through one mortal sin?

Yes, despite objections to the contrary, By mortal sin man becomes deserving of eternal death, according to Romans 6:23: "The wages of sin is death." On the other hand, whoever has charity is deserving of eternal life, for it is written (Jn 14:21): "He that loves Me, shall be loved by My Father: and I will love Him, and will manifest Myself to him," in which manifestation everlasting life consists, according to

---

[7] Like increase in the other theological virtues faith and hope, ardent prayer and reception of the sacraments are crucial for deepening supernatural charity. In addition to random acts of kindness, even more regularly repeated acts of kindness deepen love of God and neighbor. On this topic, Lawrence G. Lovasik offers much sound advice in *The Hidden Power of Kindness: A Practical Handbook for Souls Who Dare to Transform the World, One Deed at a Time* (Manchester, NH: Sophia Institute Press, 1999). Sometimes heroic opportunities to love arise: donating a kidney, saving someone's life from an attacker, facing a firing squad for standing up for persecuted people. However, for most of us, most of the time, our daily deeds of love are not newsworthy, unusual, or out of the ordinary but nevertheless are of critical importance. Each day provides numerous opportunities to perform small acts of love, strengthening the virtue of charity within us, for example, to do one's work well, to be on time, to be polite, to avoid harsh words, to refrain from gossip, to leave food for others, to run errands, to "pitch in," to pray for others, to donate money, to cheer someone up, to listen carefully, to put one's things away, to smile cheerfully. . . .

John 17:3: "This is eternal life; that they may know You the . . . true God, and Jesus Christ Whom You have sent." Now no man can be worthy, at the same time, of eternal life and of eternal death. Therefore it is impossible for a man to have charity with a mortal sin. Therefore charity is destroyed by one mortal sin.

I answer that, One contrary is removed by the other contrary supervening. Now every mortal sin is contrary to charity by its very nature, which consists in man's loving God above all things, and subjecting himself to Him entirely, by referring all that is his to God. It is therefore essential to charity that man should so love God as to wish to submit to Him in all things, and always to follow the rule of His commandments, since whatever is contrary to His commandments is manifestly contrary to charity, and therefore by its very nature is capable of destroying charity.[8]

If indeed charity were an acquired habit dependent on the power of its subject, it would not necessarily be removed by one mortal sin, for act is directly contrary, not to habit, but to act. Now the endurance of a habit in its subject does not require the endurance of its act, so that when a contrary act supervenes the acquired habit is not at once done away.[9] But charity, being an infused habit, depends on the action of God Who infuses it, Who stands in relation to the infusion and safekeeping of charity, as the sun does to the diffusion of light in the air, as stated above (a. 10, Objection 3). Consequently, just as the light would cease at once in the air, were an obstacle placed to its being lit up by the

---

8 Each commandment enjoins charity, and so all the Ten Commandments can be reduced to love of God and love of neighbor. As we will see in later questions, Thomas details the way in which charity and the commandments relate. An ethic of love and an ethic of law are not opposites for Thomas, but rather complementary. Love is first and primary; law directs and informs love.

9 Virtues that are acquired through repeated acts are not destroyed through a single act contrary to that virtue. A person who has the habit of justice may do an unjust act, but this unjust act does not destroy the habit of being just. Of course, repeated unjust acts would lead to a new habit, a vice, that would destroy the opposite virtue. If agents persist in doing unjust acts, they will develop a habit of injustice. As noted, the theological virtues, given by God, can be destroyed in us through a single act in which we turn away from God.

sun, even so charity ceases at once to be in the soul through the placing
of an obstacle to the outpouring of charity by God into the soul.[10]

Now it is evident that through every mortal sin which is contrary
to God's commandments,[11] an obstacle is placed to the outpouring of
charity, since from the very fact that a man chooses to prefer sin to
God's friendship, which requires that we should obey His will, it follows that the habit of charity is lost at once through one mortal sin.
Hence Augustine says (*Gen. ad lit.* viii, 12) that "man is enlightened
by God's presence, but he is darkened at once by God's absence,
because distance from Him is effected not by change of place but by
aversion of the will."

---

[10] Why can a single mortal sin, lasting perhaps just a few moments, lead to an
eternal, unending separation from God? Wouldn't justice demand that punishment for wrongdoing be limited to some finite amount? In the *Summa
contra Gentiles*, book three, chapter 144, Thomas provides answers to such
questions and argues that salvation of the soul is accomplished through the
body, but once body and soul are separated at death, the soul is deprived of
the means it needs to obtain the end of salvation.

   Thus, such a soul would remain outside the communion of saints, outside its heavenly reward. He also argues that equity demands that a person be
deprived of the good he acts against. Thus, heinous criminals who act against
the common good are expelled from human society either by exile, capital
punishment, or, as often today, by life imprisonment. The fact that the murder may have taken only seconds to complete is irrelevant to determining the
amount of punishment due. Whoever sins against the ultimate end, sins
against the greatest good and thereby merits to be separated from that good
eternally, even if the sin itself did not last as long. In other words, the dura-
tion of a just punishment is linked to the good the wrongdoer has acted
against rather than the length of time of the wrongdoing.

[11] Thomas explains the difference between mortal sin (which removes sanctifying grace, the charity infused by the Holy Spirit) and venial sin (which damages one's relationship with God but does not remove the charity infused by
the Holy Spirit) earlier in *ST* I–II, q. 88, a. 1. A mortal sin must have serious
matter (for instance, murder or adultery) as well as sufficient reflection and
full consent of the will of the agent. If a sin lacks any of these elements, it is
not mortal but rather venial. All sin, both mortal and venial, can be forgiven,
but mortal sin is much more serious. If one dies in a state of mortal sin, God
respects one's choice for a separation from God, and since no further acts of
repentance are possible, this choice is permanently ratified in eternal damnation, everlasting separation from God. Of course, all sins, both mortal and
venial, can be forgiven.

Objection 1. It would seem that charity is not lost through one mortal sin. For Origen[12] says (*Peri Archon* i): "When a man who has mounted to the stage of perfection, is satiated, I do not think that he will become empty or fall away suddenly; but he must needs do so gradually and by little and little." But man falls away by losing charity. Therefore charity is not lost through only one mortal sin.

Reply to Objection 1. This saying of Origen may be understood in one way, that a man who is in the state of perfection does not suddenly go so far as to commit a mortal sin, but is disposed thereto by some previous negligence, for which reason venial sins are said to be dispositions to mortal sin, as stated above (I–II, q. 88, a. 3). Nevertheless he falls, and loses charity through the one mortal sin if he commits it.

Since, however, he adds: "If some slight slip should occur, and he recover himself quickly he does not appear to fall altogether," we may reply in another way, that when he speaks of a man being emptied and falling away altogether, he means one who falls so as to sin through malice; and this does not occur in a perfect man all at once.

Objection 2. Further, Pope Leo[13] in a sermon on the Passion (60) addresses Peter thus: "Our Lord saw in you not a conquered faith, not an averted love, but constancy shaken. Tears abounded where love never failed, and the words uttered in trepidation were washed away by the fount of charity." From this Bernard (William of St. Thierry, *De Nat. et Dig. Amoris.* vi.) drew his assertion that "charity in Peter was not quenched, but cooled."[14] But Peter sinned mortally in denying Christ. Therefore charity is not lost through one mortal sin.

---

[12] Origen of Alexandria (c. 185–254) was a prolific, neo-Platonic Christian author whose powerful mind produced commentaries on Scripture, corrections of the Greek Septuagint Bible from the Hebrew, as well as more speculative-works. His most famous work is perhaps the one cited here by Thomas, the *Peri Archon* or *On First Principles.*

[13] Pope St. Leo the Great (d. 440) helped bring greater unity to the Catholic Church, wrote numerous works of great influence, and famously confronted Attila the Hun at the outskirts of Rome convincing him not to destroy the city.

[14] Thomas believed this quotation came from St. Bernard of Clairvaux, but in fact later historians have determined the quotation to have come from

Reply to Objection 2. Charity may be lost in two ways: first, directly, by actual contempt, and, in this way, Peter did not lose charity. Secondly, indirectly, when a sin is committed against charity, through some passion of desire or fear; it was by sinning against charity in this way that Peter lost charity; yet he soon recovered it.[15]

Objection 3. Further, charity is stronger than an acquired virtue. Now a habit of acquired virtue is not destroyed by one contrary sinful act. Much less, therefore, is charity destroyed by one contrary mortal sin.

Reply to Objection 3 is evident from what has been said.

Objection 4. Further, charity denotes love of God and our neighbor. Now, seemingly, one may commit a mortal sin, and yet retain the love of God and one's neighbor, because an inordinate affection for things directed to the end does not remove the love for the end, as stated above (a. 10). Therefore charity towards God can endure, though there be a mortal sin through an inordinate affection for some temporal good.

Reply to Objection 4. Not every inordinate affection for things directed to the end, i.e., for created goods, constitutes a mortal sin, but only such as is directly contrary to the Divine will; and then the inordinate affection is contrary to charity, as stated.[16]

William of St. Thierry. Such misattributions were not uncommon before the advent of the printing press. During the Middle Ages, corruption of handwritten texts, over sometimes centuries of copying, led to misattributions of authorship as well as various errors in the text itself. Indeed, Thomas himself discovered one such misattribution. The *Liber de causis* was, in Thomas's time, commonly attributed to Aristotle, but in commenting on the work Aquinas discovered that the *Liber de causis* was in fact written by an Arabic philosopher drawing on the work of Proclus.

[15] A mortal sin does not, then, require direct contempt and hatred of God. Sometimes a mortal sin is simply a preference for the sinful act and its consequences over retaining love of God. The thief steals because the love of gold overmasters the love of God, not necessarily because God is explicitly hated.

[16] The friendship between God and a human being, namely charity, may be likened to the relationship between husband and wife. Some sins, venial sins, weaken the relationship of spouses, for example being inconsiderate or rude. It is possible, however, for a single act to destroy the relationship, perhaps adultery, spouse-beating, child abuse, and certainly spouse-murder. Likewise,

Objection 5. Further, the object of a theological virtue is the last end. Now the other theological virtues, namely faith and hope, are not done away by one mortal sin, in fact they remain though lifeless. Therefore charity can remain without a form, even when a mortal sin has been committed.

Reply to Objection 5. Charity denotes union with God, whereas faith and hope do not. Now every mortal sin consists in aversion from God, as stated above (*Gen. ad lit.* viii, 12). Consequently every mortal sin is contrary to charity, but not to faith and hope, but only certain determinate sins, which destroy the habit of faith or of hope, even as charity is destroyed by every mortal sin. Hence it is evident that charity cannot remain lifeless, since it is itself the ultimate form regarding God under the aspect of last end as stated above (q. 23, a. 8).

---

a single act can, if knowingly and willing done, destroy one's relationship with God. Luckily, unlike some marital relationships, the human-divine friendship can always be restored through sincere change of heart and all that is involved in true repentance. Thomas speaks at length about this restoration and reconciliation in the third part of the *Summa* treating the Sacrament of Confession.

QUESTION 25

THE OBJECTS
OF CHARITY[1]

ARTICLE 1 ~ **Does the love of charity stop at God?**

No, despite objections to the contrary, It is written (1 Jn 4:21): "This commandment we have from God, that he who loves God loves also his brother."

I answer that, As stated above (II–II, q. 17, a. 6; q. 19, a. 3; I–II, q. 54, a. 3) habits are not differentiated except their acts be of different species. For every act of the one species belongs to the same habit. Now since the species of an act is derived from its object, considered under its formal aspect, it follows of necessity that it is specifically the same act that tends to an aspect of the object, and that tends to the object under that aspect: thus it is specifically the same visual act whereby we see the light, and whereby we see the color under the aspect of light.

Now the aspect under which our neighbor is to be loved is God, since what we ought to love in our neighbor is that he may be in God. Hence it is clear that it is specifically the same act whereby we love God, and whereby we love our neighbor. Consequently the habit of charity extends not only to the love of God, but also to the love of our neighbor.[2]

---

[1] In this question, Thomas treats the objects of charity, in other words, who is to be loved.

[2] In other words, whoever says he loves God but hates his neighbor is a liar. Charity is the love of both, but as Thomas makes clear in Objection 3, the neighbor is to be loved for God's sake. Whatever good qualities people may lack, insofar as they are human, they are in God's image and so deserve our love. The love of God is primary and gives rise to the love of neighbor.

Objection 1. It would seem that the love of charity stops at God and does not extend to our neighbor. For as we owe God love, so do we owe Him fear, according to Deuteronomy 10:12: "And now Israel, what does the Lord your God require of you, but that you fear . . . and love Him?" Now the fear with which we fear man, and which is called human fear, is distinct from the fear with which we fear God, and which is either servile or filial, as is evident from what has been stated above (q. 10, a. 2). Therefore also the love with which we love God is distinct from the love with which we love our neighbor.

Reply to Objection 1. We may fear our neighbor, even as we may love him, in two ways: first, on account of something that is proper to him, as when a man fears a tyrant on account of his cruelty, or loves him by reason of his own desire to get something from him. Such like human fear is distinct from the fear of God, and the same applies to love. Secondly, we fear a man, or love him, on account of what he has of God, as when we fear the secular power by reason of its exercising the ministry of God for the punishment of evildoers,[3] and love it for its justice: such like fear of man is not distinct from fear of God, as neither is such like love.

Objection 2. Further, the Philosopher says (*Ethic.* viii, 8) that "to be loved is to be honored." Now the honor due to God, which is known as "latria," is distinct from the honor due to a creature, and known as "dulia." Therefore again the love wherewith we love God is distinct from that with which we love our neighbor.

Reply to Objection 2. Love regards good in general, whereas honor regards the honored person's own good, for it is given to a person in recognition of his own virtue. Hence love is not differentiated specifically on account of the various degrees of goodness in various persons,

---

[3] For Thomas, a just punishment is not an evil inflicted on one person for the good of others but rather has a "medicinal" character in prompting the wrongdoer to reform, in vindicating the moral order to the community, in deterring others, and in restoring the order that was disrupted by the wrongdoing. Punishment is a good, an act of justice, so long as it is applied with prudence so that the "medicine" of justice does not turn out to be worse than the "disease" it seeks to cure.

so long as it is referred to one good common to all, whereas honor is distinguished according to the good belonging to individuals. Consequently we love all our neighbors with the same love of charity, insofar as they are referred to one good common to them all, which is God; whereas we give various honors to various people, according to each one's own virtue, and likewise to God we give the singular honor of *latria* on account of His singular virtue.

Objection 3. Further, hope begets charity, as a gloss[4] states on Matthew 1:2. Now hope is so due to God that it is reprehensible to hope in man, according to Jeremiah 17:5: "Cursed be the man that trusts in man." Therefore charity is so due to God, as not to extend to our neighbor.

Reply to Objection 3. It is wrong to hope in man as though he were the principal author of salvation, but not to hope in man as helping minister to us under God. In like manner it would be wrong if a man loved his neighbor as though he were his last end, but not if he loved him for God's sake; and this is what charity does.

ARTICLE 6 ⟿ **Should we love sinners out of charity?**

Yes, despite objections to the contrary, Augustine says (*De Doctr. Christ.* i, 30) that "when it is said: 'You shall love your neighbor,' it is evident that we ought to look upon every man as our neighbor." Now sinners do not cease to be men, for sin does not destroy nature. Therefore we ought to love sinners out of charity.

I answer that, Two things may be considered in the sinner: his nature and his guilt. According to his nature, which he has from God, he has a capacity for happiness, on the fellowship of which charity is based, as stated above (a. 3; q. 23, a. 1, a. 5), wherefore we ought to love sinners, out of charity, in respect of their nature.[5]

---

[4] As indicated earlier, a "gloss" is an interpretation or addition to the text of a manuscript written in the margins near the principle text.

[5] Since all human beings, regardless of race, nationality, religion, size, shape, sex, behavior, or belief, share in human nature, Thomas's argument would hold that we ought to have charity for every single human being.

On the other hand, their guilt is opposed to God, and is an obstacle to happiness. Wherefore, in respect of their guilt whereby they are opposed to God, all sinners are to be hated, even one's father or mother or kindred, according to Luke 12:26. For it is our duty to hate, in the sinner, his being a sinner, and to love in him, his being a man capable of bliss; and this is to love him truly, out of charity, for God's sake.[6]

Objection 1. It would seem that we ought not to love sinners out of charity. For it is written (Ps 118:113): "I have hated the unjust." But David had perfect charity. Therefore sinners should be hated rather than loved, out of charity.

Reply to Objection 1. The prophet hated the unjust, as such, and the object of his hate was their injustice, which was their evil. Such hatred is perfect, of which he himself says (Ps 138:22): "I have hated them with a perfect hatred." Now hatred of a person's evil is equivalent to love of his good. Hence also this perfect hatred belongs to charity.[7]

Objection 2. Further, "love is proved by deeds" as Gregory says in a homily for Pentecost (*In Evang.* xxx). But good men do no works of the

---

[6] Eberhard Schockenhoff puts the point this way: "One cannot love sinners and enemies insofar as they are separated from the believer, but only insofar as they coincide with one's humanity and in the common calling to live as children of God. One must hate in sinners that they are sinners, and love them as human beings who are called to beatitude." "The Theological Virtue of Charity," in *The Ethics of Aquinas*, ed. Stephen Pope (Washington DC: Georgetown University Press, 2002), 252–53. Indeed, if you truly love another person, you should hate his or her sin all the more, just as a doctor in caring for the patient hates the disease the patient suffers from.

[7] The objection is an interesting one that pits two virtues against one another: charity and justice. To be just in condemning evil appears to be uncharitable; to be charitable toward evil appears to be unjust. Thomas answers that we need to combine both virtues. We should love the sinner but hate the sin. We should always love what is loveable in all human persons, at the very least their being human and in God's image, and we should hate what is contrary to their humanity, their sinfulness. Interestingly, though one's sinfulness can change, one's humanity cannot change, so what is most permanent, lasting, and deep about us is what is always loveable about us, our being created by God and for God.

unjust: on the contrary, they do such as would appear to be works of hate, according to Psalm 100:8: "In the morning I put to death all the wicked of the land": and God commanded (Ex 22:18): "Wizards you shall not suffer to live." Therefore sinners should not be loved out of charity.

Reply to Objection 2. As the Philosopher observes (*Ethic.* ix, 3), when our friends fall into sin, we ought not to deny them the amenities of friendship, so long as there is hope of their mending their ways, and we ought to help them more readily to regain virtue than to recover money, had they lost it, for as much as virtue is more akin than money to friendship. When, however, they fall into very great wickedness, and become incurable, we ought no longer to show them friendliness. It is for this reason that both Divine and human laws command such like sinners to be put to death, because there is greater likelihood of their harming others than of their mending their ways. Nevertheless the judge puts this into effect, not out of hatred for the sinners, but out of the love of charity, by reason of which he prefers the public good to the life of the individual. Moreover the death inflicted by the judge profits the sinner, if he be converted, unto the expiation of his crime; and, if he be not converted, it profits so as to put an end to the sin, because the sinner is thus deprived of the power to sin any more.[8]

Objection 3. Further, it is part of friendship that one should desire and wish good things for one's friends. Now the saints, out of charity,

---

[8] Thomas argues here that capital punishment is an act of charity. The judge loves the good of the community and the one being punished. The idea is that the community's well-being is protected through capital punishment, and the one executed may be prompted to conversion and at the very least will not become worse by continuing to sin. For more on Thomas's view of capital punishment, see II–II, question 64, article two. John Paul II has written against the contemporary use of capital punishment in his encyclical *Evangelium Vitae*, the Gospel of Life. The pope and Thomas Aquinas would appear to be at odds. However, some scholars have argued that this tension is only an apparent contradiction. For useful accounts of these issues, see Avery Cardinal Dulles, "Catholicism and Capital Punishment," *First Things* (April 2001): 30–35, and Christopher Kaczor, "Capital Punishment and the Catholic Tradition: Contradiction, Change in Circumstance, or Development of Doctrine?" *Nova et Vetera*, 2:1 (Fall 2004): 279–304.

desire evil things for the wicked, according to Psalm 9:18: "May the wicked be turned into hell." Therefore sinners should not be loved out of charity.

Reply to Objection 3. Such like imprecations, which we come across in Holy Writ, may be understood in three ways: first, by way of prediction, not by way of wish, so that the sense is: "May the wicked be," that is, "The wicked shall be turned into hell." Secondly, by way of wish, yet so that the desire of the wisher is not referred to the man's punishment, but to the justice of the punisher, according to Psalm 57:11: "The just shall rejoice when he shall see the revenge," since, according to Wisdom 1:13, not even God "has pleasure in the destruction of the wicked (Vulg.: 'living')" when He punishes them, but He rejoices in His justice, according to Psalm 10:8: "The Lord is just and has loved justice." Thirdly, so that this desire is referred to the removal of the sin, and not to the punishment itself, to the effect, namely, that the sin be destroyed, but that the man may live.

Objection 4. Further, it is proper to friends to rejoice in and will the same things. Now charity does not make us will what sinners will, nor to rejoice in what gives them joy, but rather the contrary. Therefore sinners should not be loved out of charity.

Reply to Objection 4. We love sinners out of charity, not so as to will what they will, or to rejoice in what gives them joy, but so as to make them will what we will, and rejoice in what rejoices us. Hence it is written (Jer 15:19): "They shall be turned to you, and you shall not be turned to them."

Objection 5. Further, it is proper to friends to associate together, according to Ethic. viii. But we ought not to associate with sinners, according to 2 Corinthians 6:17: "Go out from among them." Therefore we should not love sinners out of charity.

Reply to Objection 5. The weak should avoid associating with sinners, on account of the danger in which they stand of being perverted by them. But it is commendable for the perfect, of whose perversion there is no fear, to associate with sinners that they may convert them.

For thus did Our Lord eat and drink with sinners as related by Matthew 9:11–13. Yet all should avoid the society of sinners, as regards fellowship in sin; in this sense it is written (2 Cor 6:17): "Go out from among them . . . and touch not the unclean thing," i.e. by consenting to sin.[9]

---

[9] By the "order of charity," Thomas means the degree of love, the priority of love, that is appropriate to be given to each person. We should love intelligently, taking into account whom it is we love. Were a person to love God and his neighbor equally, he would fail to recognize the proper way or mode in which we are to love, namely to love God above all things and to love the neighbor on account of God. The mode of the precept, that is, the specification that we are to love in a certain kind of way, helps to ensure human happiness by reminding us not to make human love, however good, into an idol, a rival to the one, true God. This is done not for God's good, but for our own good. For example, as C. S. Lewis noted about one powerful kind of human love, "Eros, honored without reservation and obeyed unconditionally, becomes a demon." ("Eros" in *Wing to Wing, Oar to Oar*, ed. Amy A. Kass and Leon R. Kass (Notre Dame: University of Notre Dame Press, 2000), 299.

QUESTION 26

THE ORDER
OF CHARITY

ARTICLE 2 ~ **Should God be loved more than our neighbor?**

Yes, despite objections to the contrary, A thing ought to be loved
more, if others ought to be hated on its account. Now we ought to
hate our neighbor for God's sake, if, to wit, he leads us astray from
God, according to Luke 14:26: "If any man come to Me and hate not
his father, and mother, and wife, and children, and brethren, and sis-
ters . . . he cannot be My disciple."[1] Therefore we ought to love God,
out of charity, more than our neighbor.

I answer that, Each kind of friendship regards chiefly the subject
in which we chiefly find the good on the fellowship of which that
friendship is based: thus civil friendship regards chiefly the ruler of the
state, upon whom the entire common good of the state depends;

---

[1] In this saying, Jesus is not contradicting his other injunction to love your
neighbor as yourself. We are always to love our neighbor, including especially
those who are in greatest proximity to us, such as our own parents, spouse,
children, and siblings, insofar as they are made by God and are (at least
potentially) adopted children of God. However, insofar as people, including
those most near to us, leads us away from God, in this respect we are to
"hate" them, but only insofar as their behavior damages themselves and others. We are to love all people, but hate all sin. To love a person is to wish that
person well and therefore to hate whatever undermines the well-being of the
person, be it physical evils, such as cancer or AIDS, or moral evils, such as
vices and sins. In so acting, we imitate the love of God who loves us so much
that he hates that which undermines our well-being, namely sinfulness.

hence to him before all, the citizens owe fidelity and obedience. Now the friendship of charity is based on the fellowship of happiness, which consists essentially in God, as the First Principle, whence it flows to all who are capable of happiness.

Therefore God ought to be loved chiefly and before all out of charity: for He is loved as the cause of happiness, whereas our neighbor is loved as receiving together with us a share of happiness from Him.

Objection 1. It would seem that God ought not to be loved more than our neighbor. For it is written (1 Jn 4:20): "He that loves not his brother whom he sees, how can he love God, Whom he sees not?" Whence it seems to follow that the more a thing is visible the more lovable it is, since loving begins with seeing, according to *Ethic.* ix, 5, 12. Now God is less visible than our neighbor. Therefore He is less lovable, out of charity, than our neighbor.

Reply to Objection 1. A thing is a cause of love in two ways: first, as being the reason for loving. In this way good is the cause of love, since each thing is loved according to its measure of goodness. Secondly, a thing causes love, as being a way to acquire love. It is in this way that seeing is the cause of loving, not as though a thing were lovable according as it is visible, but because by seeing a thing we are led to love it. Hence it does not follow that what is more visible is more lovable, but that as an object of love we meet with it before others: and that is the sense of the Apostle's argument. For, since our neighbor is more visible to us, he is the first lovable object we meet with, because "the soul learns, from those things it knows, to love what it knows not," as Gregory says in a homily (*In Evang.* xi). Hence it can be argued that, if any man loves not his neighbor, neither does he love God, not because his neighbor is more lovable, but because he is the first thing to demand our love: and God is more lovable by reason of His greater goodness.

Objection 2. Further, likeness causes love, according to Sirach 13:19: "Every beast loves its like." Now man bears more likeness to his neighbor than to God. Therefore man loves his neighbor, out of charity, more than he loves God.

Reply to Objection 2. The likeness we have to God precedes and causes the likeness we have to our neighbor: because from the very fact that we share along with our neighbor in something received from God, we become like to our neighbor. Hence by reason of this likeness we ought to love God more than we love our neighbor.[2]

Objection 3. Further, what charity loves in a neighbor is God, according to Augustine (*De Doctr. Christ.* i, 22, 27). Now God is not greater in Himself than He is in our neighbor. Therefore He is not more to be loved in Himself than in our neighbor. Therefore we ought not to love God more than our neighbor.

Reply to Objection 3. Considered in His substance, God is equally in all, in whomsoever He may be, for He is not lessened by being in anything. And yet our neighbor does not possess God's goodness equally with God, for God has it essentially, and our neighbor by participation.[3]

ARTICLE 6 ❧ **Should we love one neighbor more than another?**

Yes, despite objections to the contrary, One's obligation to love a person is proportionate to the gravity of the sin one commits in acting against that love. Now it is a more grievous sin to act against the love of certain neighbors than against the love of others. Hence the commandment (Lev 10:9), "He that curses his father or mother, dying let him die," which does not apply to those who cursed others than the above. Therefore we ought to love some neighbors more than others.

I answer that, There have been two opinions on this question: for some have said that we ought, out of charity, to love all our neighbors equally, as regards our affection, but not as regards the outward effect.

---

[2] God is the cause of all that is good and loveable in our neighbor. Indeed God is the cause of all that is good and loveable in the universe. It is only by participation in God's goodness that the neighbor exists to be loved. As Greatest Good and Uncaused Cause of other goods, God is the most lovable of all.

[3] God is within each human being in one sense and not in another. As an image or by participation God is in each human person. However, essentially God is not in each of us, but is only in the three Persons of the Trinity. As greatest good, God is most loveable and deserves to be loved more than anything else, and our neighbor is loved on account of the goodness he or she enjoys, which comes from God.

They held that the order of love is to be understood as applying to outward favors, which we ought to confer on those who are connected with us in preference to those who are unconnected, and not to the inward affection, which ought to be given equally to all including our enemies.

But this is unreasonable. For the affection of charity, which is the inclination of grace, is not less orderly than the natural appetite, which is the inclination of nature, for both inclinations flow from Divine wisdom. Now we observe in the physical order that the natural inclination in each thing is proportionate to the act or movement that is becoming to the nature of that thing: thus in earth the inclination of gravity is greater than in water, because it is becoming to earth to be beneath water. Consequently the inclination also of grace, which is the effect of charity, must be proportionate to those actions which have to be performed outwardly, so that, to wit, the affection of our charity be more intense towards those to whom we ought to behave with greater kindness.

We must, therefore, say that, even as regards the affection, we ought to love one neighbor more than another. The reason is that, since the principle of love is God, and the person who loves, it must be that the affection of love increases in proportion to the nearness to one or the other of those principles. For as we stated above (a. 1), wherever we find a principle, order depends on relation to that principle.[4]

---

[4] In his treatment of love, Thomas frequently states that a thing is loved more in two ways: first, because it has the character of a more excellent good, second, by reason of a closer connection. In the first way, we should love whatever is greater with a greater love, so we should love God, the most excellent good, the most. Secondly, naturally, as well as supernaturally, we should love with a greater love those nearest to us: spouse, family, relatives, friends, neighbors in close proximity. Thomas's teaching here excludes the practice of those people who claim to "love humanity" yet hate almost everyone with whom they come into personal contact. Love begins, but of course should not end, at home. Like the light and heat of a fire, love should warm and enlighten most intensely those nearest to it. Not coincidentally, to love those people placed in our path by Divine Providence can sometimes prove more challenging than to love those in far-off lands with, as Charles Dickens put it, "telescopic philanthropy." Luckily, we do not have to travel at all to exercise our vocation to love, a calling that can be discharged right in the everyday circumstances of normal life.

Objection 1. It would seem that we ought not to love one neighbor more than another. For Augustine says (*De Doctr. Christ.* i, 28): "One ought to love all men equally. Since, however, one cannot do good to all, we ought to consider those chiefly who by reason of place, time or any other circumstance, by a kind of chance, are more closely united to us." Therefore one neighbor ought not to be loved more than another.

Reply to Objection 1. Love can be unequal in two ways: first, on the part of the good we wish our friend. In this respect we love all men equally out of charity: because we wish them all one same generic good, namely everlasting happiness. Secondly, love is said to be greater through its action being more intense: and in this way we ought not to love all equally.

Or we may reply that we have unequal love for certain persons in two ways: first, through our loving some and not loving others. As regards beneficence, we are bound to observe this inequality, because we cannot do good to all; but as regards benevolence, love ought not to be thus unequal. The other inequality arises from our loving some more than others: and Augustine does not mean to exclude the latter inequality, but the former, as is evident from what he says of beneficence.

QUESTION 28

JOY

ARTICLE 1 ❧ **Is joy an effect of charity?**

Yes, despite objections to the contrary, It is written (Rom 5:5): "The charity of God is poured forth in our hearts by the Holy Spirit, Who is given to us." But joy is caused in us by the Holy Spirit according to Romans 14:17: "The kingdom of God is not meat and drink, but justice and peace, and joy in the Holy Spirit." Therefore charity is a cause of joy.[1]

I answer that, As stated above (I–II, q. 25, a. 1, a. 2, a. 3), when we were treating of the passions, joy and sorrow proceed from love, but in contrary ways. For joy is caused by love, either through the presence of the thing loved,[2] or because the proper good of the thing loved exists and endures in it; and the latter is the case chiefly in the love of benevolence,[3]

---

[1] As St. Bernard of Clairvaux explains: "All true love is without calculation and nevertheless is instantly given its reward; in fact it can receive its reward only when it is without calculation. . . . Whoever seeks as the reward of his love only the joy of love will receive the joy of love. But whoever seeks anything else in love except love will lose both love and the joy of love at the same time." Cited in Joseph Pieper, *Faith, Hope, and Love* (San Francisco: Ignatius Press, 1997), 244.

[2] Those who are in a state of grace have joy, since they have the Spirit of God living within them. Since joy is to possess what you love, and those in a state of grace do possess what they love, divine filiation, joy is an effect of being a child of God.

[3] In II–II, q. 27, a. 2, Thomas tackles the query, "Whether to love considered as an act of charity is the same as goodwill?" or more literally from the Latin,

whereby a man rejoices in the well-being of his friend, though he be absent. On the other hand sorrow arises from love, either through the absence of the thing loved, or because the loved object to which we wish well is deprived of its good or afflicted with some evil. Now charity is love of God, Whose good is unchangeable, since He is His goodness, and from the very fact that He is loved, He is in those who love Him by His most excellent effect, according to 1 John 4:16: "He that abides in charity abides in God, and God in him." Therefore spiritual joy, which is about God, is caused by charity.[4]

Objection 1. It would seem that joy is not effected in us by charity. For the absence of what we love causes sorrow rather than joy. But God, Whom we love by charity, is absent from us, so long as we are in this state of life, since "while we are in the body, we are absent from the Lord" (2 Cor 5:6). Therefore charity causes sorrow in us rather than joy.

Reply to Objection 1. So long as we are in the body, we are said to be "absent from the Lord," in comparison with that presence whereby

---

"Whether loving as an act of charity is the same as wishing well?" Thomas notes that "the love, which is in the intellective appetite, also differs from goodwill, because it denotes a certain union of affections between the lover and the beloved, in as much as the lover deems the beloved as somewhat united to him, or belonging to him, and so tends towards him. On the other hand, goodwill is a simple act of the will, whereby we wish a person well, even without presupposing the aforesaid union of the affections with him. Accordingly, to love, considered as an act of charity, includes goodwill, but such dilection or love adds union of affections, wherefore the Philosopher says (*Ethic.* ix, 5) that 'goodwill is a beginning of friendship.'" Benevolence simply wishes another person well. To be a benefactor is to go further and to procure some good for another. To love goes beyond (but includes) both wishing well and doing what is good for another, adding a unity with the other. Pieper notes further that Thomas "calls the missing element the *unio affectus*, volition directed toward the other person, the wish to be with him, to be united with him, in fact to identify with him. When the true lover says, 'It's good that you exist', he wants to be one with the person he loves." Joseph Pieper, *Faith, Hope, and Love* (San Francisco: Ignatius Press, 1997), 196–97.

4 Perhaps because life is unlivable without joy, in his novel *The Woman Who Was Poor*, Léon Bloy writes: "The only tragedy in life is not to be a saint." In order to be canonized a saint a person must have joy. Happiness and holiness go together, and as Thomas shows in this article, holiness causes happiness.

He is present to some by the vision of "sight," wherefore the Apostle goes on to say (2 Cor 5:6): "For we walk by faith and not by sight." Nevertheless, even in this life, He is present to those who love Him, by the indwelling of His grace.[5]

Objection 2. Further, it is chiefly through charity that we merit happiness. Now mourning, which pertains to sorrow, is reckoned among those things whereby we merit happiness, according to Matthew 5:5: "Blessed are they that mourn, for they shall be comforted." Therefore sorrow, rather than joy, is an effect of charity.

Reply to Objection 2. The mourning that merits happiness is about those things that are contrary to happiness, wherefore it amounts to the same that charity causes this mourning, and this spiritual joy about God, since to rejoice in a certain good amounts to the same as to grieve for things that are contrary to it.[6]

Objection 3. Further, charity is a virtue distinct from hope, as shown above (q. 17, a. 6). Now joy is the effect of hope, according to Romans 12:12: "Rejoicing in hope." Therefore it is not the effect of charity.

Reply to Objection 3. There can be spiritual joy about God in two ways: first, when we rejoice in the Divine good considered in itself; secondly, when we rejoice in the Divine good as participated by us. The former joy is the better, and proceeds from charity chiefly, while the latter joy proceeds from hope also, whereby we look forward to

---

[5] Our joy *in via*, in this life, is incomplete. Hence, Thomas speaks of the imperfect happiness possible before heaven (*beatitudo imperfecta*). In the life to come, *in patria,* our possession of God will be complete, and so therefore our joy will be complete, perfect happiness (*beatitudo perfecta*).

[6] For what shall the joyous person grieve? Thomas does not explicitly say here. However, in the supplement to the *Summa*, Thomas notes that one can grieve over one's sins—that which alone can detract or even destroy friendship with God (III-S, q. 4, a. 2). Elsewhere Thomas writes: "the sorrows of the present life lead us to the comfort of the future life. Because by the mere fact that man mourns for his sins, or for the delay of glory, he merits the consolation of eternity. In like manner a man merits it when he shrinks not from hardships and straits in order to obtain it" (I–II, q. 35, a. 3 ad 1). See also I–II, q. 39, a. 2 and I–II, q. 69, a. 4.

enjoying the Divine good, although this enjoyment itself, whether perfect or imperfect, is obtained according to the measure of one's charity.

ARTICLE 2 ⁓ Is the spiritual joy that results from charity compatible with any sorrow?

No, despite objections to the contrary, The joy of charity is joy about the Divine wisdom. Now such like joy has no admixture of sorrow, according to Wisdom 8:16: "Her conversation has no bitterness." Therefore the joy of charity is incompatible with an admixture of sorrow.

I answer that, As stated above (II–II, q. 28, a. 1, ad 3), a twofold joy in God arises from charity. One, the more excellent, is proper to charity; and with this joy we rejoice in the Divine good considered in itself. This joy of charity is incompatible with an admixture of sorrow, even as the good which is its object is incompatible with any admixture of evil:[7] hence the Apostle says (Phil 4:4): "Rejoice in the Lord always."

---

[7] If one rejoiced in God and God alone, then no mixture of sorrow would be possible. For sorrow is always of an evil, and in God there is no evil whatsoever. Certain conceptions of God, such as the "Force" in Star Wars, imagine God as a combination of "dark" and "light" sides, good and evil. This conception of God has been recurrent through history. For example, in Augustine's time the Manicheans and in Thomas's time the Cathars proposed two gods, a good one and a bad, light and dark. Thomas and his fellow Dominicans argued vigorously against any such understanding of God as contrary to both faith and reason. Thomas's understanding of God completely excludes such a misunderstanding. In his famous "five ways" arguing for God's existence, Thomas concludes that God is unmoved mover, uncaused cause, and pure actuality without potentiality (I, q. 2, a. 3). Lacking all potentiality, God is Who God is (I Am Who Am, Ex 3:12) without any sort of composition whatever. In other words, God is not a being with sections, parts, or potentiality. In Thomas's technical terminology, this truth is expressed by saying that God is "simple" (I, q. 3, especially article 7). Now all evil is a privation, a lack of due perfection. By definition, a privation is a "potency," a potentiality that is parasitic upon what is "in act," what has perfection. Consider the physical evil of suffering from blindness. Only a living being whose nature can give rise to sight can be blind. The privation of blindness is parasitic upon a certain kind of living nature with the potential to be blind. If there were no potential to be blind, the being in question would not endure the evil. All evil presupposes potentiality. God however is pure act without any potentiality; therefore there can be no evil whatsoever in God, but only goodness.

The other is the joy of charity whereby we rejoice in the Divine good as participated by us. This participation can be hindered by anything contrary to it, wherefore, in this respect, the joy of charity is compatible with an admixture of sorrow, insofar as a man grieves for that which hinders the participation of the Divine good, either in us or in our neighbor, whom we love as ourselves.[8]

Objection 1. It would seem that the spiritual joy that results from charity is compatible with an admixture of sorrow. For it belongs to charity to rejoice in our neighbor's good, according to 1 Corinthians 13:4, 6: "Charity . . . rejoices not in iniquity, but rejoices with the truth." But this joy is compatible with an admixture of sorrow, according to Romans 12:15: "Rejoice with them that rejoice, weep with them that weep." Therefore the spiritual joy of charity is compatible with an admixture of sorrow.

Reply to Objection 1. Our neighbor does not weep save on account of some evil. Now every evil implies lack of participation in the sovereign good: hence charity makes us weep with our neighbor insofar as he is hindered from participating in the Divine good.[9]

Objection 2. Further, according to Gregory (*Hom. in Ev.* xxxiv), "penance consists in deploring past sins, and in not committing again those we have deplored." But there is no true penance without charity. Therefore the joy of charity has an admixture of sorrow.

Reply to Objection 2. Our sins divide between us and God, according to Isaiah 59:2, wherefore this is the reason why we grieve for our past sins, or for those of others, insofar as they hinder us from participating in the Divine good.

---

[8] We are to love ourselves, for how else could we love our neighbor as ourselves unless we loved ourselves? Our (proper) love of ourselves should not lead to a deification or an idolization of ourselves or of the things of the world that can satisfy us in some respect. As important as each human being is, no human being, including oneself, should be treated as if he were God, the final end of all beings. To love ourselves more than God is, in a sense, to hate ourselves, for such love ruins our own happiness.

[9] Thus, it is not incompatible with divine joy or holiness to be saddened over the moral or physical evils suffered by others.

ARTICLE 3 ∾ **Can the spiritual joy that proceeds from charity be complete?**

Yes, despite objections to the contrary, Our Lord said to His disciples (Jn 15:11): "That My joy may be in you, and your joy may be complete."

I answer that, Fullness of joy can be understood in two ways: first, on the part of the thing rejoiced in, so that one rejoices in it to the degree that it is worthy to be rejoiced in, and thus God's only joy is in the fullness of himself alone, because the joy of God is infinite; and this corresponds to the infinite goodness of God: but the joy of any creature must be finite.[10] Secondly, fullness of joy may be understood on the part of the one who rejoices. Now joy is compared to desire, as rest to movement, as stated above (I–II, q. 25, a. 1, a. 2), when we were treating of the passions: and rest is full when there is no more movement. Hence joy is full, when there remains nothing to be desired. But as long as we are in this world, the movement of desire does not cease in us, because it still remains possible for us to approach nearer to God by grace, as was shown above (II–II, q. 24, a. 4, a. 7).[11] When once, however, perfect happiness has been attained, nothing will remain to be desired, because then there will be full enjoyment of God, wherein man will obtain whatever he had desired, even with regard to other

---

[10] Only an infinite intellect can fully appreciate (comprehend) the full majesty of God's glory. However, each created intellect can appreciate God as completely as it can, to the full depth of its understanding, even though this fullness could never approach the divine fullness.

[11] Much earlier in the *Summa*, Thomas distinguished between perfect and imperfect happiness. While on earth, we can be happy but only imperfectly happy. The completion or perfection of our happiness takes place only in the completion and perfection of our relationship with God. This teaching of Thomas can greatly increase our happiness here on earth. If we expect to have "heaven on earth," a utopia of constant bliss without interruption, difficulty, or set back, then we are bound to be greatly disappointed. However, approaching life with realistic expectations, such as those proposed by Thomas's frank realization that we will never be perfectly happy until heaven, can make us enjoy our lives much, much more and free us from constant "letdowns" and dashed expectations.

[12] Heavenly joy includes the satisfaction of all desires. Since God is perfect goodness, He satisfies the yearning of the human will, which restlessly seeks the

goods,[12] according to Psalm 102:5: "Who satisfies your desire with good things." Hence desire will be at rest, not only our desire for God, but all our desires: so that the joy of the blessed is full to perfection—indeed over-full, since they will obtain more than they were capable of desiring: for "neither has it entered into the heart of man, what things God has prepared for them that love Him" (1 Cor 2:9). This is what is meant by the words of Luke 6:38: "Good measure and pressed down, and shaken together, and running over shall they give into your bosom." Yet, since no creature is capable of the joy condignly due to God, it follows that this perfectly full joy is not taken into man, but, on the contrary, man enters into it, according to Matthew 25:21: "Enter into the joy of your Lord."

Objection 1. It would seem that the spiritual joy that proceeds from charity cannot be complete. For the more we rejoice in God, the more is our joy in Him complete. But we can never rejoice in Him as much as it is meet that we should rejoice in God, since His goodness, which is infinite, surpasses the creature's joy, which is finite. Therefore joy in God can never be complete.

Reply to Objection 1. This argument takes the fullness of joy in reference to the thing in which we rejoice.

Objection 2. Further, that which is complete cannot be increased. But the joy, even of the blessed, can be increased, since one's joy is greater than another's. Therefore joy in God cannot be complete in a creature.

Reply to Objection 2. When each one attains to happiness he will have reached the term appointed to him by Divine predestination, and nothing further will remain to which he may tend, although by reaching that term, some will approach nearer to God than others. Hence each one's joy will be full with regard to himself, because his desire will be fully set

---

good. Since God is perfect Truth and Being, He satisfies the yearning of the human intellect, which restlessly seeks to know. All that we desire is found in its utmost perfection in the Divine Perfection, so in heaven every aspect of us will be satisfied.

at rest; yet one's joy will be greater than another's, on account of a fuller participation of the Divine happiness.[13]

Objection 3. Further, comprehension seems to be nothing else than the fullness of knowledge. Now, just as the cognitive power of a creature is finite, so is its appetitive power. Since, therefore, God cannot be comprehended by any creature, it seems that no creature's joy in God can be complete.

Reply to Objection 3. Comprehension denotes fullness of knowledge in respect of the thing known, so that it is known as much as it can be.[14] There is however a fullness of knowledge in respect of the knower, just as we have said of joy. Wherefore the Apostle says (Col 1:9): "That you may be filled with the knowledge of His will, in all wisdom and spiritual understanding."

---

[13] All in heaven are fully happy, but they are not equally happy. Two glasses of water may be fully filled, and yet one glass of water (the bigger one) may have more water than the other.

[14] God alone has comprehension of God, for only an infinite Intellect could ever completely understand, fully appreciate, the Infinite Being of God. God will never be completely understood, appreciated, and comprehended by any finite intellect or any created being. However, as Thomas continues here, it is possible for the knowledge of any of these beings to be complete. It is possible that I know *as much as I can possibly know* about God, and this is precisely what will take place if I make it to heaven. This would be "a fullness of knowledge in respect of the knower." In knowing God perfectly, as perfectly as I ever could, the love of and enjoyment of God is also made as complete as it ever could be.

INTERIOR AND EXTERIOR ACTS OF CHARITY

QUESTION 29

PEACE

ARTICLE 2 ⤳ **Do all things desire peace?**

Yes, despite objections to the contrary, Augustine says (*De Civ. Dei* xix, 12, 14) that "all things desire peace," and Dionysius says the same (*Div. Nom.* xi).

  I answer that, From the very fact that a man desires a certain thing it follows that he desires to obtain what he desires, and, in consequence, to remove whatever may be an obstacle to his obtaining it. Now a man may be hindered from obtaining the good he desires, by a contrary desire either of his own or of some other, and both are removed by peace, as stated above.[1] Hence it follows of necessity that whoever desires anything desires peace, insofar as he who desires anything desires to attain, with tranquility and without hindrance, to that which he desires: and this is what is meant by peace, which Augustine defines (*De Civ. Dei* xix, 13) as "the tranquility of order."[2]

---

[1] There is peace, says Aquinas in question 29, article 1, when "the wills of various hearts agree together in consenting to the same thing" and when there is also "the union of the appetites even in one man." Peace is a harmony of desires both inward with respect to an individual and outward with respect to others.

[2] Even the suicide bomber desires peace, just as even the man knocking on the brothel door is, in some sense, looking for God. Both look for their final end in the wrong place, or attempt to secure means to finding happiness that are bound to fail and injure the human community. However, for Thomas, we are "hard-wired" to seek the good that is found most sublimely in God, even

Objection 2. Further, the appetite does not tend to opposite things at the same time. Now many desire war and dissension. Therefore all men do not desire peace.

Reply to Objection 2. Even those who seek war and dissension desire nothing but peace, which they deem themselves not to have. For as we stated above, there is no peace when a man concords with another man counter to what he would prefer. Consequently men seek by means of war to break this concord, because it is a defective peace, in order that they may obtain peace, where nothing is contrary to their will. Hence all wars are waged that men may find a more perfect peace than that which they had heretofore.

Objection 3. Further, good alone is an object of appetite. But a certain peace is, seemingly, evil, else Our Lord would not have said (Mt 10:34): "I came not to send peace." Therefore all things do not desire peace.

Reply to Objection 3. Peace gives calm and unity to the appetite. Now just as the appetite may tend to what is good simply, or to what is good apparently, so too, peace may be either true or apparent. There can be no true peace except where the appetite is directed to what is truly good, since every evil, though it may appear good in a way, so as to calm the appetite in some respect, has, nevertheless, many defects, which cause the appetite to remain restless and disturbed.[3] Hence true peace is only in good men and about good things. The peace of the wicked is not a true peace but a semblance thereof, wherefore it is written (Wis 14:22): "Whereas they lived in a great war of ignorance, they call so many and so great evils peace."

---

though often we mistakenly seek it. For instance, in killing others, the suicide bomber hopes to overthrow what he views as an unjust situation and thereby establish suitable living conditions. The suicide bomber uses an unjust means to do this, and, objectively speaking, he is guilty of grave wrongdoing, but even his act has an end in view that is perceived as good. Despite this good end, if done knowingly and willingly, the suicide bomber commits at least two mortal sins—killing himself and others.

[3] True peace involves the truly good, so there can never be a true peace without God, who alone is wholly good and satisfying to the rational appetite, the will.

Objection 4. Further, that which all desire is, seemingly, the sovereign good which is the last end. But this is not true of peace, since it is attainable even by a wayfarer, else Our Lord would vainly command (Mk 9:49): "Have peace among you." Therefore all things do not desire peace.

Reply to Objection 4. Since true peace is only about good things, as the true good is possessed in two ways, perfectly and imperfectly, so there is a twofold true peace. One is perfect peace. It consists in the perfect enjoyment of the sovereign good, and unites all one's desires by giving them rest in one object. This is the last end of the rational creature, according to Psalm 147:3: "Who has placed peace in your borders."[4] The other is imperfect peace, which may be had in this world, for though the chief movement of the soul finds rest in God, yet there are certain things within and without which disturb the peace.[5]

---

[4] Perfect peace is, as Thomas makes clear in continuing his comments, only possible in heaven, for it is only in heaven that we perfectly attain God in whom true peace is to be found. While here on earth, our peace, even true peace, will remain imperfect in as much as one can participate in the perfect truth of God's knowledge (faith), the life-giving power of God overcoming evil (hope), and the transcendent Beauty of God's own good nature (love); our participation is incomplete, partial, and unfinished so long as we remain "on our way" to heaven.

[5] One of the effects of the virtue of charity is peace. "Peace implies a twofold union. . . . The first is the result of one's own appetites being directed to one object, while the other results from one's own appetite being united with the appetite of another: and each of these unions is effected by charity—the first, insofar as man loves God with his whole heart, by referring all things to Him, so that all his desires tend to one object—the second, insofar as we love our neighbor as ourselves, the result being that we wish to fulfill our neighbor's will as though it were ours: hence it is reckoned a sign of friendship if people 'make choice of the same things' (*Ethic.* ix, 4), and Tully says (*De Amicitia*) that friends 'like and dislike the same things' (Sallust, *Catilin*)." (II–II, q. 29, a. 3). Peace is a direct effect of charity, for in loving God our internal desires can cease battling for supremacy, finding order in loving God, and in loving our neighbors we desire to be good to them and so are able to be in harmony with others. Charity, in other words, begets internal and external peace.

QUESTION 30

MERCY

ARTICLE 4 ── **Is mercy the greatest of the virtues?**

No, despite objections to the contrary, The Apostle after saying (Col 3:12): "Put on . . . as the elect of God . . . the bowels of mercy," etc., adds (Col 3:14): "Above all things have charity." Therefore mercy is not the greatest of virtues.[1]

I answer that, A virtue may take precedence of others in two ways: first, in itself; secondly, in comparison with its subject. In itself, mercy takes precedence of other virtues, for it belongs to mercy to be bountiful to others, and, what is more, to succor others in their wants, which pertains chiefly to one who stands above. Hence mercy is accounted as being proper to God: and therein His omnipotence is declared to be chiefly manifested.[2]

On the other hand, with regard to its subject, mercy is not the greatest virtue, unless that subject be greater than all others, surpassed by none and excelling all: since for him that has anyone above him it is better to be united to that which is above than to supply the defect of that which is beneath. Hence, as regards man, who has God above

---

[1] Mercy is a "compassionate heart [*miserum cor*] for another's unhappiness." (II–II, q, 30, a. 1.)

[2] Thomas here cites the "collect," the short prayer said before the Epistle, of the Tenth Sunday after Pentecost. For more on how prayer and liturgy influence Thomas, see David Berger, *Thomas Aquinas on the Liturgy* (Naples, FL: Sapientia Press, 2003).

him, charity, which unites him to God, is greater than mercy, whereby he supplies the defects of his neighbor. But of all the virtues that relate to our neighbor, mercy is the greatest, even as its act surpasses all others, since it belongs to one who is higher and better to supply the defect of another, insofar as the latter is deficient.[3]

Objection 1. It would seem that mercy is the greatest of the virtues. For the worship of God seems a most virtuous act. But mercy is preferred before the worship of God, according to Hosea 6:6 and Matthew 12:7: "I have desired mercy and not sacrifice." Therefore mercy is the greatest virtue.

Reply to Objection 1. We worship God by external sacrifices and gifts, not for His own profit, but for that of ourselves and our neighbor.[4] For He needs not our sacrifices, but wishes them to be offered to Him, in order to arouse our devotion and to profit our neighbor. Hence mercy, whereby we supply others' defects, is a sacrifice more acceptable to Him, as conducing more directly to our neighbor's wellbeing, according to Hebrews 13:16: "Do not forget to do good and to impart, for by such sacrifices God's favor is obtained."

Objection 2. Further, on the words of 1 Timothy 4:8: "Godliness is profitable to all things," a gloss says: "The sum total of a Christian's rule of life consists in mercy and godliness." Now the Christian rule of life embraces every virtue. Therefore the sum total of all virtues is contained in mercy.

Reply to Objection 2. The sum total of the Christian religion consists in mercy, as regards external works, but the inward love of charity, whereby we are united to God, preponderates over both love and mercy for our neighbor.

---

[3] Mercy is a virtue of the person of higher station. The judge may be merciful to the accused, not the accused to the judge.

[4] Unlike the gods depicted, for instance, by Aristophanes in Plato's *Symposium*, God does not need our worship; rather we need to worship God. Idolatry harms not God but human beings by taking them further and further from the source of true happiness and satisfaction.

Objection 3. Further, "Virtue is that which makes its subject good," according to the Philosopher. Therefore the more a virtue makes a man like God, the better is that virtue: since man is the better for being more like God. Now this is chiefly the result of mercy, since of God is it said (Ps 144:9) that "His tender mercies are over all His works," and (Lk 6:36) Our Lord said: "Be. . . merciful, as your Father also is merciful." Therefore mercy is the greatest of virtues.

Reply to Objection 3. Charity likens us to God by uniting us to Him in the bond of love: wherefore it surpasses mercy, which likens us to God as regards similarity of works.

QUESTION 31

EXTERNAL ACTS
OF BENEVOLENCE

ARTICLE 2 ·~ **Should we do good to all?**

Yes, despite objections to the contrary, The Apostle says (Gal 6:10): "While we have time, let us work good to all men."

I answer that, As stated above (a. 1, ad 1), beneficence[1] is an effect of love insofar as love moves the superior to watch over the inferior. Now degrees among men are not unchangeable as among angels, because men are subject to many failings, so that he who is superior in one respect is or may be inferior in another.[2] Therefore, since the love of charity extends to all, beneficence also should extend to all, but according as time and place require: because all acts of virtue must be modified with a view to their due circumstances.

Objection 1. It would seem that we are not bound to do good to all. For Augustine says (*De Doctr. Christ.* i, 28) that we "are unable to do good to everyone." Now virtue does not incline one to the impossible. Therefore it is not necessary to do good to all.

---

[1] Beneficence comes from the Latin "bene" and "facere" and literally means doing, acting, or making well. Beneficence is defined as doing good for others and not merely wishing them well (benevolence).

[2] For example, the physician needs help from the police officer to protect property and family from robbers; the police officer needs help from the physician to cure disease. The police officer is the superior of the doctor in one respect, namely in enforcing the law; the doctor is the superior of the police officer in another, namely in curing disease.

Reply to Objection 1. Absolutely speaking it is impossible to do good to every single one: yet it is true of each individual that one may be bound to do good to him in some particular case. Hence charity binds us, though not actually doing good to someone, to be prepared in mind to do good to anyone if we have time to spare. There is, however, a good that we can do to all, if not to each individual, at least to all in general, as when we pray for all, for unbelievers as well as for the faithful.

Objection 2. Further, it is written (Sir 12:5): "Give to the good, and receive not a sinner." But many men are sinners. Therefore we need not do good to all.

Reply to Objection 2. In a sinner there are two things, his guilt and his nature. Accordingly we are bound to succor the sinner as to the maintenance of his nature, but not so as to abet his sin, for this would be to do evil rather than good.

ARTICLE 3 ⟡ Should we do more good to those who are more closely united to us?

Yes, despite objections to the contrary, Augustine says (*De Doctr. Christ.* i, 28): "Since one cannot do good to all, we ought to consider those chiefly who by reason of place, time or any other circumstance, by a kind of chance are more closely united to us."

I answer that, Grace and virtue imitate the order of nature, which is established by Divine wisdom. Now the order of nature is such that every natural agent pours forth its activity first and most of all on the things which are nearest to it: thus fire heats most what is next to it. In like manner God pours forth the gifts of His goodness first and most plentifully on the substances which are nearest to Him,[3] as Dionysius declares (*Coel. Hier.* vii). But the bestowal of benefits is an act of charity towards others. Therefore we ought to be most beneficent towards those who are most closely connected with us.[4]

---

[3] Angels are the closest beings to God, the most akin to God's nature.

[4] Charity starts at home. Benefiting those most closely connected to us also challenges us more than focusing on those who are distant. Everyday life provides constant opportunities to act kindly in a thousand small ways, providing

Now one man's connection with another may be measured in reference to the various matters in which men are engaged together; (thus the intercourse of kinsmen is in natural matters, that of fellow-citizens is in civic matters, that of the faithful is in spiritual matters, and so forth) and various benefits should be conferred in various ways according to these various connections, because we ought in preference to bestow on each one such benefits as pertain to the matter in which, speaking simply, he is most closely connected with us. And yet this may vary according to the various requirements of time, place, or matter in hand: because in certain cases one ought, for instance, to succor a stranger, in extreme necessity, rather than one's own father, if he is not in such urgent need.[5]

Objection 1. It would seem that we are not bound to do good to those rather who are more closely united to us. For it is written (Lk 14:12): "When you make a dinner or a supper, call not your friends, nor your brethren, nor your kinsmen." Now these are the most closely united to us. Therefore we are not bound to do good to those rather who are more closely united to us, but preferably to strangers and to those who are in want: hence the text goes on: "But, when you make a feast, call the poor, the maimed," etc.

Reply to Objection 1. Our Lord did not absolutely forbid us to invite our friends and kinsmen to eat with us, but to invite them so that they may invite us in return, since that would be an act not of charity but of cupidity.[6] The case may occur, however, that one ought rather to invite strangers, on account of their greater want. For it must be understood that, other things being equal, one ought to succor those rather who are most closely connected with us. And if of two,

---

ample opportunity for growth by, for example, cleaning up small messes, listening patiently, quietly helping, etc.

[5] Practical wisdom is necessary, and no set of rules, however detailed, is sufficient to arrive at knowledge of what is to be done in each situation.

[6] The love of charity seeks what is good for the other; the love of cupidity seeks what is good for oneself. If one were to invite others to dine only in order to receive some benefit in return from them later, such an invitation would not be an act of charity.

one be more closely connected, and the other in greater want, it is not possible to decide, by any general rule, which of them we ought to help rather than the other, since there are various degrees of want as well as of connection: and the matter requires the judgment of a prudent man.[7]

Objection 2. Further, to help another in the battle is an act of very great goodness. But a soldier on the battlefield is bound to help a fellow-soldier who is a stranger rather than a kinsman who is a foe. Therefore in doing acts of kindness we are not bound to give the preference to those who are most closely united to us.

Reply to Objection 2. The common good of many is more Godlike than the good of an individual, wherefore it is a virtuous action for a man to endanger even his own life, either for the spiritual or for the temporal common good of his country. Since, therefore, men engage together in warlike acts in order to safeguard the common weal, the soldier who with this in view succors his comrade, succors him not as a private individual, but with a view to the welfare of his country as a whole: wherefore it is not a matter for wonder if a stranger be preferred to one who is a blood relation.

Objection 3. Further, we should pay what is due before conferring gratuitous favors. But it is a man's duty to be good to those who have been good to him. Therefore we ought to do good to our benefactors rather than to those who are closely united to us.

Reply to Objection 3. A thing may be due in two ways. There is one which should be reckoned, not among the goods of the debtor, but rather as belonging to the person to whom it is due: for instance, a man may have another's goods, whether in money or in kind, either

---

[7] Most rules of morality admit exceptions, such as the one under discussion here: "care first for those with whom one is most closely connected." However, there are circumstances when a complete stranger has to take first priority, even to the great inconvenience of those with whom one is most closely connected. The importance of prudence is in part to make up for what any set of rules, even the most complete, cannot supply—namely, when to invoke one rule rather than another, when two rules apparently conflict.

because he has stolen them, or because he has received them on loan or in deposit or in some other way. In this case a man ought to pay what he owes, rather than benefit his connections out of it, unless perchance the case be so urgent that it would be lawful for him to take another's property in order to relieve the one who is in need. Yet, again, this would not apply if the creditor were in equal distress: in which case, however, the claims on either side would have to be weighed with regard to such other conditions as a prudent man would take into consideration, because, on account of the different particular cases, as the Philosopher states (*Ethic.* ix, 2), it is impossible to lay down a general rule.[8]

The other kind of due is one which is reckoned among the goods of the debtor and not of the creditor; for instance, a thing may be due, not because justice requires it, but on account of a certain moral equity, as in the case of benefits received free of charge. Now no benefactor confers a benefit equal to that which a man receives from his parents: wherefore in paying back benefits received, we should give the first place to our parents before all others, unless, on the other side, there be such weightier motives, as need or some other circumstance, for instance the common good of the Church or state. In other cases we must take into account the connection and the benefit received; and here again no general rule can be laid down.

Objection 4. Further, a man ought to love his parents more than his children, as stated above (q. 26, a. 9). Yet a man ought to be more beneficent to his children, since "neither ought the children to lay up

---

[8] A proper understanding of what Aquinas states here does not exclude the possibility of exceptionless norms, such as "intentional killing of innocent human beings is always wrong" or "forced sexual intercourse is always wrong." These are not general rules stating what *should* be done but rather general rules stating what should not be done. As in the seeking of health, general rules cannot indicate what medicine a doctor should give, but general rules can exclude what should never be done in seeking to restore health, for instance, giving lethal poisons. For more, see *Summa theologiae* II–II, q. 32, a. 2 and Christopher Kaczor, "Exceptionless Norms in Aristotle? Thomas Aquinas and 20th Century Interpreters of the Nicomachean Ethics," *The Thomist* (61.1; January 1997): 33–62.

for the parents," according to 2 Corinthians 12:14. Therefore we are not bound to be more beneficent to those who are more closely united to us.

Reply to Objection 4. Parents are like superiors, and so a parent's love tends to conferring benefits, while the children's love tends to honor their parents. Nevertheless in a case of extreme urgency it would be lawful to abandon one's children rather than one's parents, to abandon whom it is by no means lawful, on account of the obligation we lie under towards them for the benefits we have received from them, as the Philosopher states (*Ethic.* iii, 14).

QUESTION 32

ALMSGIVING
(WORKS OF MERCY)[1]

ARTICLE 1 ~~ **Is almsgiving an act of charity?**

Yes, despite objections to the contrary, It is written 2 John 3:17: "He that has the substance of this world, and shall see his brother in need, and shall put up his bowels from him, how does the charity of God abide in him?"

I answer that, External acts belong to that virtue which regards the motive for doing those acts. Now the motive for giving alms is to relieve one who is in need, wherefore some have defined alms as being "a deed whereby something is given to the needy, out of compassion and for God's sake," which motive belongs to mercy, as stated above (q. 30, a. 1, a. 2). Hence it is clear that almsgiving is, properly speaking, an act of mercy. This appears in its very name, for in Greek [*eleēmosynē*] it is derived from having mercy [*eleein*] even as the Latin *miseratio* is. And since mercy is an effect of charity, as shown above (q. 30, a. 2, a. 3, obj. 3), it follows that almsgiving is an act of charity through the medium of mercy.

Objection 1. It would seem that almsgiving is not an act of charity. For without charity one cannot do acts of charity. Now it is possible to give alms without having charity, according to 1 Corinthians 13:3: "If I

---

[1] A school formerly attended is called an "alma mater" or "nourishing mother." To give alms in the broader sense used here by Thomas is to provide nourishment for another's need of body or soul.

187

should distribute all my goods to feed the poor . . . and have not charity, it profits me nothing." Therefore almsgiving is not an act of charity.

Reply to Objection 1. An act of virtue may be taken in two ways: first materially; thus an act of justice is to do what is just; and such an act of virtue can be without the virtue, since many, without having the habit of justice, do what is just, led by the natural light of reason, or through fear, or in the hope of gain. Secondly, we speak of a thing being an act of justice formally, and thus an act of justice is to do what is just, in the same way as a just man, i.e. with readiness and delight, and such an act of virtue cannot be without the virtue.

Accordingly almsgiving can be materially without charity,[2] but to give alms formally, i.e. for God's sake, with delight and readiness, and altogether as one ought, is not possible without charity.[3]

ARTICLE 2 ~~ Are the different works of mercy suitably listed?

Yes, despite objections to the contrary, Gregory says (*Nom. in Evang.* ix): "Let him that has understanding beware lest he withhold his knowledge; let him that has abundance of wealth, watch lest he slacken his merciful bounty; let him who is a servant to art be most solicitous to share his skill and profit with his neighbor; let him who has an opportunity of speaking with the worthy, fear lest he be condemned for retaining his talent, if when he has the chance he plead not with him the cause of the poor." Therefore the aforesaid works of mercy [*the seven corporal works of mercy*] namely, to feed the hungry, to give drink to the thirsty, to clothe the naked, to shelter the homeless, to visit the sick, to ransom the captive, to bury the dead and *the seven spiritual works of mercy*, namely, to instruct the ignorant, to counsel

---

[2] In other words, you could give money to the poor but not out of concern for them or out of love of God but rather merely to impress bystanders with your generosity. The real motives of deeds of kindness can remain hidden, but charity requires a pure motive.

[3] Following Aristotle's lead, Thomas holds that for an act to be virtuous it must be good in every respect. Even if the act itself, *materially considered,* is what a just or loving person would do, it is not truly a just or loving act, *formally considered,* unless it is done for the right reason, with the right interior disposition, and in all the right circumstances.

the doubtful, to comfort the sorrowful, to reprove the sinner, to forgive injuries, to bear with those who trouble and annoy us, and to pray for all] are suitably enumerated in respect of those things whereof men have abundance or insufficiency.

I answer that, The aforesaid distinction of works of mercy is suitably taken from the various needs of our neighbor:[4] some of which affect the soul, and are relieved by spiritual works of mercy, while others affect the body, and are relieved by corporal works of mercy. For corporal need occurs either during this life or afterwards. If it occurs during this life, it is either a common need in respect of things needed by all, or it is a special need occurring through some accident supervening. On the first case, the need is either internal or external. Internal need is twofold: one which is relieved by solid food, viz. hunger, in respect of which we have "to feed the hungry," while the other is relieved by liquid food, viz. thirst, and in respect of this we have "to give drink to the thirsty." The common need with regard to external help is twofold: one in respect of clothing, and as to this we have "to clothe the naked," while the other is in respect of a dwelling place, and as to this we have

---

[4] The completeness of Thomas's taxonomy of works of mercy indicates both his brilliant, synthesizing intellect as well as his trust in the reliability of what has been received in tradition. An outline of his division of the corporal and spiritual works of mercy is as follows:

(I) Needs of the human body
    a. Before death
        i. internal needs (feed the hungry, give drink to the thirsty)
       ii. external needs (clothe the naked, shelter the homeless)
      iii. special needs (visit the sick, ransom the captive)
    b. After death (bury the dead)
(II) Needs of the human soul
    a. As provided for by God answering prayer (pray for the living and the dead)
    b. As provided by other human beings in remedy of a:
        i. need of the speculative intellect (instruct the ignorant)
       ii. need of the practical intellect (counsel the doubting)
      iii. need of the appetitive power (comfort the sorrowful)
      iv. need due to an inordinate act
          1. of the one sinning (admonish the sinner)
          2. of the one sinned against (pardon the injury)
          3. of the sinner annoying others (bear wrongs patiently)

"to shelter the homeless." Again if the need be special, it is either the result of an internal cause, like sickness, and then we have "to visit the sick," or it results from an external cause, and then we have "to ransom the captive." After this life we give "burial to the dead."

In like manner spiritual needs are relieved by spiritual acts in two ways: first by asking for help from God, and in this respect we have "prayer,"[5] whereby one man prays for others; secondly, by giving human assistance, and this in three ways. First, in order to relieve a deficiency on the part of the intellect, and if this deficiency be in the speculative intellect,[6] the remedy is applied by "instructing," and if in the practical intellect, the remedy is applied by "counseling." Secondly, there may be a deficiency on the part of the appetitive power, especially by way of sorrow, which is remedied by "comforting." Thirdly, the deficiency may be due to an inordinate act; and this may be the subject of a threefold consideration. First, in respect of the sinner, inasmuch as

---

5 Some have seen a difficulty here, for if God has no potentiality, then He cannot answer any prayer of petition. In other words, if God is unchanging, then asking God in prayer to grant a request is pointless, for God cannot change his mind in response to prayer. If God is immutable, God either wills from all eternity that the proposed petition take place, or God does not will that the petition be granted, but either way prayer cannot change what God wills, so it would seem that Thomas must either admit that God does change, or admit that God does not answer prayers of petition. Thomas, so the argument goes, cannot maintain both the immutability of God and that God can answer prayer. However, God may will to bring something about on condition that someone prays for it, even as a mother may will to give a child what the child desires, but only if that child says "please." It is good for children to learn to say please, and it is good for all of us to raise our minds and hearts to God. God wills from all eternity to grant certain requests if we pray for them, and not to grant them if no prayer is made. God grants us the dignity of being "secondary causes" in the world, through our physical activities but also in the spiritual order through prayer of petition. Prayer does not change God, but it does change us, and through prayer God sometimes grants our requests.

6 Thomas draws a distinction here between the speculative and practical intellect. By the speculative intellect, he means the power to understand things that cannot be changed; the practical intellect is the intelligence used to change things in the world. Instructing the ignorant pertains only indirectly to behavior, for one could instruct another about matters that cannot be changed, while counseling is more immediately practical and implies directing human action.

the sin proceeds from his inordinate will, and thus the remedy takes the form of "reproof." Secondly, in respect of the person sinned against; and if the sin be committed against ourselves, we apply the remedy by "pardoning the injury," while, if it be committed against God or our neighbor, it is not in our power to pardon, as Jerome observes (*Super Matth.* xviii, 15). Thirdly, in respect of the result of the inordinate act, on account of which the sinner is an annoyance to those who live with him, even beside his intention, in which case the remedy is applied by "bearing with him," especially with regard to those who sin out of weakness, according to Romans 15:1: "We that are stronger ought to bear the infirmities of the weak," and not only as regards their being infirm and consequently troublesome on account of their unruly actions, but also by bearing any other burdens of theirs with them, according to Galatians 6:2: "Bear one another's burdens."

Objection 1. It would seem that the different kinds of works of mercy are unsuitably enumerated. For we reckon seven corporal works of mercy, namely, to feed the hungry, to give drink to the thirsty, to clothe the naked, to shelter the homeless, to visit the sick, to ransom the captive, to bury the dead; all of which are expressed in the following verse: "To visit, to quench, to feed, to ransom, clothe, shelter or bury."

Again we reckon seven spiritual alms, namely, to instruct the ignorant, to counsel the doubtful, to comfort the sorrowful, to reprove the sinner, to forgive injuries, to bear with those who trouble and annoy us, and to pray for all, which are all contained in the following verse: "To counsel, reprove, console, to pardon, forbear, and to pray," yet so that counsel includes both advice and instruction.

And it seems that these various works of mercy are unsuitably enumerated. For the purpose of works of mercy is to succor our neighbor. But a dead man profits nothing by being buried, else Our Lord would not have spoken truly when He said (Mt 10:28): "Be not afraid of them who kill the body, and after that have no more that they can do." [Lk 12:4] This explains why Our Lord, in enumerating the works of mercy, made no mention of the burial of the dead (Mt 25:35, 36). Therefore it seems that these works of mercy are unsuitably enumerated.

Reply to Objection 1. Burial does not profit a dead man as though his body could be capable of perception after death. In this sense Our Lord said that those who kill the body "have no more that they can do;" and for this reason He did not mention the burial of the dead with the other works of mercy, but those only which are more clearly necessary. Nevertheless it does concern the deceased what is done with his body: both that he may live in the memory of man whose respect he forfeits if he remain without burial, and as regards a man's fondness for his own body while he was yet living, a fondness which kindly persons should imitate after his death.[7] It is thus that some are praised for burying the dead, as Tobias, and those who buried Our Lord, as Augustine says (*De Cura pro Mort.* iii).

Objection 2. Further, as stated above (a. 1), the purpose of giving alms is to relieve our neighbor's need. Now there are many needs of human life other than those mentioned above; for instance, a blind man needs a leader, a lame man needs someone to lean on, a poor man needs riches. Therefore these works of mercy are unsuitably enumerated.

Reply to Objection 2. All other needs are reduced to these, for blindness and lameness are kinds of sickness, so that to lead the blind, and to support the lame, come to the same as visiting the sick. In like manner, to assist a man against any distress that is due to an extrinsic cause comes to the same as the ransom of captives. And the wealth with which we relieve the poor is sought merely for the purpose of relieving the aforesaid needs: hence there was no reason for special mention of this particular need.

Objection 3. Further, almsgiving is a work of mercy. But the reproof of the wrongdoer savors, apparently, of severity rather than of mercy. Therefore it ought not to be reckoned among the spiritual works of mercy.

---

[7] Since body and soul make up the unity that is the human person, even after death the corpse should be treated with respect. Just as a treasured possession of a deceased person is treated with care by those who loved him, so too a human corpse deserves to be treated with respect. On this account, desecration of graves is wrong, and burying the dead properly merits praise. This view is held not merely by Christians and Jews but also by the ancient Greeks, as is indicated in the story of *Antigone* by Sophocles.

Reply to Objection 3. The reproof of the sinner, as to the exercise of the act of reproving, seems to imply the severity of justice, but, as to the intention of the reprover, who wishes to free a man from the evil of sin, it is an act of mercy and loving kindness, according to Proverbs 27:6: "Better are the wounds of a friend, than the deceitful kisses of an enemy."[8]

Objection 4. Further, almsgiving is intended for the supply of a defect. But no man is without the defect of ignorance in some matter or other. Therefore, apparently, each one ought to instruct anyone who is ignorant of what he knows himself.

Reply to Objection 4. Not knowing something is not always a defect, but only when it is about what one ought to know, and it is a part of almsgiving to supply this defect by instruction. On doing this, however, we should observe the due circumstances of persons, place and time, even as in other virtuous acts.[9]

ARTICLE 3 ⤖ **Are corporal works of mercy more important than spiritual works of mercy?**

No, despite objections to the contrary, Augustine says (*De Serm. Dom. in Monte* i, 20) on the words, "Give to him that asks of you" (Mt 5:42): "You should give so as to injure neither yourself nor another, and when you refuse what another asks you must not lose sight of the claims of justice, and send him away empty; at times indeed you will give what is better than what is asked for, if you reprove him that asks unjustly."

---

[8] To admonish people who are doing wrong is, in the proper circumstances, an act of great kindness to them. Like abuse of health, wrongdoing injures the one who does wrong. It is, so to speak, a self-inflicted wound that also often harms others as well. To persuade someone to abandon vice and pursue virtue is to help that person (and normally others as well) to become happier. However, like any work of mercy, "reproof of a sinner" cannot be properly done in all times and circumstances. Perhaps, most importantly, the one who is admonished should be aware that the correction arises from love and concern rather than from haughtiness and self-righteousness.

[9] Like other works of mercy, "instruction" of others can be improperly done, for example, when it serves only to humiliate or embarrass the person.

Now reproof is a spiritual alms. Therefore spiritual works of mercy are preferable to corporal works of mercy.[10]

I answer that, There are two ways of comparing these works of mercy. First, simply; and in this respect, spiritual works of mercy hold the first place, for three reasons. First, because the offering is more excellent, since it is a spiritual gift, which surpasses a corporal gift, according to Proverbs 4:2: "I will give you a good gift; forsake not My Law." Secondly, on account of the object succored, because the spirit is more excellent than the body, wherefore, even as a man in looking after himself ought to look to his soul more than to his body, so ought he in looking after his neighbor, whom he ought to love as himself. Thirdly, as regards the acts themselves by which our neighbor is succored, because spiritual acts are more excellent than corporal acts, which are, in a fashion, servile.

Secondly, we may compare them with regard to some particular case, when some corporal alms excels some spiritual alms: for instance, a man in hunger is to be fed rather than instructed, and as the Philosopher observes (*Topic.* iii, 2), for a needy man "money is better than philosophy," although the latter is better simply.[11]

Objection 1. It would seem that corporal alms are of more account than spiritual alms. For it is more praiseworthy to give alms to one who is in greater want, since a work of mercy is to be praised because it relieves one who is in need. Now the body, which is relieved by corporal alms, is by nature more needy than the spirit, which is relieved by spiritual alms. Therefore corporal alms are of more account.

---

[10] The *prima facie* priority of spiritual over bodily aid can be seen in another way. Socrates said: "It is better to suffer evil than to do evil" (*Gorgias,* 473a–475e). Suffering evil involves a depravation of lesser goods, but doing evil involves foregoing or at least damaging a greater good—for Thomas, unity with God.

[11] Thomas's insight is reflected in much contemporary psychological research on happiness. Bodily needs, which can be met through money, are but a part of true happiness. As noted in the introduction to this volume, David Myers, in *The Pursuit of Happiness: Who is Happy—and Why,* has summarized a vast amount of empirical data on happiness that shows that once beyond poverty more money does not make people happy.

Reply to Objection 1. It is better to give to one who is in greater want, other things being equal, but if he who is less needy is better, and is in want of better things, it is better to give to him: and it is thus in the case in point.

Objection 2. Further, giving alms is less praiseworthy and meritorious if the kindness is compensated, wherefore Our Lord says (Lk 14:12): "When you make a dinner or a supper, call not you neighbors who are rich, lest perhaps they also invite you again." Now there is always compensation in spiritual works of mercy, since he who prays for another profits thereby, according to Psalm 34:13: "My prayer shall be turned into my bosom: and he who teaches another, makes progress in knowledge," which cannot be said of corporal works of mercy. Therefore corporal works of mercy are of more account than spiritual works of mercy.

Reply to Objection 2. Compensation does not detract from merit and praise if it be not intended, even as human glory, if not intended, does not detract from virtue. Thus Sallust says of Cato[12] (*Catilin.*) that "the less he sought fame, the more he became famous": and thus it is with spiritual works of mercy. Nevertheless the intention of gaining spiritual goods does not detract from merit, as does the intention of gaining corporal goods.

Objection 3. Further, a work of mercy is to be commended if the needy one is comforted by it: wherefore it is written (Job 31:20): "If his sides have not blessed me," and the Apostle says to Philemon (verse 7): "The bowels of the saints have been refreshed by you, brother." Now a corporal alms is sometimes more welcome to a needy man than a spiritual alms. Therefore bodily works of mercy are of more account than spiritual works of mercy.

---

12 Gaius Sallustius Crispus (86–34 B.C.) was a Roman historian whose most famous work, *The Conspiracy of Catiline,* chronicles the moral decline of Roman aristocrats. Marcus Porcius Cato (95–46 B.C.), also known as Cato the Younger, was a man held to have highest virtue in his time and was a relentless foe of Julius Caesar.

Reply to Objection 3. The merit of an almsgiver depends on that in which the will of the recipient rests reasonably, and not on that in which it rests when it is inordinate.[13]

ARTICLE 5 ⁓ Are works of mercy a matter of precept?[14]

Yes, despite objections to the contrary, No man is punished eternally for omitting to do what is not a matter of precept. But some are punished eternally for omitting to give alms, as is clear from Matthew 25:31–46.[15] Therefore almsgiving is a matter of precept.

---

[13] In other words, sometimes authentic benefit is given to a person even if the person does not fully appreciate it at the time. Many children do not enjoy learning how to read, but learning to read is nevertheless to their benefit. Correction of those doing wrong is also not always appreciated by those who are corrected, but it may be a work of mercy nevertheless.

[14] The question here concerns whether corporal and spiritual works are obligatory for all (a matter of precept) or, on the other hand, whether they are a heroic, supererogatory, and extraordinary option for some (a matter of counsel). All human acts are governed by precept (for instance, not stealing), but one may voluntarily go "above and beyond" the call of duty in matters of counsel (for instance, giving great sums of money to the poor).

[15] This Gospel passage reads: "When the Son of Man comes in his glory, and all the angels with him, he will sit on his throne in heavenly glory. All the nations will be gathered before him, and he will separate the people one from another as a shepherd separates the sheep from the goats. He will put the sheep on his right and the goats on his left. Then the King will say to those on his right, 'Come, you who are blessed by my Father; take your inheritance, the kingdom prepared for you since the creation of the world. For I was hungry and you gave me food, I was thirsty and you gave me drink, I was a stranger and you invited me in, I was naked and you clothed me, I was sick and you looked after me, I was in prison and you came to visit me.' Then the righteous will answer him, 'Lord, when did we see you hungry and feed you, or thirsty and give you something to drink? When did we see you a stranger and invite you in, or needing clothes and clothe you? When did we see you sick or in prison and go to visit you?' The King will reply, 'I tell you the truth, whatever you did for one of the least of these brothers of mine, you did for me.' Then he will say to those on his left, 'Depart from me, you who are cursed, into the eternal fire prepared for the devil and his angels. For I was hungry and you gave me nothing to eat, I was thirsty and you gave me nothing to drink, I was a stranger and you did not invite me in, I needed clothes and you did not clothe me, I was sick and in prison and you did not look after me.' They also will answer, 'Lord, when did we see you hungry or thirsty or a stranger or needing clothes or sick or in prison, and did not help you?' He will reply, 'I tell you the truth, what

I answer that, As love of our neighbor is a matter of precept, whatever is a necessary condition for the love of our neighbor is a matter of precept also. Now the love of our neighbor requires that not only should we be our neighbor's well-wishers, but also his well-doers,[16] according to 1 John 3:18: "Let us not love in word, nor in tongue, but in deed, and in truth." And in order to be a person's well-wisher and well-doer, we ought to succor his needs: this is done by almsgiving. Therefore almsgiving is a matter of precept.

Since, however, precepts are about acts of virtue, it follows that all almsgiving must be a matter of precept, insofar as it is necessary to virtue, namely, insofar as it is demanded by right reason. Now right reason demands that we should take into consideration something on the part of the giver, and something on the part of the recipient. On the part of the giver, it must be noted that he should give of his surplus, according to Luke 11:41: "That which remains, give alms." This surplus is to be taken in reference not only to himself, so as to denote what is unnecessary to the individual, but also in reference to those of whom he has charge, because each one must first of all look after himself and then after those over whom he has charge, and afterwards with what remains relieve the needs of others. Thus nature first, by its nutritive power, takes what it requires for the upkeep of one's own body, and afterwards yields the residue for the formation of another by the power of generation.

On the part of the recipient it is requisite that he should be in need, else there would be no reason for giving him alms: yet since it is not possible for one individual to relieve the needs of all, we are not bound to relieve all who are in need, but only those who could not be succored if we did not succor them. For in such cases the words of Ambrose apply, "Feed him that dies of hunger: if you have not fed him, you have slain him" [Cf. *Canon Pasce,* dist. lxxxvi, whence the words, as quoted, are taken]. Accordingly we are bound to give alms of

---

ever you did not do for one of the least of these, you did not do for me.' Then they will go away to eternal punishment, but the righteous to eternal life."

[16] The love of charity is not merely a matter of emotions and wishes (benevolence), but rather a matter of actions and deeds (benefacting).

our surplus, as also to give alms to one whose need is extreme: other-wise almsgiving, like any other greater good, is a matter of counsel.[17]

Objection 1. It would seem that almsgiving is not a matter of pre-cept. For the counsels are distinct from the precepts. Now almsgiving is a matter of counsel, according to Daniel 4:24: "Let my counsel be acceptable to the King; (Vulg.: 'to you, and') redeem your sins with alms." Therefore almsgiving is not a matter of precept.

Reply to Objection 1. Daniel spoke to a king who was not subject to God's Law, wherefore such things as were prescribed by the Law, which he did not profess, had to be counseled to him. Or he may have been speaking in reference to a case in which almsgiving was not a matter of precept.

Objection 2. Further, it is lawful for everyone to use and to keep what is his own. Yet by keeping it he will not give alms. Therefore it is lawful not to give alms: and consequently almsgiving is not a matter of precept.

Reply to Objection 2. The temporal goods that God grants us are ours as to the ownership, but as to the use of them, they belong not to us alone but also to such others as we are able to succor out of what we have over and above our needs.[18] Hence Basil[19] says (*Hom. super Luc.* xii, 18): "If you acknowledge them," viz. your temporal goods, "as coming from God, is He unjust because He apportions them unequally? Why are you rich while another is poor, unless it be that you may have the merit of a good stewardship, and he the reward of patience? It is the hungry man's bread that you withhold, the naked man's cloak that you have stored

---

17 In other words, we have a duty to give of our surplus and a duty to supply those in grave need. However to give still more is to go above and beyond the call of duty.

18 We have a duty, a serious duty, to aid those less fortunate than ourselves by performing corporal and spiritual works of mercy. Virtually everyone can con-tribute to the well-being of those less fortunate in some way and to fail to do so is a sinful omission. The virtue of practical wisdom helps us to take due account and care of the needs of others, our families and friends, and ourselves.

19 St. Basil the Great (329–79), Bishop of Caesarea, is a doctor of the Church who defended the divinity of Christ against the Arians.

away, the shoe of the barefoot that you have left to rot, the money of the needy that you have buried underground: and so you injure as many as you might help." Ambrose expresses himself in the same way.

Objection 3. Further, whatever is a matter of precept binds the transgressor at some time or other under pain of mortal sin, because positive precepts are binding for some fixed time. Therefore, if almsgiving were a matter of precept, it would be possible to point to some fixed time when a man would commit a mortal sin unless he gave alms. But it does not appear how this can be so, because it can always be deemed probable that the person in need can be relieved in some other way, and that what we would spend in almsgiving might be needful to ourselves either now or in some future time. Therefore it seems that almsgiving is not a matter of precept.

Reply to Objection 3. There is a time when we sin mortally if we omit to give alms: on the part of the recipient when we see that his need is evident and urgent, and that he is not likely to be succored otherwise; on the part of the giver, when he has superfluous goods, which he does not need for the time being, as far as he can judge with probability. Nor need he consider every case that may possibly occur in the future, for this would be to think about the morrow, which Our Lord forbade us to do (Mt 6:34), but he should judge what is superfluous and what necessary, according as things probably and generally occur.[20]

---

[20] It is fully permissible to have some measure of savings for emergencies that may take place. However, hoarding money, going well beyond what is needed to secure the well-being of those for whom one is responsible, is mortally sinful.

QUESTION 33

FRATERNAL
CORRECTION

ARTICLE 4 ~~ **Is a person bound to correct his prelate?**[1]

Yes, despite objections to the contrary, Augustine says in his Rule: "Show mercy not only to yourselves, but also to him who, being in the higher position among you, is therefore in greater danger." But fraternal correction is a work of mercy. Therefore even prelates ought to be corrected.

I answer that, A subject is not competent to administer to his prelate the correction which is an act of justice through the coercive nature of punishment: but the fraternal correction which is an act of charity is within the competency of everyone in respect of any person towards whom he is bound by charity,[2] provided there be something in that person which requires correction.

Now an act which proceeds from a habit or power extends to whatever is contained under the object of that power or habit: thus vision extends to all things comprised in the object of sight. Since, however, a

---

[1] By "prelate," Thomas means one's superior, ordinary, or ruler in matters pertaining to the Church, such as a bishop of a diocese.

[2] In other words, since punishment must be administered by a legitimate authority, a subject may not punish the one to whom he is subject. However, fraternal correction does not involve punishment in itself, even though it may be unpleasant for the one corrected. Thus, a layperson may admonish the local bishop for wrongdoing of various kinds, but the layperson does not have the authority to punish the bishop by removing him from his office as bishop.

virtuous act needs to be moderated by due circumstances, it follows that when a subject corrects his prelate, he ought to do so in a becoming manner, not with offensively bold behavior and harshness, but with gentleness and respect. Hence the Apostle says (1 Tim 5:1): "An ancient man rebuke not, but entreat him as a father," wherefore Dionysius finds fault with the monk Demophilus (Ep. viii), for rebuking a priest with insolence, by striking and turning him out of the church.[3]

Objection 1. It would seem that no man is bound to correct his prelate. For it is written (Ex 19:12): "The beast that shall touch the mount shall be stoned," (Vulg.: 'Everyone that shall touch the mount, dying he shall die') and (2 Kgs 6:7) it is related that the Lord struck Oza for touching the ark. Now the mount and the ark signify our prelates. Therefore prelates should not be corrected by their subjects.

Reply to Objection 1. It would seem that a subject touches his prelate inordinately when he upbraids him with insolence, as also when he speaks ill of him: and this is signified by God's condemnation of those who touched the mount and the ark.[4]

Objection 2. Further, a gloss on Galatians 2:11, "I withstood him to the face," adds: "as an equal." Therefore, since a subject is not equal to his prelate, he ought not to correct him.

Reply to Objection 2. To withstand anyone in public exceeds the mode of fraternal correction, and so Paul would not have withstood

---

3 Fraternal correction should be done after the manner of a loving son correcting his father. Indeed, it is in this spirit that the correction is most likely to be effective. Few people, when rebuked harshly, listen carefully and openly. In addition, even when they are in error, a due respect should be given to Church officials on account of their office. However, as Thomas notes here, due respect does not mean a slavish agreement with all that a bishop, for example, may say or do.

4 Like all good acts, fraternal correction must be administered in a due manner and out of love. If not, then what otherwise could have been a good act, all things considered, is not. For an action as a whole to be good, the act done must be good (or at least morally indifferent), the motive must be good, and the circumstances (to whom, what, where, by what aids, why, how, and when) must be fitting (I–II, q. 7).

Peter then, unless he were in some way his equal as regards the defense of the faith. But one who is not an equal can reprove privately and respectfully. Hence the Apostle in writing to the Colossians (4:17) tells them to admonish their prelate: "Say to Archippus: Fulfill your ministry [Vulg.: 'Take heed to the ministry which you have received in the Lord, that you fulfill it' (Cf. 2 Timothy 4:5).]" It must be observed, however, that if the faith were endangered, a subject ought to rebuke his prelate even publicly. Hence Paul, who was Peter's subject, rebuked him in public, on account of the imminent danger of scandal concerning faith, and, as the gloss of Augustine says on Galatians 2:11, "Peter gave an example to superiors, that if at any time they should happen to stray from the straight path, they should not disdain to be reproved by their subjects."

Objection 3. Further, Gregory says (*Moral.* xxiii, 8) that "one ought not to presume to reprove the conduct of holy men, unless one thinks better of oneself." But one ought not to think better of oneself than of one's prelate. Therefore one ought not to correct one's prelate.

Reply to Objection 3. To presume oneself to be simply better than one's prelate would seem to savor of presumptuous pride; but there is no presumption in thinking oneself better in some respect, because, in this life, no man is without some fault. We must also remember that when a man reproves his prelate charitably, it does not follow that he thinks himself any better, but merely that he offers his help to one who, "being in the higher position among you, is therefore in greater danger," as Augustine observes in his Rule quoted above.[5]

---

[5] Indeed, to think oneself "better," absolutely speaking, than another is rather difficult on Thomas's account. Although outward conduct can be judged as in accord or not in accord with faith and morals, the degree to which someone responds or fails to respond to grace is utterly hidden to all but God. It may well turn out that many who appear to be "sinners" or "saints" to us in fact relate to God in ways that surprise human expectation.

QUESTION 34

HATRED

ARTICLE 1 ⚬ Is it possible for anyone to hate God?

Yes, despite objections to the contrary, It is written (Ps 73:23): "The pride of them that hate You ascends continually," and (Jn 15:24): "But now they have both seen and hated both Me and My Father."

   I answer that, As shown above (I–II, q. 29, a. 1), hatred is a movement of the appetitive power, which power is not set in motion save by something apprehended. Now God can be apprehended by man in two ways: first, in Himself, as when He is seen in His Essence; secondly, in His effects, when, to wit, "the invisible things" of God . . . "are clearly seen, being understood by the things that are made" (Rom 1:20). Now God in His Essence is goodness itself, which no man can hate—for it is natural to good to be loved. Hence it is impossible for one who sees God in His Essence to hate Him.[1]

   Moreover some of His effects are such that they can nowise be contrary to the human will, since "to be, to live, to understand," which are effects of God, are desirable and lovable to all, wherefore again God cannot be an object of hatred if we consider Him as the Author of such like effects. Some of God's effects, however, are contrary to an inordinate will, such as the infliction of punishment, and the prohibition of sin by the Divine Law. Such like effects are repugnant to a will debased

---

   [1] However, only the blessed in heaven see God's essence, so although it is impossible for anyone in heaven ever to hate God, it is nevertheless possible for human beings on earth to hate God's condemnation and punishment of sin.

by sin, and as regards the consideration of them, God may be an object of hatred to some, insofar as they look upon Him as forbidding sin, and inflicting punishment.

Objection 1. It would seem that no man can hate God. For Dionysius says (*Div. Nom.* iv) that "the first good and beautiful is an object of love and dilection to all." But God is goodness and beauty itself. Therefore He is hated by none.

Reply to Objection 1. This argument is true of those who see God's Essence, which is the very essence of goodness.[2]

Objection 2. Further, in the Apocryphal books of 3 Esdras 4:36, 39 it is written that "all things call upon truth . . . and (all men) do well like of her works." Now God is the very truth according to John 14:6. Therefore all love God, and none can hate Him.

Reply to Objection 2. This argument is true insofar as God is apprehended as the cause of such effects as are naturally beloved of all, among which are the works of Truth who reveals herself to men.

ARTICLE 2 ~ Is hatred of God the greatest of sins?

Yes, despite objections to the contrary, The best is opposite to the worst, according to the Philosopher (*Ethic.* viii, 10). But hatred of God is contrary to the love of God, wherein man's best consists. Therefore hatred of God is man's worst sin.[3]

I answer that, The defect in sin consists in its aversion from God, as stated above (q. 10, a. 3): and this aversion would not have the character of guilt, were it not voluntary. Hence the nature of guilt consists in a voluntary aversion from God.

Now this voluntary aversion from God is directly implied in the hatred of God, but in other sins, by participation and indirectly. For just as the will cleaves directly to what it loves, so does it directly shun what it hates. Hence when a man hates God, his will is directly averted

---

[2] To see God's essence is to enjoy the beatific vision in heaven.

[3] Since charity is the greatest of all the virtues, the opposite of charity, namely, hatred for God, is the greatest of all sins.

from God, whereas in other sins, fornication for instance, a man turns away from God, not directly, but indirectly, insofar, namely, as he desires an inordinate pleasure, to which aversion from God is connected.[4] Now that which is so by itself, always takes precedence of that which is so by another. Wherefore hatred of God is more grievous than other sins.

Objection 1. It would seem that hatred of God is not the greatest of sins. For the most grievous sin is the sin against the Holy Spirit, since it cannot be forgiven, according to Matthew 12:32. Now hatred of God is not reckoned among the various kinds of sin against the Holy Spirit, as may be seen from what has been said above (q. 14, a. 2). Therefore hatred of God is not the most grievous sin.

Reply to Objection 1. According to Gregory (*Moral.* xxv, 11), "it is one thing not to do good things, and another to hate the giver of good things, even as it is one thing to sin indeliberately, and another to sin deliberately." This implies that to hate God, the giver of all good things, is to sin deliberately, and this is a sin against the Holy Spirit. Hence it is evident that hatred of God is chiefly a sin against the Holy Spirit, insofar as the sin against the Holy Spirit denotes a special kind of sin, and yet it is not reckoned among the kinds of sin against the Holy Spirit, because it is universally found in every kind of that sin.

Objection 2. Further, sin consists in withdrawing oneself from God. Now an unbeliever who has not even knowledge of God seems to be further away from Him than a believer, who though he hate God, nevertheless knows Him. Therefore it seems that the sin of unbelief is graver than the sin of hatred against God.

---

[4] The one who fornicates, that is, has premarital sex, loves the pleasure more than he loves cleaving to God, so the very choosing of the fornication is turning away from a right relationship with God and neighbor. For more on why fornication involves turning from proper love of God and neighbor, see Christopher Kaczor, "Marital Acts without Marital Vows: Social Justice and Premarital Sex," *Josephinum Journal of Theology* 9 (2002): 310–19.

Reply to Objection 2. Even unbelief is not sinful unless it be voluntary:[5] wherefore the more voluntary it is, the more it is sinful. Now it becomes voluntary by the fact that a man hates the truth that is proposed to him, wherefore it is evident that unbelief derives its sinfulness from hatred of God, Whose truth is the object of faith; and hence just as a cause is greater than its effect, so hatred of God is a greater sin than unbelief.

Objection 3. Further, God is an object of hatred, only by reason of those of His effects that are contrary to the will: the chief of which is punishment. But hatred of punishment is not the most grievous sin. Therefore hatred of God is not the most grievous sin.

Reply to Objection 3. Not everyone who hates his punishment hates God the author of punishments. For many hate the punishments inflicted on them, and yet they bear them patiently out of reverence for the Divine justice. Wherefore Augustine says (*Confess.* x) that God commands us to bear with penal evils, not to love them. On the other hand, to break out into hatred of God when He inflicts those punishments is to hate God's very justice, and that is a most grievous sin.

---

[5] At least in some cases, atheism is not arrived at reluctantly, but rather voluntarily is held. As J. Budziszewski notes in "The Second Tablet Project," *First Things* (June/July 2002): 27, "The reason it is so difficult to argue with an atheist is that he is not being honest with himself. He knows that there is a God; he only tells himself that he doesn't. One need not take this from a theist like me. Consider the remarks of the Harvard population biologist Richard Lewontin—an atheist who thinks matter is all there is—in the *New York Review of Books* (January 9, 1997): 'Our willingness to accept scientific claims that are against common sense is the key to an understanding of the real struggle between science and the supernatural. We take the side of science *in spite of* the patent absurdity of some of its constructs, *in spite of* its failure to fulfill many of its extravagant promises of health and life, *in spite of* the tolerance of the scientific community for unsubstantiated just-so stories, because we have a prior commitment, a commitment to materialism.' He continues, 'It is not that the methods and institutions of science somehow compel us to accept a material explanation of the phenomenal world but, on the contrary, that we are forced by our a priori adherence to material causes to create an apparatus of investigation and a set of concepts that produce material explanations, no matter how counterintuitive, no matter how mystifying to the uninitiated. Moreover, that materialism is absolute, for we cannot allow a divine foot in the door.' "

Hence Gregory says (*Moral.* xxv, 11): "Even as sometimes it is more grievous to love sin than to do it, so is it more wicked to hate justice than not to have done it."[6]

ARTICLE 3 ⁓ Is hatred of one's neighbor always a sin?

Yes, despite objections to the contrary, It is written (1 Jn 2:9): "He that . . . hates his brother, is in darkness." Now spiritual darkness is sin. Therefore there cannot be hatred of one's neighbor without sin.

I answer that, Hatred is opposed to love, as stated above (I–II, q. 29, a. 2), so that hatred of a thing is evil according as the love of that thing is good. Now love is due to our neighbor in respect of what he holds from God, i.e. in respect of nature and grace, but not in respect of what he has of himself and from the devil, i.e. in respect of sin and lack of justice.

Consequently it is lawful to hate the sin in one's brother, and whatever pertains to the defect of Divine justice, but we cannot hate our brother's nature and grace without sin. Now it is part of our love for our brother that we hate the fault and the lack of good in him, since desire for another's good is equivalent to hatred of his evil. Consequently the hatred of one's brother, if we consider it simply, is always sinful.[7]

Objection 1. It would seem that hatred of one's neighbor is not always a sin. For no sin is commanded or counseled by God, according to Proverbs 8:8: "All My words are just; there is nothing wicked nor perverse in them." Now, it is written (Lk 14:26): "If any man come to Me, and hate not his father and mother . . . he cannot be My disciple." Therefore hatred of one's neighbor is not always a sin.

---

[6] Passages such as this reflect the profound "interiority" of Thomistic ethics, indeed Christian ethics, which concerns itself not merely with external violations of law but also with the interior passions, loves, and desires of the human heart.

[7] *Summa contra Gentiles* III, chapter 117 notes that whoever loves God should love what God loves, and in creating and offering redemption to each human person, God shows a great love for every human being. Thus, love of God demands love of neighbor. As Jesus said just before his passion and death: "This is my commandment: that you love one another" (Jn 15:12).

Reply to Objection 1. By the commandment of God (Ex 20:12) we must honor our parents—as united to us in nature and kinship. But we must hate them insofar as they prove an obstacle to our attaining the perfection of Divine justice.

Objection 2. Further, nothing wherein we imitate God can be a sin. But it is in imitation of God that we hate certain people: for it is written (Rom 1:30): "Detractors, hateful to God." Therefore it is possible to hate certain people without committing a sin.

Reply to Objection 2. God hates the sin that is in the detractor, not his nature: so that we can hate detractors without committing a sin.[8]

Objection 3. Further, nothing that is natural is a sin, for sin is a "wandering away from what is according to nature," according to Damascene (*De Fide Orth.* ii, 4, 30; iv, 20). Now it is natural to a thing to hate whatever is contrary to it, and to aim at its undoing. Therefore it seems that it is not a sin to hate one's enemy.

Reply to Objection 3. Men are not opposed to us in respect of the goods that they have received from God: wherefore, in this respect, we should love them. But they are opposed to us insofar as they show hostility towards us, and this is sinful in them. In this respect we should hate them, for we should hate in them the fact that they are hostile to us.[9]

ARTICLE 4 ⁓ Is hatred of our neighbor the most grievous sin against our neighbor?

No, despite objections to the contrary, A thing is said to be evil because it hurts, as Augustine observes (*Enchiridion* xii). Now there are

---

[8] We are to hate the sin, but love the sinner; hate the wrongdoing, but love the person who does wrong. Indeed, the hating of sin and wrongdoing arises out of the love of the sinner and wrongdoer. To do wrong is to thwart happiness, in the agent and often also in others. So, a love of others gives rise to a hating of that which impedes or undermines the well-being of others. Just as we hate the disease because we love the person who has the disease, so too from love of each human being a hatred of injustice, vice, and sin naturally arises.

[9] Properly speaking we should not hate any person but love all people. From this love, a hatred of what is corrupting of them and often harmful to us arises.

sins by which a man hurts his neighbor more than by hatred, e.g. theft, murder and adultery. Therefore hatred is not the most grievous sin.

Moreover, Chrysostom [Hom. x in the *Opus Imperfectum*, falsely ascribed to St. John Chrysostom] commenting on Matthew 5:19, "He that shall break one of these least commandments," says: "The commandments of Moses, You shall not kill, You shall not commit adultery, count for little in their reward, but they count for much if they be disobeyed. On the other hand the commandments of Christ such as, You shall not be angry, You shall not desire, are reckoned great in their reward, but little in the transgression." Now hatred is an internal movement like anger and desire. Therefore hatred of one's brother is a less grievous sin than murder.

I answer that, Sins committed against our neighbor are evil on two counts: first by reason of the disorder in the person who sins, secondly by reason of the hurt inflicted on the person sinned against. On the first count, hatred is a more grievous sin than external actions that hurt our neighbor, because hatred is a disorder of man's will, which is the chief part of man, and wherein is the root of sin, so that if a man's outward actions were to be inordinate, without any disorder in his will, they would not be sinful, for instance, if he were to kill a man, through ignorance or out of zeal for justice: and if there be anything sinful in a man's outward sins against his neighbor, it is all to be traced to his inward hatred.[10]

On the other hand, as regards the hurt inflicted on his neighbor, a man's outward sins are worse than his inward hatred.

---

[10] Without an action being voluntary, it cannot be sinful or meritorious. To kill another person may not in any way be sinful, if the agent did not realize, and could not have realized, what was done. Only human actions, actions coming from an agent's reason and will, are subject to moral evaluation as sinful or meritorious. That which is done by accident, though often tragic, is not *morally* right or wrong.

QUESTION 36

ENVY

ARTICLE 4 ～ **Is envy a capital vice?**

Yes, despite objections to the contrary, Stands the authority of Gregory (*Moral.* xxxi, 45) who states that envy is a capital sin and assigns the aforesaid offspring (hatred, gossip,[1] detraction, joy at our neighbor's misfortunes, and grief for his prosperity) thereto.

I answer that, Just as sloth is grief for a Divine spiritual good, so envy is grief for our neighbor's good.[2] Now it has been stated above (q. 35, a. 4) that sloth is a capital vice for the reason that it incites man to do certain things, with the purpose either of avoiding sorrow or of satisfying its demands. Wherefore envy is accounted a capital vice for the same reason.

Objection 1. It would seem that envy is not a capital vice. For the capital vices are distinct from their offspring. Now envy is the daughter of

---

[1] Not simply any kind of gossip is meant here but gossip intended to stir people against one another by telling each that which will alienate the other (II–II, q. 74, a. 1).

[2] Jealousy and envy are not the same. Jealousy is the desire to exclusively possess someone or something. Envy is sorrow at another's good, a hoping that this good will be lost whether or not we are able to have it. In II–II, q. 36, a. 2, Thomas remarks: "[W]e grieve over a man's good, insofar as his good surpasses ours; this is envy properly speaking, and is always sinful, as also the Philosopher states (*Rhet.* ii, 10), because to do so is to grieve over what should make us rejoice, viz. over our neighbor's good." In opposition to envy, charity rejoices at the neighbor's good.

vainglory; for the Philosopher says (*Rhet.* ii, 10) that "those who love honor and glory are more envious." Therefore envy is not a capital vice.

Reply to Objection 1. As Gregory says (*Moral.* xxxi, 45), "the capital vices are so closely akin to one another that one springs from the other. For the first offspring of pride is vainglory, which by corrupting the mind it occupies begets envy, since while it craves for the power of an empty name, it recoils in fear lest another should acquire that power." Consequently the notion of a capital vice does not exclude its originating from another vice, but it demands that it should have some principal reason for being itself the origin of several kinds of sin. However it is perhaps because envy manifestly arises from vainglory, that it is not reckoned a capital sin, either by Isidore *(De Summo Bono)* or by Cassian[3] (*De Instit. Caenob.* v, 1).

Objection 2. Further, the capital vices seem to be less grave than the other vices which arise from them. For Gregory says (*Moral.* xxxi, 45): "The leading vices seem to worm their way into the deceived mind under some kind of pretext, but those which follow them provoke the soul to all kinds of outrage, and confuse the mind with their wild out-cry." Now envy is seemingly a most grave sin, for Gregory says (*Moral.* v, 46): "Though in every evil thing that is done, the venom of our old enemy is infused into the heart of man, yet in this wickedness the serpent stirs his whole bowels and discharges the bane of spite fitted to enter deep into the mind." Therefore envy is not a capital sin.

Reply to Objection 2. It does not follow from the passage quoted that envy is the greatest of sins, but that when the devil tempts us to envy, he is enticing us to that which has its chief place in his heart, for as quoted further on in the same passage, "by the envy of the devil, death came into the world" (Wis 2:24).

There is, however, a kind of envy which is accounted among the most grievous sins, viz. envy of another's spiritual good, which envy is a sorrow for the increase of God's grace, and not merely for our neigh-

---

[3] St. John Cassian (c. 360–435) is known as a "desert father" and was an ally and disciple of St. John Chrysostom. From his travels in Egypt, he exported monasticism to the West.

bor's good. Hence it is accounted a sin against the Holy Spirit, because thereby a man envies, as it were, the Holy Spirit Himself, Who is glorified in His works.

Objection 3. Further, it seems that its offspring are unfittingly assigned by Gregory (*Moral.* xxxi, 45), who says that from envy arise "hatred, gossip, detraction, joy at our neighbor's misfortunes, and grief for his prosperity." For joy at our neighbor's misfortunes and grief for his prosperity seem to be the same as envy, as appears from what has been said above (art. 3). Therefore these should not be assigned as off-spring of envy.

Reply to Objection 3. The number of envy's offspring may be under-stood for the reason that in the struggle aroused by envy there is some-thing by way of beginning, something by way of middle, and something by way of term. The beginning is that a man strives to lower another's reputation, and this either secretly, and then we have "gossip," or openly, and then we have "detraction."[4] The middle consists in the fact that when a man aims at defaming another, he is either able to do so, and then we have "joy at another's misfortune," or he is unable, and

---

[4] Slander and detraction should also be distinguished. The *Catholic Encyclope-dia* (1917) notes: "Slander is the attributing to another of a fault of which one knows him to be innocent. It contains a twofold malice, that which grows out of damage unjustly done to our neighbor's good name and that of lying as well." Slander is also known as calumny. Unlike calumny or slander, detraction is not a sin against the truth but rather against charity. The *Catholic Encyclopedia* (1917) observes: "Detraction is the unjust damaging of another's good name by the revelation of some fault or crime of which that other is really guilty or at any rate is seriously believed to be guilty by the defamer." The detractor does not lie but rather states the truth. However, not all truths should be revealed to all people. Sometimes, often it is very hurtful and wrong to reveal a hidden and embarrassing truth about another, to air "dirty laundry." It is not detraction, however, if one has a just reason for revealing the fault of others, such as informing police about dangerous crim-inal activity or testifying under oath in court. However, since most "gossip" does not involve information that people need to know for the good of safety, public order, or communal flourishing, detraction is a rather common and potentially serious vice. Unless a serious reason justifies revealing the information, charity demands discretion and confidentiality about the weak-nesses, faults, and sins of others.

then we have "grief at another's prosperity." The term is hatred itself, because just as good which delights causes love, so does sorrow cause hatred, as stated above (II–II, q. 34, a. 6). Grief at another's prosperity is in one way the very same as envy, when namely a man grieves over another's prosperity, insofar as it gives the latter a good name, but in another way it is a daughter of envy, insofar as the envious man sees his neighbor prosper notwithstanding his efforts to prevent it. On the other hand, "joy at another's misfortune" is not directly the same as envy, but is a result thereof, because grief over our neighbor's good, which is envy, gives rise to joy in his evil.

QUESTION 38

CONTENTION

ARTICLE 1 ⟿ Is contention a mortal sin?

Yes, despite objections to the contrary, It is against the precept of the Apostle who says (2 Tim 2:14): "Contend not in words." Moreover (Gal 5:20) contention is included among the works of the flesh, and as stated there (Gal 5:21) "they who do such things shall not obtain the kingdom of God." Now whatever excludes a man from the kingdom of God and is against a precept, is a mortal sin. Therefore contention is a mortal sin.

I answer that, To contend is to tend against some one. Wherefore just as discord denotes a contrariety of wills,[1] so contention signifies

---

[1] In the previous question (q. 37, a. 1), not included here, Thomas asks whether discord is a sin. One of the objections and the reply are reproduced here: "Objection 3. Further, sin, especially mortal sin, is not to be found in a holy man. But discord is to be found even among holy men, for it is written (Acts 15:39): 'There arose a dissension' between Paul and Barnabas, 'so that they departed one from another.' Therefore discord is not a sin and least of all a mortal sin. Reply to Objection 3. The discord between Paul and Barnabas was accidental and not direct: because each intended some good, yet the one thought one thing good, while the other thought something else, which was owing to human deficiency: for that controversy was not about things necessary to salvation. Moreover all this was ordained by Divine providence, on account of the good which would ensue." Thomas makes an important point. Not all disagreements constitute discord. Nor can all disagreements be traced back to wrongdoing on the part of one or more participants. Tensions, misunderstandings, and difficulties between people can arise entirely apart from any sin whatever; such was the case between Jesus and Mary when Jesus was

contrariety of speech. For this reason when a man contrasts various contrary things in a speech, this is called *contentio*, which Tully calls one of the rhetorical colors (*De Rhet. ad Heren.* iv), where he says that "it consists in developing a speech from contrary things," for instance: "Adulation has a pleasant beginning, and a most bitter end."

Now contrariety of speech may be looked at in two ways: first, with regard to the intention of the contentious party; secondly, with regard to the manner of contending. As to the intention, we must consider whether he contends against the truth, and then he is to be blamed, or against falsehood, and then he should be praised. As to the manner, we must consider whether his manner of contending is in keeping with the persons and the matter in dispute, for then it would be praiseworthy—hence Tully says (*De Rhet. ad Heren.* iii) that "contention is a sharp speech suitable for proof and refutation"—or whether it exceeds the demands of the persons and matter in dispute, in which case it is blameworthy.

Accordingly if we take contention as denoting a disclaimer of the truth and an inordinate manner, it is a mortal sin. Thus Ambrose (Cf. Gloss. *Ord. in Rom.* i, 29) defines contention: "Contention is a disclaimer of the truth with clamorous confidence." If, however, contention denote a disavowal of what is false, with the proper measure of acrimony, it is praiseworthy: whereas, if it denote a disavowal of falsehood, together with an inordinate manner, it can be a venial sin, unless the contention be conducted so inordinately as to give scandal to others.[2] Hence the Apostle, after saying (2 Tim 2:14): "Contend not in words," adds, "for it is to no profit, but to the subverting of the hearers."[3]

---

twelve and lost for three days (see Lk 3:41–50). Even among the very best of people, the human condition is such that disagreements will arise. The best people disagree agreeably.

[2] It is possible, Thomas notes here, to oppose error or to defend the truth, and nevertheless to do wrong if the defense is given at the wrong time, for the wrong reason, in the wrong way, for example, in a mean or vindictive spirit.

[3] A practical application of what Thomas says would include "naysayers" and those who instinctively and acrimoniously disagree with virtually everything others says, sometimes even to the point of contradicting themselves. When one cannot even discuss the weather with someone without fear of contradiction, the failure is not just social but, for Thomas, also moral.

Objection 1. It would seem that contention is not a mortal sin. For there is no mortal sin in spiritual men: and yet contention is to be found in them, according to Luke 22:24: "And there was also a strife amongst" the disciples of Jesus, "which of them should . . . be the greatest." Therefore contention is not a mortal sin.

Reply to Objection 1. The disciples of Christ contended together, not with the intention of disclaiming the truth, since each one stood up for what he thought was true. Yet there was inordinateness in their contention, because they contended about a matter which they ought not to have contended about, viz. the primacy of honor; for they were not spiritual men as yet, as a gloss says on the same passage; and for this reason Our Lord checked them.

Objection 2. Further, no well disposed man should be pleased that his neighbor commit a mortal sin. But the Apostle says (Phil 1:17): "Some out of contention preach Christ," and afterwards he says (Phil 1:18): "In this also I rejoice, yea, and will rejoice." Therefore contention is not a mortal sin.

Reply to Objection 2. Those who preached Christ "out of contention," were to be blamed, because, although they did not gainsay the truth of faith, but preached it, yet they did gainsay the truth, by the fact that they thought they would "raise affliction" to the Apostle who was preaching the truth of faith. Hence the Apostle rejoiced not in their contention, but in the fruit that would result therefrom, namely that Christ would be made known—since evil is sometimes the occasion of good results.[4]

---

[4] That good can come out of evil or evil can come out of good does not change good into evil or evil into good. An act of adultery can produce the good of a child, but adultery remains an evil act. The torture and imprisonment of a person because of his faith can lead that person and others to even greater fidelity to God, and yet denying a person's religious liberty is evil. Likewise, something good, like education, can lead to something evil, like using one's intelligence to plan mass murder. Evil is evil and good is good, even if sometimes good leads to evil or evil leads to good. Evil acts are evil precisely because they lack a due perfection. However, because they are not entirely evil, evil acts are not nothing but rather something, a deficient something.

Objection 3. Further, it happens that people contend either in the courts or in disputations, without any spiteful purpose, and with a good intention, as, for example, those who contend by disputing with heretics. Hence a gloss on 1 Kings 14:1, "It came to pass one day," etc. says: "Catholics do not raise contentions with heretics, unless they are first challenged to dispute." Therefore contention is not a mortal sin.

Reply to Objection 3. Contention is complete and is a mortal sin when, in contending before a judge, a man gainsays the truth of justice, or in a disputation, intends to impugn the true doctrine. In this sense Catholics do not contend against heretics, but the reverse. But when, whether in court or in a disputation, it is incomplete, i.e. in respect of the acrimony of speech, it is not always a mortal sin.

Objection 4. Further, Job seems to have contended with God, according to Job 39:32: "Shall he that contends with God be so easily silenced?" And yet Job was not guilty of mortal sin, since the Lord said of him (Job 42:7): "You have not spoken the thing that is right before me, as my servant Job has." Therefore contention is not always a mortal sin.

Reply to Objection 4. Contention here denotes an ordinary dispute. For Job had said (13:3): "I will speak to the Almighty, and I desire to reason with God": yet he intended not to impugn the truth, but to defend it, and in seeking the truth thus, he had no wish to be inordinate in mind or in speech.

QUESTION 39

SCHISM

ARTICLE 1 ⚬⚬ Is schism a special sin?

Yes, despite objections to the contrary, Augustine (*Contra Faust.* xx, 3; *Contra Crescon.* ii, 4) distinguishes between schism and heresy, for he says that a "schismatic is one who holds the same faith, and practices the same worship, as others, and takes pleasure in the mere disunion of the community, whereas a heretic is one who holds another faith from that of the Catholic Church."

I answer that, As Isidore says (*Etym.* viii, 3),[1] schism takes its name "from being a scission of minds," and scission is opposed to unity. Wherefore the sin of schism is one that is directly and essentially opposed to unity. For in the moral, as in the physical order, the species is not constituted by that which is accidental.[2] Now, in the moral order, the essential is that which is intended, and that which results

---

[1] St. Isidore of Seville's *Etymologiae,* cited here by Thomas, was one of the most popular books throughout the middle ages. This work provided an almost encyclopedic summary of Pagan and Christian wisdom, citing more than 150 Latin and Greek authors on a wide range of subjects including education, medicine, zoology, agriculture, war, theology, languages, peoples, and road making.

[2] For example, having white hair, black hair, or brown hair is accidental to being a human being. We do not mark a difference in species on account of hair color. Rather the human species is distinguished by being a rational animal, an essential nature shared by all humans regardless of hair color. Likewise, the moral order is not constituted by what is accidental. To steal is to steal: whether it is rubies, cash, or credit cards that are stolen is accidental to the act being theft.

beside the intention is, as it were, accidental. Hence the sin of schism is, properly speaking, a special sin, for the reason that the schismatic intends to sever himself from that unity which is the effect of charity: because charity unites not only one person to another with the bond of spiritual love, but also the whole Church in unity of spirit.

Accordingly schismatics properly so called are those who willfully and intentionally separate themselves from the unity of the Church; for this is the chief unity, and the particular unity of several individuals among themselves is subordinate to the unity of the Church, even as the mutual adaptation of each member of a natural body is subordinate to the unity of the whole body. Now the unity of the Church consists in two things: namely, in the mutual connection or communion of the members of the Church, and again in the subordination of all the members of the Church to the one head, according to Colossians 2:18, 19: "Puffed up by the sense of his flesh, and not holding the Head, from which the whole body, by joints and bands, being supplied with nourishment and compacted, grows unto the increase of God." Now this Head is Christ Himself, Whose vicar in the Church is the Sovereign Pontiff. Wherefore schismatics are those who refuse to submit to the Pope, and to hold communion with those members of the Church who acknowledge his supremacy.[3]

Objection 1. It would seem that schism is not a special sin. For "schism," as Pope Pelagius I says (*Epist. ad Victor. et Pancrat.*), "denotes a division."[4] But every sin causes a division, according to Isaiah 59: "Your sins have divided between you and your God." Therefore schism is not a special sin.

Reply to Objection 1. The division between man and God that results from sin is not intended by the sinner: it happens beside his

---

3 See *Summa theologiae* II–II, q. 1, a. 10: "Does it belong to the pope to draw up a creed of faith?" The ministry of the papacy is in the service of Christian unity as noted in chapter one of this book.

4 Thomas R. Heath notes that the word schism comes: "From the Greek *schizo*, to split, cleave, rend: *schisma*, a dissension, division: *schisma sonat scissuram*, schism sounds like scissoring. Pope Pelagius II (579–90), in St. Thomas Aquinas, *Summa theologiae* XXXV (New York: Blackfriars 1975), 67.

intention as a result of his turning inordinately to a mutable good, and so it is not schism properly so called.[5]

Objection 2. Further, a man is apparently a schismatic if he disobeys the Church. But every sin makes a man disobey the commandments of the Church, because sin, according to Ambrose (*De Parad.* viii) "is disobedience against the heavenly commandments." Therefore every sin is a schism.

Reply to Objection 2. The essence of schism consists in rebelliously disobeying the commandments: and I say "rebelliously," since a schismatic both obstinately scorns the commandments of the Church and refuses to submit to her judgment. But every sinner does not do this, wherefore not every sin is a schism.

Objection 3. Further, heresy also divides a man from the unity of faith. If, therefore, the word schism denotes a division, it would seem not to differ, as a special sin, from the sin of unbelief.

Reply to Objection 3. Heresy and schism are distinguished in respect of those things to which each is opposed essentially and directly. For heresy is essentially opposed to faith, while schism is essentially opposed to the unity of ecclesiastical charity. Wherefore just as faith and charity are different virtues, although whoever lacks faith lacks charity, so too schism and heresy are different vices, although whoever is a heretic is also a schismatic, but not conversely. This is what Jerome says in his commentary on the Epistle to the Galatians (*In Ep. ad Tit.* iii, 10): "I consider the difference between schism and heresy to be that heresy holds false doctrine while schism severs a man from the

---

[5] That which is intended defines the human action in a way that what is merely foreseen does not. If I go jogging, my activity is not best described as "perspiring," although it is true that I do perspire when running. To sweat is, however, merely an accidental or foreseen effect of what I am really trying to do, namely get some exercise. On the other hand, if I go into a sauna, I may very well be intending to perspire, and this would define my act. The intention/foresight distinction is an extremely important one in ethics. For more, see "How is the Dignity of the Person as Agent Realized? Distinguishing Intention from Foresight," in Christopher Kaczor, *The Edge of Life: Human Dignity and Contemporary Bioethics* (New York: Kluwer Academic Publishers/Springer, 2005).

Church." Nevertheless, just as the loss of charity is the road to the loss of faith, according to 1 Timothy 1:6: "From which things," i.e. charity and the like, "some going astray, are turned aside into vain babbling," so too, schism is the road to heresy. Wherefore Jerome adds (*In Ep. ad Tit.* iii, 10) that "at the outset it is possible, in a certain respect, to find a difference between schism and heresy: yet there is no schism that does not devise some heresy for itself, that it may appear to have had a reason for separating from the Church."

ARTICLE 2 ~ Is schism a graver sin than unbelief?

No, despite objections to the contrary, That which results from an addition to something else surpasses that thing either in good or in evil. Now heresy results from something being added to schism, for it adds corrupt doctrine, as Jerome declares in the passage quoted above (a. 1, ad 3). Therefore schism is a less grievous sin than unbelief.

I answer that, The gravity of a sin can be considered in two ways: first, according to the species of that sin; secondly, according to its circumstances.[6] And since particular circumstances are infinite in number, so too they can be varied in an infinite number of ways: wherefore if one were to ask in general which of two sins is the graver, the question must be understood to refer to the gravity derived from the sin's genus. Now the genus or species of a sin is taken from its object, as shown above (I–II, q. 72, a. 1; I–II, q. 73, a. 3).[7] Wherefore the sin

---

[6] So various "species" differentiate various kinds of sins such as theft, murder, or adultery. Various circumstances make a difference in assessing the action as a whole. For example, stealing from a poor person is worse than stealing from a wealthy person. Stealing a large sum of money is worse than stealing a small sum. Stealing from a family member is worse than stealing from a stranger. Kinds of acts share a common species but differ, often a great deal, in terms of their circumstances.

[7] The "object" of the human act is tremendously important in Thomistic ethics, for habits are defined in terms of acts, and acts are defined in terms of their objects. In *Veritatis Splendor*, Pope John Paul II writes: "*The morality of the human act depends primarily and fundamentally on the 'object' rationally chosen by the deliberate will,* as is borne out by the insightful analysis, still valid today, made by Saint Thomas [Cf. *ST* I–II, q. 18, a. 6]. In order to be able to grasp the object of an act that specifies that act morally, it is therefore necessary to place oneself *in the perspective of the acting person.* The object of the act of willing is in

which is opposed to the greater good is, in respect of its genus, more grievous; for instance, a sin committed against God is graver than a sin committed against one's neighbor.

Now it is evident that unbelief is a sin committed against God Himself, according as He is Himself the First Truth, on which faith is founded; whereas schism is opposed to ecclesiastical unity, which is a participated good, and a lesser good than God Himself. Wherefore it is manifest that the sin of unbelief is generically more grievous than the sin of schism, although it may happen that a particular schismatic sins more grievously than a particular unbeliever, either because his contempt is greater, or because his sin is a source of greater danger, or for some similar reason.

---

fact a freely chosen kind of behavior. To the extent that it is in conformity with the order of reason, it is the cause of the goodness of the will; it perfects us morally, and disposes us to recognize our ultimate end in the perfect good, primordial love. By the object of a given moral act, then, one cannot mean a process or an event of the merely physical order, to be assessed on the basis of its ability to bring about a given state of affairs in the outside world. Rather, that object is the proximate end of a deliberate decision that determines the act of willing on the part of the acting person. Consequently, as the *Catechism of the Catholic Church* teaches, 'there are certain specific kinds of behavior that are always wrong to choose, because choosing them involves a disorder of the will, that is, a moral evil' (*Catechism of the Catholic Church,* No. 1761). And Saint Thomas observes that 'it often happens that man acts with a good intention, but without spiritual gain, because he lacks a good will. Let us say that someone robs in order to feed the poor: in this case, even though the intention is good, the uprightness of the will is lacking. Consequently, no evil done with a good intention can be excused. "There are those who say: And why not do evil that good may come? Their condemnation is just" (Rom 3:8)' *In Duo Praecepta Caritatis et in Decem Legis Praecepta. De Dilectione Dei: Opuscula Theologica* II, No. 1168, Ed. Taurinen. (1954), 250." John Paul II, *Veritatis Splendor,* 78. Scholars dispute what should or should not count as the object of the human act, a matter of great importance in various cases of applied ethics, such as treating pregnancies endangering the life of the mother. See, for example, John Finnis, Germain Grisez, Joseph Boyle's " 'Direct' and 'Indirect': A Reply to Critics of Our Action Theory," *The Thomist* 65 (2001): 1–44, as well as three articles in the January 2003 issue of *The Thomist.* See also chapter four of Christopher Kaczor, *Proportionalism and the Natural Law Tradition* (Washington, DC: The Catholic University of America Press, 2002). Finally, see the Symposium on Moral Action in *Nova et Vetera* 6:1, Winter 2008.

Objection 2. Further, "The good of the multitude is greater and more godlike than the good of the individual," as the Philosopher states (*Ethic.* i, 2). Now schism is opposed to the good of the multitude, namely, ecclesiastical unity, whereas unbelief is contrary to the particular good of one man, namely the faith of an individual. Therefore it seems that schism is a graver sin than unbelief.

Reply to Objection 2. Just as the good of the multitude is greater than the good of a unit in that multitude, so is it less than the extrinsic good to which that multitude is directed, even as the good of a rank in the army is less than the good of the commander-in-chief. In like manner, the good of ecclesiastical unity, to which schism is opposed, is less than the good of Divine truth, to which unbelief is opposed.

Objection 3. Further, a greater good is opposed to a greater evil, according to the Philosopher (*Ethic.* viii, 10). Now schism is opposed to charity, which is a greater virtue than faith, to which unbelief is opposed, as shown above (q. 10, a. 2; q. 23, a. 6). Therefore schism is a graver sin than unbelief.

Reply to Objection 3. Charity has two objects: one is its principal object and is the Divine goodness, the other is its secondary object and is our neighbor's good. Now schism and other sins against our neighbor are opposed to charity in respect of its secondary good, which is less than the object of faith, for this is God Himself; and so these sins are less grievous than unbelief. On the other hand, hatred of God, which is opposed to charity in respect of its principal object, is not less grievous than unbelief. Nevertheless, of all sins committed by man against his neighbor, the sin of schism would seem to be the greatest, because it is opposed to the spiritual good of the multitude.

QUESTION 40

WAR

ARTICLE 1 ⸺ Is it always sinful to wage war?[1]

No, despite objections to the contrary, Augustine says in a sermon on the son of the centurion (*Ep. ad Marcel.* cxxxviii): "If the Christian Religion forbade war altogether, those who sought salutary advice in the Gospel would rather have been counseled to cast aside their arms, and to give up soldiering altogether. On the contrary, they were told: 'Do violence to no man . . . and be content with your pay' (Lk 3:14). If he commanded them to be content with their pay, he did not forbid soldiering."

---

[1] This article is one of the most influential and important in the entire *Summa*, and it is also the subject of scholarly dispute. Was Thomas implying that all wars are *prima facie* evils in need of justification? Or might some wars be not evil but rather a positive good of defending justice and innocent life? For one view of this debate, see James Turner Johnson, "Just War, As It Was and Is," *First Things* 149 (January 2005): 14–24. Despite this debate, there is widespread agreement that Aquinas aims for a mean between pacifism and realism. Pacifism rejects all war as morally evil to wage for a variety of reasons, some secular (violence breeds violence) and some religious (Jesus acted non-violently). Realism, in the context of the ethics of war, denotes the view that war has no rules whatsoever, aside, perhaps, from survival of the fittest. Thomas's just war theory is a mean between pacifism and realism, a mean that has been explicitly adopted and appealed to by most contemporary governments. One may only wage war if strict criteria are met both before (*jus ad bellum*) and in the process of carrying out warfare (*jus in bello*).

I answer that, In order for a war to be just, three things are necessary.[2] First, the authority of the sovereign by whose command the war is to be waged. For it is not the business of a private individual to declare war, because he can seek for redress of his rights from the tribunal of his superior. Moreover it is not the business of a private individual to summon together the people, which has to be done in wartime. And as the care of the common weal is committed to those who are in authority, it is their business to watch over the common weal of the city, kingdom or province subject to them. And just as it is lawful for them to have recourse to the sword in defending that common weal against internal disturbances, when they punish evil-doers, according to the words of the Apostle (Rom 13:4): "He bears not the sword in vain: for he is God's minister, an avenger to execute wrath upon him that does evil," so too, it is their business to have recourse to the sword of war in defending the common weal against external enemies. Hence it is said to those who are in authority (Ps 81:4): "Rescue the poor: and deliver the needy out of the hand of the sinner"; and for this reason Augustine says (*Contra Faust.* xxii, 75): "The natural order conducive to peace among mortals demands that the power to declare and counsel war should be in the hands of those who hold the supreme authority."[3]

---

[2] Just war theory distinguishes between two sets of criteria: one set for the right to wage war—*jus ad bellum;* another set for how to behave in carrying out a war—*jus in bello.* Thomas in this article writes of the *jus ad bellum* conditions needed to justify going to war. Sometimes others have added that there must be a likelihood of success in addition to a just cause, declaration by legitimate authority, and right intention. The *jus in bello* criteria include proportionality and discrimination in the waging of war. Proportionality, as in individual self-defense (see II–II, q. 64, a. 7), means that no more force should be used than is needed to restore peace. Discrimination denotes that civilians should not be targeted, but only soldiers and military targets. Recent discussions have also addressed the question of whether a "preemptive" war, a war launched in order to prevent attack, could be justified according to traditional just war teaching.

[3] The necessity of having the authority for the common good to declare war is sometimes a difficult one to realize, as in the case of civil wars for instance. However, Thomas's point is that a just war is not merely a private vendetta of one individual against another. Such private disagreements should be adjudicated by other means, such as courts. This condition excludes applying the notion of just war to, for example, rival mafia gangs.

Secondly, a just cause is required, namely that those who are attacked should be attacked because they deserve it on account of some fault.[4] Wherefore Augustine says (QQ. in *Hept.*, qu. x, super Jos.): "A just war is to be described as one that avenges wrongs, when a nation or state has to be punished, for refusing to make amends for the wrongs inflicted by its subjects, or to restore what it has seized unjustly."[5]

Thirdly, it is necessary that the belligerents should have a rightful intention, so that they intend the advancement of good, or the avoidance of evil. Hence Augustine says (*De Verb. Dom.*)[6] "True religion looks upon as peaceful those wars that are waged not for motives of aggrandizement, or cruelty, but with the object of securing peace, of punishing evil-doers, and of uplifting the good." For it may happen that the war is declared by the legitimate authority, and for a just cause, and yet be rendered unlawful through a wicked intention. Hence Augustine says (*Contra Faust.* xxii, 74): "The passion for inflicting harm, the cruel thirst for vengeance, an unpacific and relentless spirit, the fever of revolt, the lust of power, and such like things, all these are rightly condemned in war."[7]

---

[4] This fault must not be a trivial matter, but rather one of grave public concern. In 1993, the U.S. Catholic Bishops wrote: "Force may be used only to correct a grave, public evil, i.e., aggression or massive violation of the basic human rights of whole populations." This view would seem to justify military interventions to stop genocide even if the offending country did not aggressively attack other countries.

[5] What constitutes a "just cause" remains somewhat under-specified here. Obviously, a war would not be justified to take over the land of others or simply for economic gain. St. Augustine considered just cause for war to include defending against invaders, recovering stolen property, and punishing those who have done grave wrong. Later scholastics added that it is permissible to go to war to aid one's allies or innocent persons who cannot defend themselves.

[6] The words quoted are to be found not in St. Augustine's works, but *Can. Apud. Caus.* xxiii, qu. 1.

[7] Wrongful intention, in war as well as in any other act, renders the entire action blameworthy even if other elements are not. Thus, for example, a war motivated by ethnic hatred would not be just, even if the other two conditions (legitimate authority and just cause) were met. However, one may be motivated out of love. Since few would deny that an individual may use violence in self-defense, "now there is much more reason for safeguarding the common good (whereby many are saved from being slain, and innumerable

Objection 1. It would seem that it is always sinful to wage war. Because punishment is not inflicted except for sin. Now those who wage war are threatened by Our Lord with punishment, according to Matthew 26:52: "All that take the sword shall perish with the sword." Therefore all wars are unlawful.

Reply to Objection 1. As Augustine says (*Contra Faust.* xxii, 70): "To take the sword is to arm oneself in order to take the life of anyone, without the command or permission of superior or lawful authority." On the other hand, to have recourse to the sword (as a private person) by the authority of the sovereign or judge, or (as a public person) through zeal for justice, and by the authority, so to speak, of God, is not to "take the sword," but to use it as commissioned by another, wherefore it does not deserve punishment. And yet even those who make sinful use of the sword are not always slain with the sword, yet they always perish with their own sword, because, unless they repent, they are punished eternally for their sinful use of the sword.

Objection 2. Further, whatever is contrary to a Divine precept is a sin. But war is contrary to a Divine precept, for it is written (Mt 5:39): "But I say to you not to resist evil"; and (Rom 12:19): "Not revenging yourselves, my dearly beloved, but give place unto wrath." Therefore war is always sinful.

Reply to Objection 2. Such like precepts, as Augustine observes (*De Serm. Dom. in Monte* i, 19), should always be borne in readiness of mind, so that we be ready to obey them, and, if necessary, to refrain from resistance or self-defense. Nevertheless it is necessary sometimes for a man to act otherwise for the common good, or for the good of those with whom he is fighting.[8] Hence Augustine says (*Ep. ad Marcel.*

---

evils both temporal and spiritual prevented), than the bodily safety of an individual" (II–II, q. 40, a. 4).

[8] Perhaps this is another reason why Thomas includes his treatment of just war under the aegis of charity. In order to defend the common good, charity itself may impel a person to take up arms, just as the father of a house may have to resort to violence to preserve the safety of his family. Such use of violence, in both cases, arises from love of the common good of the community or of a family.

cxxxviii): "Those whom we have to punish with a kindly severity, it is necessary to handle in many ways against their will. For when we are stripping a man of the lawlessness of sin, it is good for him to be vanquished, since nothing is more hopeless than the happiness of sinners, whence arises a guilty impunity, and an evil will, like an internal enemy."

Objection 3. Further, nothing, except sin, is contrary to an act of virtue. But war is contrary to peace. Therefore war is always a sin.

Reply to Objection 3. Those who wage war justly aim at peace, and so they are not opposed to peace, except to the evil peace, which Our Lord "came not to send upon earth" (Mt 10:34). Hence Augustine says (*Ep. ad Bonif.* clxxxix): "We do not seek peace in order to be at war, but we go to war that we may have peace. Be peaceful, therefore, in warring, so that you may vanquish those whom you war against, and bring them to the prosperity of peace."9

Objection 4. Further, the exercise of a lawful thing is itself lawful, as is evident in scientific exercises. But warlike exercises which take place in tournaments are forbidden by the Church, since those who are slain in these trials are deprived of ecclesiastical burial. Therefore it seems that war is a sin in itself.

Reply to Objection 4. Manly exercises in warlike feats of arms are not all forbidden, but those which are inordinate and perilous, and end in slaying or plundering. In olden times warlike exercises presented no such danger, and hence they were called "exercises of arms" or "bloodless wars."

---

9 Surprisingly, Thomas's teaching about just war is found within his treatment of the virtue of charity rather than the virtue of justice. War is opposed to peace, an interior act of charity. But this peace is not merely the absence of external conflict. As Thomas reminds us in question 22, article 2: Augustine defines peace as "the tranquility of order" (*De Civ. Dei* xix, 13). If this tranquility of order has been disturbed, then peace is already missing even if arms are not being used.

QUESTION **42**

REBELLION AGAINST THE AUTHORITY OF THE STATE (SEDITION)

ARTICLE 2 ⤐ **Is rebellion against the authority of the state always a mortal sin?**

Yes, despite objections to the contrary, The Apostle forbids seditions[1] together with other things that are mortal sins (2 Cor 12:20).

I answer that, As stated above (a. 1, ad 2), sedition[2] is contrary to the unity of the multitude, viz. the people of a city or kingdom. Now

---

[1] In the previous article, Thomas talks about the nature of sedition as follows: "Sedition is a special sin, having something in common with war and strife, and differing somewhat from them. It has something in common with them, insofar as it implies a certain antagonism, and it differs from them in two points. First, because war and strife denote actual aggression on either side, whereas sedition may be said to denote either actual aggression, or the preparation for such aggression. Hence a gloss on 2 Corinthians 12:20 says that 'seditions are tumults tending to fight,' when, to wit, a number of people make preparations with the intention of fighting. Secondly, they differ in that war is, properly speaking, carried on against external foes, being as it were between one people and another, whereas strife is between one individual and another, or between few people on one side and few on the other side, while sedition, in its proper sense, is between mutually dissentient parts of one people, as when one part of the state rises in tumult against another part. Wherefore, since sedition is opposed to a special kind of good, namely the unity and peace of a people, it is a special kind of sin."

[2] Sedition is rebellion or insurrection against the authority of a state.

Augustine says (*De Civ. Dei* ii, 21) that "wise men understand the word people to designate not any crowd of persons, but the assembly of those who are united together in fellowship recognized by law and for the common good." Wherefore it is evident that the unity to which sedition is opposed is the unity of law and common good: whence it follows manifestly that sedition is opposed to justice and the common good. Therefore by reason of its genus it is a mortal sin, and its gravity will be all the greater according as the common good which it assails surpasses the private good which is assailed by strife.

Accordingly the sin of sedition is first and chiefly in its authors, who sin most grievously; and secondly it is in those who are led by them to disturb the common good. Those, however, who defend the common good, and withstand the seditious party, are not themselves seditious, even as neither is a man to be called quarrelsome because he defends himself, as stated above (q. 41, a. 1).

Objection 1. It would seem that sedition is not always a mortal sin. For sedition denotes "a tumult tending to fight," according to the gloss quoted above (a. 1). But fighting is not always a mortal sin; indeed it is sometimes just and lawful, as stated above (q. 40, a. 1). Much more, therefore, can sedition be without a mortal sin.

Reply to Objection 1. It is lawful to fight, provided it be for the common good, as stated above (q. 40, a. 1). But sedition runs counter to the common good of the multitude, so that it is always a mortal sin.

Objection 2. Further, sedition is a kind of discord, as stated above (a. 1, ad 3). Now discord can be without mortal sin, and sometimes without any sin at all. Therefore sedition can be also.

Reply to Objection 2. Discord from what is not evidently good may be without sin, but discord from what is evidently good cannot be without sin: and sedition is discord of this kind, for it is contrary to the unity of the multitude, which is a manifest good.

Objection 3. Further, it is praiseworthy to deliver a multitude from a tyrannical rule. Yet this cannot easily be done without some dissension in the multitude, if one part of the multitude seeks to retain the tyrant, while the rest strive to dethrone him. Therefore there can be sedition without mortal sin.

Reply to Objection 3. A tyrannical government is not just, because it is directed, not to the common good, but to the private good of the ruler, as the Philosopher states (*Polit.* iii, 5; *Ethic.* viii, 10). Consequently there is no sedition in disturbing a government of this kind, unless indeed the tyrant's rule be disturbed so inordinately that his subjects suffer greater harm from the consequent disturbance than from the tyrant's government. Indeed it is the tyrant rather that is guilty of sedition, since he encourages discord and sedition among his subjects, that he may lord over them more securely; for this is tyranny, being conducive to the private good of the ruler, and to the injury of the multitude.

QUESTION **44**

PRECEPTS OF CHARITY

ARTICLE 1 ⚬ **Should any precept be given about charity?**

Yes, despite objections to the contrary, Whatever God requires of us is included in a precept. Now God requires that man should love Him, according to Deuteronomy 10:12. Therefore it behooved precepts to be given about the love of charity, which is the love of God.[1]

I answer that, As stated above (q. 16, a. 1; I–II, q. 99, a. 1), a precept implies the notion of something due. Hence a thing is a matter of precept, insofar as it is something due. Now a thing is due in two ways, for its own sake, and for the sake of something else. In every affair, it is the end that is due for its own sake, because it has the character of a good for its own sake: while that which is directed to the end is due for the sake of something else: thus for a physician, it is due for its own sake, that he should heal, while it is due for the sake of something else that he should give a medicine in order to heal. Now the end of the spiritual life is that man be united to God, and this union is effected by charity, while all things pertaining to the spiritual life are ordained to this union, as to their end. Hence the Apostle says (1 Tim 1:5): "The

---

[1] Here Thomas connects law and love, for the purpose of God's written law, command, or precept is to secure that the demands of love are not violated. The moral law helps us to get what we really want, a happiness that can only be had through a true love of God and neighbor. As the rules of health (e.g. eating well, getting enough sleep) help us to attain physical well-being, the rules of morality help us to attain the virtues and authentic human freedom and happiness.

end of the commandment is charity from a pure heart, and a good con-science, and an unfeigned faith." For all the virtues, about whose acts the precepts are given, are directed either to the freeing of the heart from the whirl of the passions—such are the virtues that regulate the passions[2]—or at least to the possession of a good conscience—such are the virtues that regulate operations[3]—or to the having of a right faith[4]—such are those which pertain to the worship of God: and these three things are required of man that he may love God. For an impure heart is with-drawn from loving God, on account of the passion that inclines it to earthly things; an evil conscience gives man a horror for God's justice, through fear of His punishments; and an untrue faith draws man's affec-tions to an untrue representation of God, and separates him from the truth of God. Now in every genus that which is for its own sake takes precedence of that which is for the sake of another, wherefore the great-est precept is that of charity, as stated in Matthew 22:39.

Objection 1. It would seem that no precept should be given about charity. For charity imposes the mode on all acts of virtue, since it is the form of the virtues as stated above (q. 23, a. 8), while the precepts are about the virtues themselves. Now, according to the common say-ing, the mode is not included in the precept. Therefore no precepts should be given about charity.

Reply to Objection 1. As stated above (I–II, q. 100, a. 10) when we were treating of the commandments, the mode of love does not come under those precepts which are about the other acts of virtue: for instance, this precept, "Honor your father and your mother," does not prescribe that this should be done out of charity.[5] The act of love does, however, fall under special precepts.

---

[2] For example, temperance governs the passion for bodily pleasure, and forti-tude governs the passion driving us away from what is perceived as harmful.

[3] Justice, for example, regulates our external operations in dealing with others.

[4] The theological virtue of faith supplies this need.

[5] Thomas explains in this earlier article that the "commandment, 'Honor your father,' does not mean that a man must honor his father from charity, but merely that he must honor him. Wherefore he that honors his father, yet has not charity, does not break this precept: although he does break the precept

Objection 2. Further, charity, which "is poured forth in our hearts by the Holy Spirit" (Rom 5:5), makes us free, since "where the Spirit of the Lord is, there is liberty" (2 Cor 3:17). Now the obligation that arises from a precept is opposed to liberty, since it imposes a necessity. Therefore no precept should be given about charity.

Reply to Objection 2. The obligation of a precept is not opposed to liberty, except in one whose mind is averted from that which is prescribed, as may be seen in those who keep the precepts through fear alone.[6] But the precept of love cannot be fulfilled save of one's own will, wherefore it is not opposed to charity.

Objection 3. Further, charity is the foremost among all the virtues, to which the precepts are directed, as shown above (I–II, q. 90, a. 2; I–II, q. 100, a. 9). If, therefore, any precepts were given about charity, they should have a place among the chief precepts which are those of the decalogue. But they have no place there. Therefore no precepts should be given about charity.

Reply to Objection 3. All the precepts of the decalogue are directed to the love of God and of our neighbor: and therefore the precepts of charity had not to be enumerated among the precepts of the decalogue, since they are included in all of them.[7]

---

concerning the act of charity, for which reason he deserves to be punished." It is a matter of precept that we should love our neighbor as ourselves, but other precepts concern other matters and do not include that we must fulfill the precept out of the motivation of charity.

6 The relationship of freedom and precept, liberty and law, was a recurring theme in the pontificate of John Paul II. Mere absence of constraint is not the same as true human freedom that is ordered to human flourishing. True human freedom must therefore correspond to the truth about humanity and God, and the truth about humanity and God is revealed in part through the moral law. Moral wrongdoing is not merely a matter of disobeying arbitrary rules. Rather, violating the rights of others emaciates the authentic freedom of the violator. The saint enjoys the greatest freedom, and the sinner is a slave to sin. See Avery Dulles, "John Paul II and the Truth about Freedom," *First Things* 55 (August/September 1995): 36–41.

7 The Ten Commandments can be divided into two tablets. The first tablet treats commandments that forbid acting contrary to the love of God. One cannot love God properly if other things are loved in God's place (first commandment,

ARTICLE 2 ~ **Should two precepts of love have been given?**

Yes, despite objections to the contrary, It is written (1 Jn 4:21): "This commandment we have from God, that he who loves God, love also his brother."

I answer that, As stated above (I–II, q. 91, a. 3; I–II, q. 94, a. 2) when we were treating of the commandments, the precepts are to the Law what propositions are to speculative sciences, for in these latter, the conclusions are virtually contained in the first principles. Hence whoever knows the principles as to their entire virtual extent has no need to have the conclusions put separately before him. Since, however, some who know the principles are unable to consider all that is virtually contained therein, it is necessary, for their sake, that scientific conclusions should be traced to their principles. Now in practical matters wherein the precepts of the Law direct us, the end has the character of principle, as stated above (q. 23, a. 7, ad 2; q. 26, a. 1, ad 1): and the love of God is the end to which the love of our neighbor is directed. Therefore it was beneficial to us to receive precepts not only

---

you shall have no god before me), if things related to God such as his name and other holy things are not treated with due respect (second commandment, you shall not take the name of the Lord your God in vain), and if adequate time is not devoted to giving God the honor, respect, and worship due to Him (third commandment, you shall keep holy the Sabbath). The second tablet treats commandments that forbid acting against the authentic love of neighbor. Our neighbor is not being loved properly if honor and respect are not paid to those who have benefited us (fourth commandment, honor your father and mother). Our neighbor is not being loved if his bodily life and health are unjustly violated by our actions (fifth commandment, you shall not murder). Our neighbor is not being loved properly if we violate the bonds of marriage (sixth commandment, you shall not commit adultery). Our neighbor is not being loved if we steal his property (seventh commandment, you shall not steal). Our neighbor is not being loved if we lie and tear down his reputation and honor (eighth commandment, you shall not bear false witness). Finally, our neighbor is not being authentically loved if we stir desire in our hearts to make our own that which belongs to another (ninth commandment, you shall not covet your neighbor's spouse; tenth commandment, you shall not covet your neighbor's goods). For a great medieval treatment of the Ten Commandments as the demands of love, see St. Bonaventure, *Collations on the Ten Commandments. Works of Bonaventure VI* (St. Bonaventure, NY: The Franciscan Institute, 1995).

of the love of God but also of the love of our neighbor, on account of those who are less intelligent, who do not easily understand that one of these precepts is included in the other.[8]

Objection 1. It would seem that there should not have been given two precepts of charity. For the precepts of the Law are directed to virtue, as stated above (a. 1, Objection 3). Now charity is one virtue, as shown above (q. 33, a. 5). Therefore only one precept of charity should have been given.

Reply to Objection 1. Although charity is one virtue, yet it has two acts, one of which is directed to the other as to its end. Now precepts are given about acts of virtue, and so there had to be several precepts of charity.

Objection 2. Further, as Augustine says (*De Doctr. Christ.* i, 22, 27), charity loves none but God in our neighbor. Now we are sufficiently directed to love God by the precept, "You shall love the Lord your God." Therefore there was no need to add the precept about loving our neighbor.

Reply to Objection 2. God is loved in our neighbor, as the end is loved in that which is directed to the end; and yet there was need for an explicit precept about both, for the reason given above.

Objection 3. Further, different sins are opposed to different precepts. But it is not a sin to put aside the love of our neighbor, provided we put not aside the love of God; indeed, it is written (Lk 14:26): "If any man come to Me, and hate not his father, and mother . . . he cannot be My disciple." Therefore the precept of the love of God is not distinct from the precept of the love of our neighbor.

---

8 If a person loves God and understands what loving God really demands, he will follow the Ten Commandments. Loving God leads to loving the image of God in our neighbor, and loving the image of God in our neighbor excludes acts contrary to this charity such as murder, theft, and adultery. The whole of the law can be summed up in the love of God and the love of neighbor. However, as a mercy for those who fail to see the full implications of love, the Ten Commandments are given to make explicit what loves requires.

Reply to Objection 3. The means derive that which is toward an end has (its) reason of goodness from (its) order to the end, and according to this, also, to go away from it [the end, presumably] has the reason of evil and not otherwise.[9]

Objection 4. Further, the Apostle says (Rom 13:8): "He that loves his neighbor has fulfilled the Law." But a law is not fulfilled unless all its precepts be observed. Therefore all the precepts are included in the love of our neighbor: and consequently the one precept of the love of our neighbor suffices. Therefore there should not be two precepts of charity.

Reply to Objection 4. Love of our neighbor includes love of God, as the end is included in the means, and vice versa: and yet it behooved each precept to be given explicitly, for the reason given above.[10]

ARTICLE 3 ↝ **Are two precepts of love sufficient?**

Yes, despite objections to the contrary, Our Lord said (Mt 22:40): "On these two commandments depend the whole Law and the prophets."

I answer that, Charity, as stated above (q. 23, a. 1), is a kind of friendship. Now friendship is between one person and another, wherefore Gregory says (*Hom. in Ev.* xvii): "Charity is not possible between less than two": and it has been explained how one may love

---

[9] Elsewhere, Thomas more directly responds to the objection about hating father and mother. "By the commandment of God (Ex 20:12) we must honor our parents—as united to us in nature and kinship. But we must hate them insofar as they prove an obstacle to our attaining the perfection of divine justice" (*ST* II–II, q. 34, a. 3, ad 1).

[10] Eberhard Schockenhoff explains this mutuality as follows: "Charity is aimed at the Triune God, who destines human beings to friendship with Himself, and, along with this aspect directed to its inmost center, encompasses as its concrete object the neighbor, who is called to the very same end. The human being's responsive love of God necessarily includes the love for all those put on the path alongside us to the same final goal, who are called to share in the same beatitude. In caritas, the neighbors are loved for God's sake, . . . because God is in the neighbors, and so that they can be in God and God can be in them." E. Schockenhoff, "The Theological Virtue of Charity," in *The Ethics of Aquinas*, ed. Stephen Pope (Washington DC: Georgetown University Press, 2002), 252.

oneself out of charity (q. 25, a. 4).[11] Now since good is the object of dilection and love, and since good is either an end or a means, it is fitting that there should be two precepts of charity, one whereby we are induced to love God as our end, and another whereby we are led to love our neighbor for God's sake, as for the sake of our end.

Objection 1. It would seem that two precepts of charity do not suffice. For precepts are given about acts of virtue. Now acts are distinguished by their objects. Since, then, man is bound to love four things out of charity, namely, God, himself, his neighbor and his own body, as shown above (q. 25, a. 12; q. 26), it seems that there ought to be four precepts of charity, so that two are not sufficient.

Reply to Objection 1. As Augustine says (*De Doctr. Christ.* i, 23), "though four things are to be loved out of charity, there was no need of a precept as regards the second and fourth," i.e. love of oneself and of one's own body. "For however much a man may stray from the truth, the love of himself and of his own body always remains in him."[12] And

---

[11] Here Thomas writes: "[W]e may speak of charity in respect of its specific nature, namely as denoting man's friendship with God in the first place, and, consequently, with the things of God, among which things is man himself who has charity. Hence, among these other things which he loves out of charity because they pertain to God, he loves also himself out of charity."

[12] A difficulty may be raised here. It does not seem apparent that everyone loves himself or loves his body. Persons who commit suicide appear to hate themselves, and people with a 'body image' problem appear to hate their own bodies. These examples do not in fact show a lack of love of self or body, however misguided that love may be. A suicide might be explained in terms of a misguided love for self. It is not that the one committing suicide wishes he did not exist simply for the sake of not existing. Rather he so detests whatever situation has arisen that in order to escape the situation he chooses to die. He loves himself, but he would love to get out of the horrible situation even more. Thus, suicide is compatible with self-love, although not compatible with a well-ordered self-love that arises from a charity that would view life as a good from God that in innocence should never be deliberately taken. The person with the body image problem likewise loves her body, for if she had no love of her body she would not care about the (allegedly) unacceptable appearance of her body. It is of no concern to her that unshapely rocks exist for she does not love the rocks. It is love that leads to the desire for improvement of the beloved object, albeit in this case a misguided desire.

yet the mode of this love had to be prescribed to man, namely, that he should love himself and his own body in an ordinate manner, and this is done by his loving God and his neighbor.

Objection 2. Further, love is not the only act of charity, but also joy, peace and beneficence. But precepts should be given about the acts of the virtues. Therefore two precepts of charity do not suffice.

Reply to Objection 2. As stated above (q. 28, a. 4; q. 29, a. 3), the other acts of charity result from the act of love as effects from their cause. Hence the precepts of love virtually include the precepts about the other acts. And yet we find that, for the sake of the slow minded, special precepts were given about each act—about joy (Phil 4:4): "Rejoice in the Lord always"—about peace (Heb 12:14): "Follow peace with all men"—about beneficence (Gal 6:10): "Whilst we have time, let us work good to all men"—and Holy Writ contains precepts about each of the parts of beneficence, as may be seen by anyone who considers the matter carefully.

Objection 3. Further, virtue consists not only in doing good but also in avoiding evil. Now we are led by the positive precepts to do good, and by the negative precepts to avoid evil. Therefore there ought to have been not only positive, but also negative precepts about charity; and so two precepts of charity are not sufficient.

Reply to Objection 3. To do good is more than to avoid evil, and therefore the positive precepts virtually include the negative precepts.[13] Nevertheless we find explicit precepts against the vices contrary to charity: for, against hatred it is written (Lev 12:17): "You shall not hate your brother in your heart"; against sloth (Sir 6:26): "Be not grieved with her bands"; against envy (Gal 5:26): "Let us not be made desirous of vainglory, provoking one another, envying one another"; against dis-

---

[13] For this reason, Jesus said that the whole of the law could be reduced to love of God and love of neighbor. If one truly and properly loves God and neighbor, then precepts about not killing, not committing adultery, and not committing idolatry will be followed. Hence, Augustine famously said: "Love, and do what you will" (Homily 7 on the First Epistle of John)—a demanding injunction, not permission for license.

cord (1 Cor 1:10): "That you all speak the same thing, and that there be no schisms among you"; and against scandal (Rom 14:13): "That you put not a stumbling-block or a scandal in your brother's way."

Article 4 ⤚ Is it fittingly commanded that man should love God with his whole heart?

Yes, despite objections to the contrary, It is written (Dt 6:5): "You shall love the Lord your God with your whole heart."

I answer that, Since precepts are given about acts of virtue, an act is a matter of precept according as it is an act of virtue. Now it is requisite for an act of virtue that not only should it fall on its due matter, but also that it should be endued with its due circumstances, whereby it is adapted to that matter. But God is to be loved as the last end, to which all things are to be referred. Therefore some kind of totality was to be indicated in connection with the precept of the love of God.[14]

Objection 2. Further, "A thing is whole and perfect when it lacks nothing" (Aristotle, *Phys.* iii, 6). If therefore it is a matter of precept that God be loved with the whole heart, whoever does something not pertaining to the love of God acts counter to the precept, and consequently sins mortally. Now a venial sin does not pertain to the love of God. Therefore a venial sin is a mortal sin, which is absurd.

Reply to Objection 2. To love God with one's whole heart has a twofold signification. First, actually, so that a man's whole heart be always actually directed to God: this is the perfection of heaven. Secondly, in the sense that a man's whole heart be habitually directed to God, so that it consent to nothing contrary to the love of God, and this is the perfection of the way.[15] Venial sin is not contrary to this latter

---

[14] In other words, a precept merely to "love God," lacking more circumstantial description, would not function as well as the more specific precept "love God with your whole heart" because the first precept would not properly inform a person about the manner in which God is to be loved, namely as the final, ultimate, most important end. A person might follow this command and love God with the love appropriate for a possession or an idol and thereby fail to achieve happiness.

[15] It is not possible on earth, even for the most saintly of contemplatives, to be constantly thinking about God and dwelling consciously and explicitly in his

perfection, because it does not destroy the habit of charity, since it does not tend to a contrary object, but merely hinders the use of charity.

Objection 3. Further, to love God with one's whole heart belongs to perfection, since according to the Philosopher (Aristotle, *Phys.* iii, text. 64), "to be whole is to be perfect." But that which belongs to perfection is not a matter of precept, but a matter of counsel. Therefore we ought not to be commanded to love God with our whole heart.

Reply to Objection 3. That perfection of charity to which the counsels are directed is between the two perfections mentioned in the preceding reply: and it consists in man renouncing, as much as possible, temporal things, even such as are lawful, because they occupy the mind and hinder the actual movement of the heart towards God.

ARTICLE 6 ⁓ **Is it possible in this life to fulfill this precept of the love of God?**

No, despite objections to the contrary, Augustine says (*De Perfect. Justit.* viii), "In the fullness of heavenly charity this precept will be fulfilled: You shall love the Lord your God. . . ." For as long as any carnal concupiscence remains that can be restrained by continence man cannot love God with all his heart.

I answer that, A precept can be fulfilled in two ways: perfectly, and imperfectly. A precept is fulfilled perfectly when the end intended by the author of the precept is reached. It is fulfilled imperfectly when although the end intended by its author is not reached, the order to that end is, nevertheless, not departed from. Thus if the commander of an army order his soldiers to fight, his command will be perfectly obeyed by those who fight and conquer the foe, which is the commander's intention; it is fulfilled, albeit imperfectly, by those who

---

love. However, love of God, like knowledge of geometry, can be dispositionally or habitually with a person even when a person is not thinking at that moment or actually about God or geometry. You know that the interior angles of a triangle add up to 180 degrees, even when that bit of knowledge is not at the time in your mind. Similarly, a person in a state of grace loves God habitually even when consciously working at something that is not immediately and obviously connected with love of God.

fight without gaining victory, provided they do nothing contrary to military discipline. God intends by this precept that man should be entirely united to him, and this will be realized in heaven, when God will be "all in all," according to 1 Corinthians 15:28. Hence this precept will be observed fully and perfectly in heaven;—yet it is fulfilled, though imperfectly, on the way. Nevertheless on the way one man will fulfill it more perfectly than another, and so much the more, as he approaches by some kind of likeness to the perfection of heaven.

Objection 1. It would seem that in this life it is possible to fulfill this precept of the love of God. For according to Jerome (Pelagius, *Exposit. Cath. Fid.*), "accursed is he who says that God has commanded anything impossible." But God gave this commandment, as is clear from Deuteronomy 6:5. Therefore it is possible to fulfill this precept in this life.

Reply to Objection 1. This argument proves that the precept can be fulfilled after a fashion on the way, but not perfectly.[16]

Objection 2. Further, whoever does not fulfill a precept sins mortally, since according to Ambrose (*De Parad.* viii) sin is nothing else than "a transgression of the Divine Law, and disobedience of the heavenly commandments." If therefore this precept cannot be fulfilled by wayfarers, it follows that in this life no man can be without mortal sin, and this is against the saying of the Apostle (1 Cor 1:8): "(Who also) will confirm you unto the end without crime," and (1 Tim 3:10): "Let them minister, having no crime."

Reply to Objection 2. Even as the soldier who fights legitimately without conquering is not blamed nor deserves to be punished for this, so too he that does not fulfill this precept on the way, but does nothing against the love of God, does not sin mortally.

---

[16] It would seem that this could be cause for despair, but only for those so proud as to wish to deny their own weakness. Although we continually need God's mercy, this should continually bring to mind the great kindness, compassion, and forgiveness of God. Rather than simply depressing us, our weakness should remind us that others too share in an inability to love God or neighbor as they should, a reminder that can lead to greater compassion and willingness to promptly and fully forgive others.

Objection 3. Further, precepts are given in order to direct man in the way of salvation, according to Psalm 18:9: "The commandment of the Lord is lightsome, enlightening the eyes." Now it is useless to direct anyone to what is impossible. Therefore it is not impossible to fulfill this precept in this life.

Reply to Objection 3. As Augustine says (*De Perfect. Justit.* viii), "why should not this perfection be prescribed to man, although no man attains it in this life? For one cannot run straight to the goal unless one knows in which direction to run. And how would one know this if no precept pointed it out?"[17]

ARTICLE 7 ∽ Is the precept of love of our neighbor fittingly expressed?

Yes, despite objections to the contrary, It is written (Mt 22:39): "The second commandment is like to this: You shall love your neighbor as yourself."

I answer that, This precept is fittingly expressed, for it indicates both the reason for loving and the mode of love. The reason for loving is indicated in the word "neighbor," because the reason why we ought to love others out of charity is because they are nigh to us, both as to the natural image of God, and as to the capacity for glory. Nor does it matter whether we say "neighbor," or "brother" according to 1 John 4:21, or "friend" according to Leviticus 19:18, because all these words express the same affinity.

The mode of love is indicated in the words "as yourself." This does not mean that a man must love his neighbor equally as himself, but in like manner as himself, and this in three ways. First, as regards the end, namely, that he should love his neighbor for God's sake, even as he loves himself for God's sake, so that his love for his neighbor is a "holy" love. Secondly, as regards the rule of love, namely, that a man should not give way to his neighbor in evil, but only in good things, even as he

---

[17] Our lack of reaching the goal does not obstruct the importance of the goal for directing us. Indeed, it is important to note that one day all those who are saved will love God and neighbor with absolute perfection, but such perfection will always elude us while we are still on our way to heaven.

ought to gratify his will in good things alone, so that his love for his neighbor may be a "righteous" love. Thirdly, as regards the reason for loving, namely, that a man should love his neighbor, not for his own profit, or pleasure, but in the sense of wishing his neighbor well, even as he wishes himself well, so that his love for his neighbor may be a "true" love: since when a man loves his neighbor for his own profit or pleasure, he does not love his neighbor truly, but loves himself.[18]

---

[18] In addition to the works cited in the notes, readers interested in looking more deeply into the virtue of love according to Thomas should also read his *On Charity* (*De caritate*), trans. J. P. Reid (Providence, RI: Providence College Press, 1951), Paul J. Wadell, *The Primacy of Love: An Introduction to the Ethics of Thomas Aquinas* (New York: Paulist, 1992), and especially Michael S. Sherwin, *By Knowledge and By Love: Charity and Knowledge in the Moral Theology of St. Thomas Aquinas* (Washington, DC: The Catholic Univeresity of American Press, 2005).

GENERAL INDEX

251

Scripture Index

Old Testament

Genesis
 2:24, 40

Exodus
 3:12, 168*n7*
 6:2, 3, 18
 19:12, 202
 20:12, 210, 242*n9*
 22:18, 155

Leviticus
 10:9, 161
 12:17, 244
 19:18, 248

Deuteronomy
 4:2, 21
 6:5, 245, 247
 10:12, 152, 237

1 Kings
 14:1, 220

2 Kings
 6:7, 202

3 Esdras
 4:36, 39, 206

Judith
 6:15, 120
 9:17, 122

Job
 12:11, 36
 13:3, 220
 15:22, 101
 19:25, 43
 28:28, 110
 31:20, 195
 35:11, 44
 39:32, 220
 40:18, 101
 40:28, 101
 42:7, 220

Psalms
 9:18, 156
 10:8, 156
 18:9, 248
 23:8, 41
 30:2, 98

 34:13, 195
 36:5, 90
 36:39, 36
 57:11, 156
 72:28, 137
 73:23, 205
 81:4, 228
 100:8, 155
 102:5, 171
 110:10, 108
 118:100, 18
 118:113, 154
 138:22, 154
 144:9, 179
 147:3, 175

Proverbs
 4:2, 194
 4:6–8, 109*n7*
 8:8, 209
 27:6, 193

Wisdom
 1:13, 156
 1:13, 15, 107
 2:24, 214

271